Doctor Who and History

Critical Essays on Imagining the Past

Edited by CAREY FLEINER
and DENE OCTOBER

McFarland & Company, Inc., Publishers
Jefferson, North Carolina

ISBN (print) 978-1-4766-6656-3
ISBN (ebook) 978-1-4766-2981-0

Library of Congress cataloguing data are available

British Library cataloguing data are available

Front cover images of Kublai Khan, Queen Boudicca, Nero, Winston Churchill and Nefertiti © 2017 iStock

Printed in the United States of America

McFarland & Company, Inc., Publishers
  Box 611, Jefferson, North Carolina 28640
    www.mcfarlandpub.com

Table of Contents

Acknowledgments   vii

Introduction   1

Part 1. Television as History: Inform and Entertain

Journeys through Cathay: Remediation and Televisuality   13
  in "Marco Polo"
  DENE OCTOBER

"O tempora, o mores": Class(ics) and Education in *Doctor Who*   35
  AVEN MCMASTER *and* MARK SUNDARAM

Remixing the Imperial Past: *Doctor Who*, British Slavery   47
  and the White Savior's Burden
  SUSANA LOZA

Part 2. Historical Drama: Genre and Conventions

Doctor, Go Roman: "The Romans," Emperor Nero   61
  and Historical Comedy in *Doctor Who*
  CAREY FLEINER

History as Genre, Aesthetic and Context in "The Gunfighters"   78
  RAMIE TATEISHI

A Rude Awakening: Metafiction in Eric Pringle's   92
  "The Awakening"
  ANDREW O'DAY

Part 3. Historical Constructions/Reconstructions

Playing with History: Terrance Dicks, Fans and Season 6B   102
  RHONDA KNIGHT

Doctor Who Unbound and Alternate History   118
    KAREN HELLEKSON

The Vikings at the End of the Universe: *Doctor Who*, Norsemen   132
    and the End of History
    MARCUS K. HARMES

Part 4. History and Identity

Ape-Man or Regular Guy? Depictions of Neanderthals   148
    and Neanderthal Culture in *Doctor Who*
    KRISTINE LARSEN

The Dark Heart of the Village: *Doctor Who* in the 1970s   168
    and the Problematic Idyll
    PETER LOWE

Doctor Who and Environmentalism in the 1960s
    and Early 1970s   186
    MARK WILSON

Appendix: Adventures Referenced   204

About the Contributors   207

Index   209

Doctor Who and History

Acknowledgments

Like Barbara Wright and Ian Chesterton, we two are putting our feet up having enjoyed many enjoyable *adventures historical*. We have many people to celebrate, those who helped with the long research sojourns in ancient Cathay and Rome (the focus of our respective essays) and those who offered their support and wisdom, who took our travels seriously and assisted in bringing this collection to fruition.

Thanks to our contributors, of course, without whom we wouldn't have such a diverse and exciting bunch of essays to share. And to the many more who wished to contribute, and who submitted abstracts—we received far too many to use in a single volume, for we could only choose a dozen out of the five dozen or so proposals we received.

A special shout out also to James Jordan at the University of Southampton, who worked closely with us at the outset, offering ideas, and helping to hammer out the proposal. Thanks also to the anonymous reviewers whose quiet diligence gave us cause to revise our thoughts.

Thanks go to those archives and libraries who allowed us access to their *Doctor Who* holdings and answered our many queries and requests, including the folk at the awesome BBC Written Archives Centre in Caversham, England. Thanks also to those in our respective university research departments and libraries for your skills and services.

To our teaching colleagues at the University of the Arts London and the University of Winchester—thanks to all for your support and understanding, and especially for standing in for us while *we* got to spend study leave in the TARDIS. Although we weren't gone too long, we could perhaps have learned from Barbara and Ian's error, and arranged to arrive back at the precise moment we left. You live and, thankfully, you learn.

Finally, enormous thanks to the Doctor, without whom there may never have been any inspiration to time-travel. Doctor, you don't just observe the past … for us, you make it happen.

Introduction

"Historians," writes Penelope J. Corfield, "are often asked: what is the use or relevance of studying History?" Her reply, that "the study of the past is essential for 'rooting' people in time," could have been written with *Doctor Who* in mind. While some lack a sense of their history, for others "the inherited legacy may even be too powerful and outright oppressive" (Corfield n.d.). So it is with the central character of the show, whose own past and mythos is itself long and winding, part of broader broadcast history and fan folklore; his lives not only cross paths with historical characters but also the line between fact and fiction. Through such a figure we might learn a great deal about history, and how we approach it. These are issues we seek to explore in *Doctor Who and History*.

Fifty years after its initial transmission on the BBC, *Doctor Who* has become part of the cultural history of Britain itself, and its many stories have played out across the medium of television, audio plays and books. Whether set in the past or populated with the inevitable bug-eyed monsters, these adventures in time and space have engaged with important contemporary and historical issues and events. While many recent publications have celebrated the show's longevity, or reflected on the program as a product of the BBC as British institution, *Doctor Who and History* is the first volume of essays to focus on the topic of history as it is expressed thematically in the show itself, as well as how its program-makers and audience are situated within that history. The diverse essays here promote a scholarly and interdisciplinary approach, exploring how *Doctor Who* reflects on and contributes to notions of history.

The story of the Doctor's character development is well-documented; he is a mysterious being traveling through the "past, future, and sideways" in his TARDIS, a time machine stuck in the shape of a British police phone box, itself now an icon of post-war London but one the Metropolitan Police thankfully failed to trademark. In addition to his young granddaughter, the Doctor initially travels with a pair of comprehensive schoolteachers, science instructor Ian Chesterton and history teacher Barbara Wright. BBC Head of Drama Sydney Newman and *Doctor Who* producer Verity Lambert envisioned the show as being, in former BBC Director-General John Reith's terms, something that would "educate, inform, and entertain" especially in terms of science and history (Tulloch and Alvarado 1983, 42–43). During William Hartnell's tenure especially the show presented what were referred to in-house as "adventures-historical" and are now referred to as "pure historicals," that is, stories which take place during a particular historical event with no science fiction elements or anachronisms aside from those brought by the Doctor and his companions (1964's "The Reign of Terror" being one example). Sydney Newman also insisted that the four travelers in the TARDIS would only observe history rather than act as agents of it and possibly become the source of myth. Newman was particularly sensitive concerning the direction of the show, and his penciled comments on early drafts and promotional material reveal this insistence. For example, he criticized an early proposal that suggests the Doctor was an impish time traveler whose meddling perhaps became the basis for the Tooth Fairy or Jacob Marley. On this in-house memo, he commented that such ideas were "silly and condescending … it doesn't get across the basis of teaching or educational experience—drama based upon and stemming from factual material and scientific phenomenon and actual social history of past and future."[1] The Doctor has, consequently, observed quite a bit of Earth's history over the course of the program: he's seen the origins of life on the planet (e.g., "City of Death," 1977), witnessed the destruction of the Earth ("End of the World," 2005) and discovered the source of the meteor that destroyed the dinosaurs ("Earthshock," 1982). Sometimes, his interference is accidental: we learn, for example, that he caused the Great Fire of London in 1666 in his haste to escape the locals after he's saved them from a Terileptil invasion ("The Visitation," 1982). Despite Newman's initiative, from quite early on, the Doctor has been quite pleased to discover that his presence has influenced historical events: in "The Romans" (1965), he realizes that Nero was inspired to set Rome aflame after seeing the Doctor burn a map of the city; in the same serial, he brags to companion Vicki that he gave Hans Christian Anderson the idea for *The Emperor's New Clothes*. Vicki herself becomes the basis for the myth of Troilus and Cressida when she stays behind at the end of 1965's "The Myth Makers"—and the *Doctor* becomes an integral part of folklore and mythology, from England's Merlin ("Battlefield," 1989) to the folkloric, inspirational hero to the rebels in "Timelash" (1985), and even, albeit by well-meaning accident, corrupts a malfunctioning computer which uses the image of the Fourth Doctor as an avatar of its divinity ("Face of Evil," 1977). Indeed, from the reboot of the series especially, the Doctor's role in the history of Earth and other planets and cultures becomes so encompassing that he acquires the sorts of nicknames one associates normally with the desert gods of Bronze Age cultures—"The Oncoming Storm" and "Destroyer of Worlds"; at the same time, he becomes a symbol of hope as his name is whispered across the earth by his companion Martha (2006's "Sound of Drums"/"Last of the Time Lords")—despite the fear he brings to the hearts of his enemies and the many deaths he leaves in his wake, his own death would bring inconceivable loss across the universe. River Song tells him passionately in "The Big Bang" of the importance of his life and well-being to so many who know, love, and depend on him, making canon Emma's 1999 elegy in the BBC charity telethon for *Red Nose Day* "The Curse of the Fatal Death": "Doctor, listen to me. [W]e all need you to listen to me […] we all need you, and you simply cannot die." In 1963, Sydney Newman envisioned a wanderer amongst the stars; the Doctor quickly became a proactive character who balks against the Time Lords' strict policy of non-interference—by 2015, showrunner Steven Moffat has given us a chap who, simply put, saves people.

Early efforts of the program and its production team at teaching history were earnest, and the production crew expected writers and script-editors to do their homework, even in comedies. Several of *Doctor Who*'s writers have had degrees or a background in history, including John Lucarotti ("Marco Polo," 1964) and Louis Marks ("Masque of Mandragora," 1976), who had a Ph.D. from Oxford. Lack of formal education did not preclude historical knowledge among the writers, however, and reflects, too, what could be appreciated by the audience: although Dennis Spooner was forced to leave school at a young age, his initial draft-script for the serial "The Reign of Terror" was praised by David Whitaker for its excellence and depth in the treatment of the subject matter. His follow-up script of "The Romans" hit all the marks required for a screen-version of Rome and assumes the audience is conversant in the general history of the period. Similarly, history enthusiast Donald Cotton drew up a detailed crib sheet outlining the timeline and information on contemporary Greek culture that accompanied his drafts and script of "The Myth Makers" (1965), a document that is preserved in the BBC Written Archives. The BBC were pleased to receive mostly positive feedback from schoolteachers at the time of the early serials; there were, however, some complaints from viewers of too many liberties taken and too much frivolity in the storytelling as well, something Sydney Newman had been quite against. Presenting history to the masses, however, has always been a tricky business, as the first century AD Roman historian Tacitus himself observes complaining that one's audience is far more eager to hear (and to believe) scandal and crime, and distrusts the historian who "curries favor" (Tac., *Hist.* 1.1).

In December 1963 Donald Baverstock, BBC's chief of programs, authorized the making of an additional ten episodes of *Doctor Who*, meaning that there would be 36 in total in the first series. He used this as an opportunity both to request an outline of the future stories and to criticize what he had already seen, asking Sydney Newman to "brighten up the logic and inventiveness of the scripts." In particular, he concluded, "I suggest that you should make efforts in future episodes to reduce the amount of slow prosaic dialogue and to centre the dramatic movement much more on historical and scientific hokum" (WAC T5/647/1). Yet after "The Romans," *Doctor Who* would screen only seven more "pure" historicals: four of them during William Hartnell's era, two in Patrick Troughton's, and the last during Peter Davison's tenure, 1982's two-part "Black Orchid," touted as the first "pure historical" since "The Highlanders" in 1966. Pseudo-historicals became, and have remained, the norm—the travelers land in the midst of a well-known historical era where they might interfere (or not) in the course of events as the storyline requires it. In addition, they might meet up with someone famous (as seen far more in the revival of the series)—Tom Baker's Doctor was almost ever meeting Leonardo ("Masque of Mandragora," 1976 and "City of Death," 1979); Colin Baker, who had H.G. Wells as a stowaway in the TARDIS in 1985's "Timelash," got to work side-by-side with George Stephenson in "The Mark of the Rani" (1985). Historical settings become sometimes merely the backdrop for the story so that a sinister plan of alien meddling in human history might be revealed; sometimes, however, the plot hinges on disruption of the timeline, and the Doctor and his companions must heroically and responsibly set straight history as it is known at the time of transmission (despite the Time Lord code of non-intervention), otherwise chaos will ensue: hence the Fourth Doctor shows Sarah Jane the apocalyptic wasteland of her home-era 1970s Earth if the evil Sutekh is left to run amok in 1911 in "Pyramids of Mars" (1975); the Fifth Doctor must sort out the Master's plan to prevent the Magna Carta from ever being sealed (even as he admits it's a rather petty and small-minded bit of terrestrial interference on the part of the Master) in 1983's "The Kings Demons." The first real instance of the Doctor dealing with a meddler in history comes, however, during the First Doctor's tenure in 1965's "The Time Meddler," when a rogue member of the Doctor's people (we don't learn they're called Time Lords until 1969's "The War Games") amuses himself simply by messing about in 11th-century England: his grand scheme is to equip Harold II's army with modern weapons so that they can not only easily defeat the Vikings at Stamford Bridge in September 1066, but then wipe out William of Normandy's invading force at Hastings two weeks later—for no other reason it seems than to behave as a naughty schoolboy. His light-hearted twist to time travel intrigued and delighted viewers (BBC Audience Research quoted in Howe and Walker 1998, 63) and, like the Daleks, he makes a quick return to the program (in "The Daleks' Master Plan," 1965–1966). The Monk's approach to history is in contrast to the arguably dull and worthy one put forward by the Doctor in "The Aztecs" (1964) when he tells Barbara that they must not interfere in the progress of history. Later on in the program's own history, this sideline career as the protector of Earth's past is circumnavigated by the argument that certain elements are fixed in time and cannot be disrupted or interfered with. Which ones? The ones most convenient to the plot. Poor Adric.[2]

In 2015, a decade into the reboot of the program, figures from both history and folklore populate "celebrity historicals." Russell T. Davies envisioned that the inclusion of real people from the past would lend not only continuity but legitimacy to the series as a whole. As a consequence, Christopher Eccleston's Doctor teamed up with Charles Dickens in a story conjoined with Dickens' real-life predilections with the supernatural in "The Unquiet Dead" (2005), rationalizing strange, ghostly doings as in fact a rift between dimensions; David Tennant's Doctor hobbed with nobs such as Shakespeare ("The Shakespeare Code," 2007), and enjoyed dallying with not only Madame de Pompadour ("The Girl in the Fireplace," 2006) but also Queen Elizabeth I—apparently quite intimately judging from his *braggadocio* in "The End of Time" (2009) if not actually following through with his courtship in "Day of the Doctor" (2013). His relationships with Queen Victoria ("Tooth and Claw," 2006) and Agatha Christie ("The Unicorn and the Wasp," 2008) were, on the other hand, strictly platonic. Matt Smith's Doctor has brought on board as a companion Egyptian queen Nefertiti (with hints that she's traveled with him for a while in "Dinosaurs on a Spaceship," 2012), and has befriended Winston Churchill ("Asylum of the Daleks," 2012) and Vincent Van Gogh ("Vincent and the Doctor," 2010), and he has accidently married Marilyn Monroe ("A Christmas Carol," 2010). Peter Capaldi's Doctor has had an adventure with Robin Hood, much to his annoyance, insisting throughout that Robin was *not* a real person, and consequently there must be a more sinister force behind the scenes in "Robot of Sherwood" (2014)—neatly tying the show back to the 1966 Patrick Troughton serial set in the Land of Make-Believe, 1968's "The Mind Robber." The knowing argument here, of course, is how a folkloric character is created from bits and pieces culled from historical sources, and the "search for Robin Hood" much like the search for the real King Arthur (his relatives, at least, who appear in 1989's "Battlefield"), inquires after the creation of historical and cultural narrative as a reflection of the author's own setting.

But there is far more to *Doctor Who* than historical name-dropping. The program engages with history in multifarious ways and can therefore reveal much about how history is practiced, produced, consumed and remediated. The essays in this volume cover a diverse range of academic approaches including media studies, reception theory, fan studies, and education. They engage not only with the content of televised episodes and serials, but also other media including original fiction, audio plays and fan reconstructions. The goal of this collection is that it speaks both to the program and to history as a subject area, drawing on and identifying appropriate historiographical methods and debates, and encouraging further thoughtful debate and discussion. The volume is divided into four themed parts.

The essays in the first part, "Television as History: Inform and Entertain," evaluate how the program affords education to audiences through entertainment and distinguishes between the dissemination of classical history through school and books and that of "public history." Dene October's essay considers *Doctor Who*'s depiction of "Marco Polo," the fourth serial in the show's history and the first "lost" one; he explores the decision to present the story of the Doctor and his companions as observers in the company of, and through the narrative focus upon, the explorer Marco Polo in China, asking after the historical process of remediation in piecing together how audiences adapt and retell the story through different media. The essay asks how fan reconstructions use media as an immersive tool in re-experiencing television nostalgically or alternatively to wake viewers to how media shapes historical content and, indeed, memory of missing stories. The second essay in this part by Aven McMaster and Mark Sundaram examines the use of classical history and mythology in the show and how it reflects changing educational practices and its relationship to class structure in Britain from the 1960s through to the present day; the authors explore how the show relies on the audience having some pre-knowledge of events, how reference to classical history can be seen as a means to understand connections between class and education in Britain, and British attitudes towards imperialism and its own history. History is never neutral but always framed by the ways that particular histories are intentionally and unintentionally remembered and forgotten. The final essay in this part considers the implications of British colonialism in light of the program's 50-year history. Susana Loza's essay examines how the show has been fabricating and exporting British fears and fantasies to the rest of the world. The discussion here looks at how the program's ideas and imagery related to Empire and post-colonialism have evolved and changed since the 1960s, particularly in the context of attitudes towards race and immigration in post-colonial and multicultural Britain, taking as its case study modern episodes featuring the characters of the Ood. All three essays in part one reflect on how the use of historical reference reinforces popular British historical worldviews if not its self-image.

Part two, "Historical Drama: Genre and Conventions," examines how television drama negotiates issues of historical fidelity through literary and artistic conventions. In particular, the essays here reflect on the shift to genre as *pure historicals* that inevitably give way to *pseudo* ones. The first essay in this part by Carey Fleiner looks as 1965's "The Romans," an early historical that reflects this transition: Nero is the key figure here, and he is played more as a folkloric, comedic villain than an historical character; the serial's author relies not so much on the audience's academic knowledge of the Julio-Claudian period, but rather what they have gleaned from recent popular portrayals of the Romans, including Peter Ustinov's Nero of *Quo Vadis* (1956), HollyRome blockbuster *Cleopatra* (1963), and the West End debut of *A Funny Thing Happened on the Way to the Forum* (1963). Ramie Tateishi's essay on 1966's "The Gunfighters" continues the theme of how audience expectation of a particular historical era and genre of storytelling affect the portrayal of its historical-cum-folkloric figures. If the adventure with Nero and the Doctor was played as a farce, here Tateishi demonstrates how "The Gunfighters" continues the slippage away from the original directive of "pure historicals," framing the story with a narrative ballad, and expands on the typical depiction of the American West as an already-mythologized version of real-life events. The final essay in this part by Andrew O'Day looks at 1984's "The Awakening" in which a modern-day village takes a traditional May Day festival and subverts it into something more sinister due to the outside influence of an alien being. The story and the essay consider the use and misuse of history in storytelling, a compelling meta-fictional reflection of the show's treatment of history, as there is presented a conflict between a history teacher (who is terrified of the misuse of history by her fellow villagers) and the villagers compelled to act out a deadly version of an historic tradition. O'Day ties the themes of this part together as he reflects on how history, popular conception, and the influence of an alien outside of that history are interwoven in a single story.

The historical timeline established by *Doctor Who* on television is not entirely secure from reimagining by new episodes or via the paratextual and transmedia environment within which alternative books and audios challenge the canon. The third part in this volume considers "Historical Constructions/Reconstructions." Rhonda Knight's essay looks at the theoretical "Season 6B" where the Second Doctor does not regenerate immediately, but rather goes on to have adventures as a Gallifreyan agent. Rather than the televised adventures, her essay explores novels that, while officially outside of the *Doctor Who* canon, place the Doctor in an alternate history in which Germany won World War II, in which the Doctor prevents the assassination of Winston Churchill, and in which he visits the Napoleonic era; all three case studies explore the use of history as a means of the powerful to exploit their positions and power. Karen Hellekson also explores the idea of alternate history in her essay: she complements Knight in that she illustrates how science fiction uses history to create and explore alternative timelines. In her essay, she looks at "what ifs" that occur in the Doctor's own history, again using as her case studies media outside of the televised adventures—what if the Sixth Doctor had lost his trial? What if the Doctor and Susan had never left Gallifrey? What if the program *Doctor Who* itself had never been made? All of these questions are supported by material taken from novels and audio adventures. Finally, the third essay in this part considers the adaptation of myth—in this case, that of the Norse—into the history and shaping of the Doctor's own mythology within the program. Here Marcus K. Harmes looks at how Viking history is adapted into the *Doctor Who* canon in "The Greatest Show in the Galaxy" (1988) and "Curse of Fenric" (1989)—a key difference being that Norse myth is preoccupied with the destruction of the world, but that the Doctor always saves the day, subverting if not averting the ultimate fulfillment of Norse belief.

Finally, history is personal. It narrates who we have been, presents a mirror for our reflection, and offers us a glimpse of our potential. The essays in this final part, "History and Identity," consider the reflection of image and self-awareness within *Doctor Who* in both the original era of the series and its subsequent reboot. Kristine Larsen's essay looks at the depictions of Neanderthal culture in *Doctor Who*, especially in the removal of Neanderthal man from his historical context and placing of him within another: her case studies from both televised adventures as well as novels and comics demonstrate how the show wrestles with such questions as what it means to be human, what it means to be "the other" or the "outsider." Peter Lowe's examination of the village and its symbolism of England and Englishness continues this idea of identity and considers what might lie beneath the surface of our safest self-images: the idea of the village idyll under threat by industrialization has been the subject of popular culture in Britain in, for example, the writings of J. B. Priestley in the 1930s and of the lyrics of popular music groups such as The Kinks in the late 1960s and 1970s: Lowe examines this phenomenon in the context of the adventures of the Third Doctor. The *Doctor Who* of the 1970s, he argues, deconstructs the cultural-historical myth of the quiet order of the village to reveal darker forces at work—and, as O'Day also notes, these forces are the work of outsiders. Outsiders are not the only agency that might meddle with our homes and hearth; we humans ourselves have the potential to ignore the effects of our invention and meddling with nature on our own well-being. Thus the final essay in this part is Mark Wilson's look at 1963's "Planet of the Giants" and how it fits in the environmental history and changing self-image of post-war Britain; as he notes, it is especially significant that the story takes place on Earth, since it reflects an early instance of the Doctor "going green" and a response to contemporary environmental themes brought to the public consciousness by works such as Rachel Carson's *Silent Spring* (1962).

Doctor Who's stories and characters not only consider history, but itself also has a long history and has become part of our collective identity. The essays here join and complement a rich and growing field of study and exploration. There have been many histories written about the program. Indeed, the fortnightly part-work *Doctor Who—The Complete History* (Hachette) examines its production and reception, however most of the material has been taken and modified from *Doctor Who Magazine* back issues (1980 onwards) and the themed *DWM bookazines* (Panini, 2013 onwards). This resource tends to focus on an episode at a time and rarely attempts to understand material as part of the wider broadcast, cultural or historical context. The fan interest in production history is demonstrated by BBC DVD releases frequently containing extra filmed material relevant to the specific serial or the series; these have been documented by *The Classic Doctor Who DVD Compendium* (Wonderful Books, 2014). Many other books attempt to critically evaluate 50 years of programs by creating lists or "best of" selections. A good example of this is *Who's 50: 50 Doctor Who Stories to Watch Before You Die* (ECW Press, 2013) which focuses its critical lens on the thematic content and production notes for episodes. Critically acclaimed "guides" include Sandifer's *Tardis Eruditorum* series (CreateSpace, 2014), which began life as a blog, Shearman and Hadoke's *Running Through Corridors* series, written by program insiders, and Woods and Miles *About Time* series (Mad Norwegian Press, 2006), which attempts to situate episodes retrospectively in relation to other episodes and paratexts. Occasionally, such publications are able to stitch in wider cultural comment but do not develop critiques of broadcast histories nor attempt rigorous or methodologically focused examination of the cultural contexts of episodes.

Tulloch and Alvarado's *The Unfolding Text* (St. Martin's Press, 1983) was the first serious analysis of the program which sought to examine it through an institutional lens. Of the many program guides available, John Kenneth Muir's *A Critical History of Doctor Who on Television* (McFarland, 1999/2008) also reflects critically on the themes that shape the program's stories. Other such titles include *Contents & Contexts of Doctor Who* (Pop Matters, 2016) which includes Dene October's essay "That's Not Right: Television, History and Education during the Hartnell Era" on the BBC audience as a critical witness to "public history." The program as media history is investigated through particular media contexts such as narrative, adaptations studies, soundtracks, and so forth, for example, Harmes' *Doctor Who and the Art of Adaptation* (Rowman & Littlefield, 2014). From the perspectives of audience and reception studies, there is an increase in titles such as Tulloch and Jenkins' *Science Fiction Audiences: Watching Doctor Who and Star Trek* (Routledge, 1995) particularly in the area of fan studies. Booy's *Love and Monsters* (I.B. Tauris, 2012), for example, attempts a historical account of *Doctor Who* fandom as it changes and influences the program.

Since Tulloch's *The Unfolding Text*, many academic titles have sought to study how social forces operate on the program. The issues of class and gender have since been investigated by titles such as Britton's *Tardisbound* (I.B. Tauris, 2011) while race, imperialism and colonization are tackled in Orthia's collection *Doctor Who and Race* (Intellect, 2013). Decker's *Who Is Who* (I.B. Tauris, 2013) and Lewis and Smithka's *Bigger on the Inside* (Open Court, 2011) place the themes of the program into metaphysical and philosophical considerations while psychoanalytical treatments of episodes are provided by MacRury and Rustin's *The Inner World of Doctor Who: Psychoanalytic Reflections in Time and Space* (Karnac, 2013). David Layton's *The Humanism of Doctor Who: A Critical Study in Science Fiction and Philosophy* (McFarland, 2012) makes a strong case for challenging any notion that the Doctor is a mythic or magical being.

History as a tool of analysis is occasionally employed by individual authors within edited volumes. Edited volumes are targeted more obviously toward undergraduates, such as Butler's *Time and Relative Dissertations in Space* (Manchester University Press, 2007). These volumes usually have quite broad academic interests, such as Hansen's *Ruminations, Peregrinations, and Regeneration* (Cambridge, 2010) and Garner and Beattie's *Impossible Worlds, Impossible Things: Cultural Perspectives on Doctor Who, Torchwood and The Sarah Jane Adventures* (Cambridge, 2010). Else they may focus on specific themes, such as language, but employ a range of approaches and methodologies, e.g., Barr and Mustachio's *The Language of Doctor Who: From Shakespeare to Alien Tongues* (Rowman & Littlefield, 2014), including Dene October's examination of the language used by the original Doctor in "What's He Talking About: Performativity and the First Doctor."

Finally, it will surely not have escaped the reader's attention that there is a great deal of publishing activity surrounding *Doctor Who*, particularly responding to the 50th anniversary of the program in 2013. Books aimed at the general audience of the 2005 reboot of the program tend to be summative evaluations of specific seasons or auteur tenures, such as Russell T. Davies' *The Writer's Tale* (BBC, 2008). Books targeting fans include titles from independent publishers—such as *Companion Piece: Women Celebrate the Aliens, Humans and Tin Dogs of Doctor Who* (Mad Norwegian Press, 2015)—and mainstream ones such as *Doctor Who Fan Phenomena* (Intellect, 2013). Besides the continuing publishing activity, a further importance of such books lies in the considerable crossover appeal between *Doctor Who* fans and academics for material aiming to put the program into wider cultural contexts. The term *acafan*, popularized by Hills' monograph *Fan Cultures* (Routledge, 2002), itself points to the shared interests of academics and fans both as writers and readers of critical material for cult programs like *Doctor Who*. Critical celebrations of the program, such as the upcoming *Twelfth Night* (Andrew O'Day, ed., I.B. Tauris, 2017) appeal to fans and academics and offer a range of approaches and critical viewpoints on an aspect of the show (here, seasons eight to 10). That fans are increasingly encouraged to make relationships between fictional texts and the wider culture is evidenced by Guerrier and Kukula's *The Scientific Secrets of Doctor Who* (BBC, 2015) where short stories are accompanied by critical commentaries.

Doctor Who had as part of its original plan historical stories—stories set in the past—to enlighten and entertain its audience. But it is unfair to dismiss the program as a budget-busting pastiche with the conceit of a time-traveling main character whose adventures represent a rummage through the BBC's props and costumes. *Doctor Who* has used history and historical characters as creatively as any of its science fiction and fantasy-orientated stories have created new worlds and new creatures for the Doctor and his companions to experience and explore. But the program is, after all, a drama and one of its strengths lies in adapting from sources not with the intention of fidelity but to tell a good story, one that sometime subverts the original source (as the Troughton story "The Evil of the Daleks," 1967, does with the much mythologized—and frequently revisited by the program—Victorian period). The idea of a "pure historical," that is, a story with no science fiction elements at all, was quickly superseded by so-called pseudo-historicals in the classic era of the program and then by the "celebrity-historicals" of the modern incarnation of the show. Nevertheless, as the show has evolved, so too has its dynamic engagement with historical elements. *Doctor Who* continues to educate and inform audiences 50-plus years since its first broadcast in November 1963, one day after John F. Kennedy's assassination which destabilized the audience's sense of time and order and connected the cultural with the televisual (since events meant the first episode had to be quickly repeated). Yet the relationship of broadcast history to history as theme and methodology is in need of scholarly appraisal. This collection brings together several authors under the common goal of extrapolating one of the major themes of the show and exploring what it means to travel historically, to engage with and debate the historical, and to discuss what *Doctor Who* can do with and for history.

We invite our readers to join with us on our adventures in history—perhaps it is impossible simply to observe dispassionately. The Eleventh Doctor (Matt Smith) once insisted to his companion Amy Pond (Karen Gillan), "We are observers only. That's the one rule I've always stuck to, in all my travels. I never get involved in the affairs of other peoples or planets" ("The Beast Below," 2010). He immediately, of course, gets stuck into the affairs of other people. The goal of this collection is that its essays speak both to the program and to history as a subject area, draw on and identify appropriate historiographical methods and debates, and encourage further meddling by our readers through thoughtful debate and discussion. These 12 essays are also a gateway to adventures with "this man … [who] has a time machine. Up and down history he goes, zip, zip, zip, zip, zip—getting into scrapes" ("Before the Flood," 2015). Time, then, to travel back in history, and get stuck in.

NOTES

1. Newman's reactions to the "Doctor-as-Santa" proposal and other writers' pipedreams are penciled into the margins of one document in the BBC Written Archive; he comments that such ideas are "silly and condescending ... it doesn't get across the basis of teaching or educational experience—drama based upon and stemming from factual material and scientific phenomenon and actual social history of past and future" (WAC T5/647/1 Dr Who General 1963).

2. The sadly fated companion of the Fifth Doctor, who sacrificed himself in "Earthshock" (1982) by manning his station on a doomed spaceship, hijacked by the Cybermen to crash into the earth and wipe out the dinosaurs. Despite the sorrow of his companions, who beg him to go back in time to rescue the teenager, the Doctor refuses and admonishes them for asking him to abuse his capabilities of traveling in time and space, even for a noble cause.

BIBLIOGRAPHY

Corfield, Penelope J. n.d. "Why History Matters." Making History. http://www.history.ac.uk/makinghistory/resources/articles/why_history_matters.html. Accessed July 2015.

Howe, David, J., and Stephen James Walker. 1998. *Doctor Who: The Television Companion*. London: BBC Books.

Tacitus. 1992. *The Histories*. Trans. C.H. Moore. Cambridge: Harvard University Press.

Tulloch, J., and M. Alvarado. 1983. *Doctor Who: The Unfolding Text*. New York: St. Martin's Press.

WAC T5/647/1 Dr Who General 1963.

Wood, T., and L. Miles. 2006. *About Time: The Unauthorized Guide to Doctor Who: 1963–1966, Seasons 1 to 3*. Des Moines: Mad Norwegian Press.

Journeys through Cathay
Remediation and Televisuality in "Marco Polo"

DENE OCTOBER

Introduction: "Through the air" (Ian)

In 1964, *Doctor Who* presented its first historical serial, only four stories into the show's run. As episode one opens, an interloper threatens to abduct the Doctor's spaceship, unsettle narrative conventions and steal the scenes. "How does it move?" he asks, mistaking the TARDIS for a caravan. "Through the air," answers the Doctor's companion, science teacher Ian Chesterton (William Russell). This conversation parallels the serial's real-life transmission through media: first as the broadcast episode and then, as the tapes were lost from the archives, through fans' off-air audio recordings and reconstructions. It also exemplifies what 1960s media theorist Marshall McLuhan means in coining the phrase "the medium is the message" (1964); different media delivers—and shapes—content differently. Just as the narratives of historical events shape how the past is told and received, so, too, does the medium alter the shape of the account and our perception of events—whether it is a documented historical occurrence or the presentation of a now-lost television show. The reconstruction of fact and fiction changes not only its content but how we are able to make sense of and recall it; media changes content and also changes us. This essay tackles the idea of the *nachleben* of an historical event, its re-presentation in media forms as shedding light on its presentation as part of family entertainment on the BBC in the 1960s, as well as how audiences respond to and use that media—how immersed within or critically aware of it they are—and how memory mediates these relationships. The remediation of "Marco Polo" as "public history" and subsequent official and fan reconstructions of an episode now physically lost, make this *Doctor Who* serial equally as fascinating as those of the Venetian merchant himself.

13

The aforementioned conversation between the TARDIS intruder and Ian reveal that the intruder is indeed the famed explorer Marco Polo (1254–1324), whose travels from Italy to China have been of great public interest since being co-written in collaboration with Rustichello da Pisa (1272–1300) some seven hundred years ago. Marco Polo's *Travels* have themselves traveled across media and culture. They have been translated, redacted and remediated as biographies, films, music and television dramas. There is much value in studying all manifestations of Marco Polo's *Travels* across their various oral, print and digital forms as remediation is defined as the logic by which media refashion each other (Bolter and Grusin 1999), but is not exclusively concerned with moving content from old to new media (e.g., analogue to digital transfer). This is a particularly useful definition given that "Marco Polo" (a.k.a. and hereafter referred to as "Serial D")[1] only exists today in the forms of script, novelization, "tele-photos" and audio soundtrack, media which fans have exploited in their attempts to reconstruct the serial in televisual form. Meanwhile, the remediation of Marco Polo's travelogue as a *time-travelogue* draws attention to travel as both trope and metaphor, prompting us to reflect upon how media-specificity shapes audience experience. When Ian tells Marco (Mark Eden) that their "caravan" travels in time and space he reminds us of the First Doctor's (William Hartnell) comparison of TARDIS to television: "by showing an enormous building on your television screen, you can do what seemed impossible" ("An Unearthly Child," 1963).

Along with the TARDIS, the Venetian consequently usurps center stage away from the time-traveler to become the principal narrator for much of "Serial D"; he and the television Doctor become what Jacobs (2003) calls "reflector pairs," that is, characters who articulate "dimensions of their predicament, identity or situation that is reflected back" acutely to others (Jacobs 2003, 14). Both are nomadic exiles as well as instruments of public history in that they beguile audiences with improbable tales; as such they are afforded ambiguous narrative agencies in critically engaging their audience through stylized delivery of content. These stylizations, realized through redactions and new medialities, such as from television script to camera-work,[2] shape audience experience and, considered as part of the wider pan-cultural "Travels," identify "Marco Polo" as an unfolding history, one that enables critical engagement and narrative adaptation.

"Ping-Cho is a good story-teller" (Marco): History and Narrative

In the third episode of "Serial D," "Five Hundred Eyes," comes a dramatic hiatus in the unfolding narrative. After Mongol warlord Tegana (Darren Nesbitt) purposely spills the gourds of water that the traveling caravan (which now includes the time-travelers) is reliant upon, and Marco requisitions the TARDIS, the narrative flow comes to an abrupt halt as Ping-Cho (Zienia Merton) recounts the tale of "Ala-eddin and the Hashashins," a performance which mixes poetry recital with intricate body gestures. This interruption is unusual in the midst of viewers' expectations of typical television storytelling. Ping-Cho's carefully planned dance illuminates the teller as much as the tale, something Ian picks up on immediately in quizzing Susan (Carole Ann Ford) about the English derivation of the word "Hashashins." Ian's teacherly question is in many ways a remediation of the Chinese girl's poem, one he perhaps feels improves, remedies or corrects the previous version (to apply the term's common use); that is, it repeats the content but through a familiar medium. Ping-Cho and Ian are both educators yet each explore different media which reflects the program's challenges in delivering historical content to a mixed family audience.

Doctor Who's commitment to historical awareness followed the spirit of John Reith, the first Director-General of the BBC (1927 to 1938), whose vision of a national consensus included the use of television as an emergent public agency where broadcast awakened people to consider their own point of view rather than simply to absorb "the dictated and partial versions of others" (Reith 1925, 4). Yet, outside the corporation, others distrusted visual media such as television (Williams 2004, 31) and feared the dumbing down of content—frequently educators were quick to complain where they felt the BBC undermined "the lessons given at school" (Bignell 2009, 11). Although the *Doctor Who* writers' guide urged writers to pursue the latest historical (and indeed scientific) research,[3] the program was a particular focus for ire because of its mission statement to alternate between stories of science fiction and those that were categorized as the so-called "pure historical" (i.e., a story that places the TARDIS crew into an historical event with no science fiction elements). Even if the BBC appeared to proffer a purist view of the latter, educators feared the program's seriality, populism, adaptive tendency and latent transmediality; they worried that historical accuracy would be diluted if retold for entertainment purposes.[4]

The logic of teaching history through television would eventually lead (beginning with the 1965 serial "The Time Meddler") to what fans have dubbed the "pseudo-historical" where anachronistic elements are not only acknowledged by characters, but are also incorporated into the serial's adaptation of history. Consequently, the Doctor increasingly abandons his role of historical gate-keeper and takes up the narrative function of hero—frequently he even instigates historical change. Indeed, like the Meddling Monk (Peter Butterworth) in the aforementioned serial, audiences came to demand more science fiction elements. Viewer letters to the BBC at the time were mainly about the Daleks (BBC WAC T5/649/1), and serials featuring these fearsome beings tended to trump "the boring detail of maps and commentary."[5] In this respect, the early version of Hartnell's Doctor embodies BBC Head of Drama Sydney Newman's traditional view of history as unmediated, immutable and faithful to the historical record. Ironically, it is this conservative position which burdened Reith's hopes for audience agency, stalling an active engagement by presenting television history as evidence of history and failing to recognize how its representations arise in "specific production" and "reception contexts" (Wheatley 2007, 4).

"Serial D," the first *Doctor Who* historical, is an odd model of adaptive fidelity because what we know about the merchant traveler is almost exclusively mediated through the hybridized and stylized chronicle of his travels, one disputed immediately upon its reception, and obscured further by scholarly intervention over the years. The medieval vernacular text itself has been widely disseminated through various translations, redactions and popular remediation (opera, films, television drama) and therefore subject to revisions and cultural insertions that left academic history prone to the inaccuracies and narrative inflation long before Edison and Logie-Baird ever realized their inventions. Nevertheless, there has been a tendency in scholarship to fence the past off from public engagement (Ellis 1997, 22), taking an elitist academic stance in determining issues of canon construction (Creeber 2004, xv), "models of historical thinking" and the veracity of "the individual historian's thesis" (Turnock 2007, 9). When television is made in this sneering view, it may on the one hand promote engaging historical content, but on the other, it also occludes material considered irrelevant to the non-scholar, such as how programs source and research history, masking historiographical controversy, and giving prominence to the authority of the expert and apparently "omniscient presenter" (Stearn 2002, 26).

Whereas the Doctor embodies the traditional view of asserting a constative history, that is, where he states and describes an unequivocal view of past events, we may nevertheless discern from other characters, such as Ping-Cho (and Barbara in historical stories such as "The Aztecs," 1964 and "The Reign of Terror," 1964—see October 2016) that history is performative, and therefore revised through its retelling. For John Hartley, television is a transmodern mode of teaching "lay" audiences "television knowledge" (Hartley 1999, 41). The gathering of populations to witness history (Turnock 2007, 5) "by seeing" promotes experiential learning (Williams 1990, 74) and, as "public history" (drama), helps viewers perceive the world anew in a way that factual programming cannot, foregrounding emotional engagements with the past that are "complex and unstable" (de Groot 2009, 3–4). Television history, as a public mode of consumption, observes the need for "social" knowledge (Samuel 1994, 8), and exploration of narrative causality (Ellis 2014, 13–14), in making structural coherence of "a web of historical meanings and experiences" (de Groot 2009, 13).

As Hegel says in "Lectures on the Philosophy of History," history is a narration of the past; "it means both *res gestae* (the things that happened) and *historia rerum gestarum* (the narration of things that happened)" (1984, 97). Ping-Cho's performed poetry and Ian's formal teaching both qualify as history through Hegel's definition, yet only the former medium really conforms to Hartley's transmodernism. When Ping-Cho asks the travelers to "pray attend me while I tell my tale" (Lucarotti 1964, episode 4/shot 14)[6] she invites the viewers to understand her role as mediator in organizing narrative events into a media-specific—in this case, stylized dance and poetry—coherence. As Sorlin says of the media documentary, the narrator's voice functions to "remind viewers that somebody is telling this story, and telling it in a certain way" (Sorlin 1990, 32). Remediation, when it discloses how it shapes content, acknowledges itself as media. As with Ping-Cho's dance, "Serial D" can be viewed as a self-conscious construction, an attempt to show the past expressed through different voices.

"Like a familiar voice" (Marco):
Remediating Stories

In the novelization of the serial, Marco Polo identifies Ping-Cho as a good storyteller. This may be true but it is more precise to argue that she provides a convenient medium for emphasizing particular content in the story. Furthermore, this switch in narrative device alerts the audience that the TARDIS travelers are in a different time and a different culture to their own. This is a fact brought home to the audience in episode two, "The Singing Sands," when Susan and Ping-Cho become disorientated during a storm in the Gobi Desert, their own voices lost in an affective piece of sound design comprised of string tremolos and distorted radio noise (reminiscent of the *BBC Radiophonic Workshop*, who rendered Ron Grainer's theme music and provided much of the familiar electronic incidental music and sound effects to *Doctor Who*). At this point, the sands themselves demand to be heard, sounding like "all the devils in hell were laughing" and then "musical instruments being played" (Lucarotti 1964, 2/16).[7] Each character interprets the sound as a familiar voice, and subsequently becomes lost. Similarly, for the audience at home, it is Marco's guiding narrative voice which acts as an anchor in this strange historical time and place. In truth, stories may be conveyed in many different forms, some adding weight to particular dramatic or discursive purposes. Similarly, characters are convenient mediums for communicating particular messages: just as Ping-Cho articulates a 1960s Western outlook on arranged marriage[8] so Marco is the mediator between East and West. As in the sandstorm, our perception of events may be led by the familiarity of a voice.

Marco Polo was and is a familiar and inspirational figure, whose story was chosen for *Doctor Who* because it brought to life and gave a narrative voice to the character said to have captured the imagination of Kublai Khan and stirred the young Christopher Columbus to travel. The tales of his journey have fascinated the general public in the West from the 13th century onwards and been a popular subject with medieval historians—inspiring monographs, biographies, period studies, translations and philological studies. He remains firmly entrenched in modern popular culture thanks to the merchandising industry which has used him—and audience familiarity with his story—to brand an array of modern commercial products and services ranging from travel companies through to cars. His name is part of American culture in the form of a popular swimming game in which one child attempts a blind search for the missing explorer crying out "Marco" while the other children respond by calling "Polo." He's been the subject of films and television shows such as Archie Mayo's *The Adventures of Marco Polo* (1938) starring Gary Cooper, Guliano Montaldo's television mini-series *Marco Polo* (1982) with Burt Lancaster, and most recently the Netflix series *Marco Polo* (2014) which, like *Doctor Who*, deployed a transient team of writers and directors to put together as lush and epic a story as their respective budgets would allow.

Doctor Who's treatment of the explorer's story is part of a long and rich tradition of study and interpretation. Marco Polo's chronicles have appeared in various editions with titles such as *The Travels of Marco Polo* and *The Description of the World*. There survive more than 140 medieval manuscripts which have been recopied, set in text, and translated into numerous European languages; it is still readily available in print, an example of a medieval vernacular text with a continuous reception over the past seven centuries. Simon Gaunt, one of Marco's many medievalist scholars, has noted that most scholarly attention paid to the traveler has focused on the content of the stories rather than on style of presentation (Gaunt 2013, 10). Studying the French-Italian redaction in particular, he argues that *Le Devisement du Monde* exploits narrative styles and techniques to "create its own textual dynamic" (Gaunt 2013, 11). The form that the narrative takes in the *Devisement* has largely been attributed to Rustichello da Pisa, the Italian writer of romantic prose with whom Marco was imprisoned in Genoa on his return to Europe in 1298, and with whom he collaborated, writing in French—an interesting choice, as neither man were native speakers, but regarded French as the language best suited to international mobility (*ibid.*, 36). The *Devisement*'s genre has been widely debated—it has been variously described as a merchant's manual, an encyclopedia, a travel journal, a book of marvels and a crusading tract—marking it as a *protean* and *chameleon* text (*ibid.*, 33). This genre-blurring, along with stylistic treatments like language hybridity and mixed-authorship, with its implications for who speaks and when, for Gaunt, creates an ambiguous narrative experience and intervening agency, one that enables an active and critical readership.

Doctor Who's serial similarly invites and instantiates a critical audience interaction through its ambiguities of narrative voice, blurring of genres, compromised authorship, and inconsistent pattern of identification. Indeed, like the fan-reconstructions of it, it is already a hybrid text, the product of constant revisions and patchwork of available material ("bricolage"), as well as refashioning itself from an unavailable original source. This reconstruction or reshaping of the television broadcast can be called "remediation." In their influential study, Bolter and Grusin identify remediation as "the formal logic by which new media refashion prior media forms" (1999, 273). For the authors, the practice of remediation dates from the Renaissance, when artists used perspective to "dissolve" the surface of the painting and oil paint to "erase" brush strokes thereby satisfying a desire for immediacy; in the 19th century, one sees it as some artists used the new medium of photography to create artistic portraits, and then in the 20th and 21st century how film and television makers use their new medium to recreate stories that started life centuries ago simply as poetry recited around the fire. The core of the stories and audience expectation remain; the impact of the new media affects the story not only by reshaping its details to fit the current audience's expectations, but to affect the presentation through the particular physical characteristics of that medium itself. Remediation complements reception as both are forms through which media reproduce and comment upon and replace each other—and it is a process which adds as well as subtracts as the new medium replaces the old: Christian monks copied only those ancient texts which they felt were of use to their own needs (models of good grammar, for example, or sources of metaphor to use in religious dialogue), changing the original classical meanings; similarly, analogue purists argue that digital technology replaces the warmth and depth of analogue with sterile sound and picture. The process of remediation is governed by a "double logic" of the two seemingly paradoxical cultural logics of "immediacy" and "hypermediacy," that is, a dialectic produced by the cultural need to both multiply media and erase all signs of mediation (1999, 5).

In the context of its use here, remediation describes both the transfer of histories into *Doctor Who* television stories and *Doctor Who* television stories into alternative media, including the fan-reconstruction. As a process it highlights the dialectic between transparency, that is, an unmediated experience of the original, and hypermediacy, or an experience which causes the

medium to become visible. The tapes of the original serial have been wiped—
yet the legend of the serial itself lives on in the memories of those (including
this author) lucky enough to have seen and still remember the program on
original transmission, along with the many surviving tele-snaps (a mix of
black and white and color photographs) made at the time of production. Current fans have attempted to reproduce and reconstruct the lost serial through
modern media, such as YouTube, by marrying together these still images
with surviving, fan-made, off-air recordings of the serial's soundtrack. Such
reconstructions can be difficult for casual fans to watch, particularly those
who are hoping for an "authentic" viewing experience. Yet it is this very lack
of immediacy which keeps it within the purview of other fans, who participate
in discussion of such reconstructions at conventions, and through social
media, thereby distinguishing themselves from casual viewers. This hypermediacy also elevates "Marco Polo" from its originally intended purpose of
educating as well as entertaining its BBC audience more than 50 years ago
and takes the production and reconstruction of the broadcast to a different
level of appreciation if not appropriation. This approach brings us back to
the seminal work of media theorist Marshall McLuhan who coined the familiar phrase "the medium is the message" to identify how characteristics of the
medium, as well as content, communicate affects (1999, 9). Media are "make
happen" agents rather than "make aware" agents operating under closed systems and placing users into numb and narcotic states (McLuhan 1999, 47–
50); however, their multiplication—e.g. through reconstructions of missing
stories—draws attention to media and audience interactions.

"You stay here Susan" (Ian): Remediating the Static Image

I vividly recall watching this story back in 1964. It is not my memory
that Susan grimaces her way through "Serial D," yet, watching the (2002) *Loose
Cannon* version of "Marco Polo," this becomes my perception of her character.
Drawing from a relatively small image pool to create composite shots, and
editing them by appropriating the grammar of moving image, using pans and
zooms to repurpose the still images, this fan reconstruction is ultimately unable
to fully reform the static camera into the moving image it seeks to recapture
the essence of. Susan cringes understandably when the Doctor snaps at Ian
during the opening scene of episode one, "The Roof of the World," and again,
less explicably, when reunited with Barbara (Jacqueline Hill) and Ian after
getting lost in the desert storm in episode two, "The Singing Sands." The
effect of this is to promote viewer consciousness through an uncanny recognition, a repurposing that works against immediacy and "televisuality."

Traveling across Cathay required a particularly ambitious commitment to spectacle and camera-mobility putting extra pressure on the efficiency of Waris Hussein's camera runs and Barry Newbury's set design within BBC's smallest studio, Lime Grove D. The consequence is a storytelling that is always in the process of remediating static conventions and studio space. The mobile camera, for example, is only unobtrusive when it is "motivated," where its movement is triggered by actions, appropriately paced and purposefully directed towards the target action or actor (Holland 1997, 62); otherwise it risks drawing attention to the camera as the mediator of viewing agency. One instance of this is when the camera collides with a Zarbi in "Escape to Danger," episode three of "The Web Planet" (1965).[9] Media that draws attention to itself wakes the viewer from their immersion in content and serves rather as an agent to "make aware" those organizing voices of style and presentation.

The remediated *Doctor Who* text offers users modes of affective-engagement in the context of conscious nostalgia, that is, as a replacement "television event" for the lost serial. Like the great majority of *Doctor Who* serials, "Marco Polo" is available through a variety of medial forms such as Lucarotti's self-penned novelization (Target Books, 1984)—which remediates lost images into text form, allowing the travelogue aspects of *Marco Polo's Travels* to come to the fore in detailed descriptions of places and journeys— and the audio soundtrack, released on CD as part of *Doctor Who*'s 40th anniversary in 2003, which is presented with a choice of listening modes: with or without William Russell's added narrative links. While using these media, I often feel conflicted between desires of abandoning myself to the fantasy of televisuality and that of fan-academic vigilance (critical attention to style as well as content). The reproduction of media, and cultural desire to hide it, are "two seemingly contradictory logics [which] not only coexist … but are mutually dependent" (Bolter and Grusin 1999, 6). The soundtrack is at once memory site and amnesia, promising both documentation of the absent referent and immersion into a nostalgic televisuality.

Of the fan reconstructions, the version by *Whoflix* attempts to immerse audiences by "picking up the pace," eliminating the long silences where actors engage each other visually, focusing on Marco's narration and thereby reducing the seven episodes to just one hour. A condensed 30-minute reconstruction on "The Beginning" (DVD box set, 2006) also attempts to remediate what is often considered a slow, discursive storytelling, especially from the perspective of those audiences more conventionalized into post-classical editing with its time and space discontinuities and faster non-linear story-telling (Dancyger 2006). Such attempts to create immersive televisual experience operate through a contradictory logic, the alleviation of boredom a conscious indicator of an intrusive presentism. Nevertheless, this version by Derek

Handley, whose reconstructions for *Loose Cannon* are discussed below, is a nod to how fan-practices (and indeed fans themselves) inform "official" remediation practices.

Loose Cannon's (2002) reconstruction uses a range of photographic archive including composites from other stories and off-air color images,[10] a distraction according to some fans who are nevertheless struck by how the images situate viewers in television history: "the quality of these Sets are that good, that Colour is the best way to see them" says one reviewer on *The Doctor Who Ratings Guide*, an online site dedicated to fan reviews. A second *Loose Cannon* production (2013) made use of the newly discovered telesnaps,[11] photographs of the actual transmission which lend their aura to televisual immersion. Whereas the photograph is "a neat slice of time," as Sontag puts it, and "not a flow" (1977, 17), the reconstruction must somehow reverse this, borrowing the language of frame mobility and "focalization"[12] to restore the viewer's position in time and space. Using careful editing and image matching, zooms into and across the photographic frame, and synching of sound to image and story vicissitudes, the reconstruction attempts to erase itself as media but is unable to restore the viewer's embodiment of the mobile-camera and point-of-view shot. This interruption to immersion can be understood by reference to French philosopher Gilles Deleuze's (1925–1995) study of film which draws on his philosophies of repetition and difference. Deleuze's notion of "time-image" describes how film shapes time by splitting the present simultaneously into two directions, the future and the past, a split in time "that we see in the crystal" (Deleuze 2005, 81). The remediation of static-image into *faux* moving image cannot escape the memory of media-specificity where time is frozen rather than flows, drawing the viewer into a consciousness of mediality rather than immersion. Television continuity is immersive where the narrative runs smoothly, unfolding over the implied time thus extending the viewer's imaginative movement in and of the frame.

Not all reconstructions use post-production techniques to simulate camera-mobility. The *Who Recons* CGI version uses animation to reform the camera script into a *faux* video game environment. Many original camera operations in "Serial D" intended to sweep the viewer along through "motivated" camera movements, and establish "objective" point-of-view shots as a corrective to Marco's controlling, yet often mistaken, narratory observations (e.g., he is wrong in his support for Tegana and camera movement often undermines his subjective point-of-view in favor of the objective one of the audience). The medium of the video game emphasizes the embodied viewer and *Who Recons* uses additional shots, swaps the original's close-ups for mid to long shots to extend space, and adds new choices of camera angles. Looked at in light of the original, the advantages to this approach include being able to move characters freely and "create any set imaginable with no constraints

… which would not have been within the budget of *Doctor Who* at the time."[13] The efficacy of remediating the characters as game avatars is undermined, however, by the jerky motion of the images that distracts from the viewers' immersion in the story.

Regardless of their technical capabilities in repurposing the static photo, fans who repurpose may be caught between two impulses: on the one hand fan affective engagement often emerges as nostalgic and driven by the desire to restore the authentic televisual experience. On the other, however, fans also take up the responsibility to history and memory, in particular by using digital technologies to restore the archive that "official" keepers have dilapidated. Film footage for "Serial D" has been fully lost from the BBC archives since BBC Enterprises issued wipe/junk forms in 1967, meaning that the two-inch videotapes would no longer be retained; this and a later directive to overseas television stations to dispose of all film copies means that, despite sales to 25 countries (Molesworth 2013), the only footage that survives of "Marco Polo" is the reprise from "The Brink of Disaster" ("The Edge of Destruction," 1964). The use of archive images can therefore be understood as a reversal of the fan as resistant reader and illegal poacher, the figure popularized by books such as Henry Jenkins's *Textual Poachers* (1992), into fans as loyalists legitimately "rescuing essential elements" abused by those entrusted to maintain the text (Jenkins 2006, 41).

The assumption that viewers prefer immersion is tested by a survey of fans carried out by *Nothing at the End of the Lane*—a fanzine which describes itself as *The Magazine of Doctor Who Research & Restoration*. Fans' viewing practices were identified as varied, some preferring reconstructions which organized material around the heightening of immersive experience whereas others preferred to treat the reconstruction as a simulation, one that only adds "subtle touches to enhance watchability" (Robinson 1998, 20). Fans were divided over the degree of preferred televisuality with some seeking high production qualities and seamless editing—allowing them to imagine they are watching the "real thing"—and others motivated by the mediated and memorial qualities of the reconstruction, seeing the fanzine aesthetic as drawing attention to and activating the amateur historian's gaze, albeit through enhanced televisuality.

Nor is the activation of fan agency restricted to the pursuit of history and fan communication over archive management. Remediation reproduces content in new media regardless of factual or fictional credentials and can be made to serve partial or polemical purposes in the service of fan interests and critiques of official gatekeepers. Since its rediscovery, one tele-snap of TARDIS strapped upright to Marco's caravan (from "The Wall of Lies") has been used adaptively across several contexts, accompanying articles about missing stories in *Doctor Who Magazine*, videos about filming in Lime Grove

Studio D (Hussein 2005), online blog reviews, and of course fan reconstructions where the image is a reusable sign for the journey across Cathay. One example of this fan appropriation remediates the original tele-snap into a virtual postcard adding the following legend: "It's been a long ride but we'll soon be home from Cathay.... The Doctor."[14] This subversive use of the image in a new media context draws attention both to the diegetic journey within the story and extra-diegetic commentary upon how the story came to be lost. This fan-made image was distributed as a tweet, added to hashtag searches and threads, and spread by other fans in the context of conspiracy theories and spurious press reports suggesting "Marco Polo" was due for imminent release (Watts 2013). This fan remediation turns the trope of the journey into a meta-textual journey, where media, content and fan-memory are entangled in a nostalgic repurposing.

The "double logic of remediation" creates a scene of agency for the viewer which is at once the scene of erasure. *Doctor Who* fan reconstructions perhaps exhibit this logic more keenly by recreating the televisual event through a pluri-medial recycling of archival content—tele-snaps, audio, theme music, and so forth—in an attempt to harness the transparency, and therefore "unmediated" enjoyment of the missing serial. Yet the very multiplication of remedial agents also presents the viewer with the signs of memory as media. Simultaneous to their immersion, viewers catch themselves looking in the very window through which content is constructed. As with those singing sands, it is the media rather than the content that produces this opportunity for self-reflexivity and remembrance.

"A perfectly normal print" (Ian): Memory as Media

When TARDIS materializes on the Plain of Pamir in 13th-century imperial China, mysterious footprints are found in the snow, tracks leading to our misidentification of genre. For Susan, the prints belong to giants, to Barbara, they are from monsters, whereas the Doctor states blankly they make no impression on him at all. It is left to scientist Ian Chesterton to remind the audience they are not in a science fiction serial and posit that culture has already contaminated the simple record in the snow. In doing so, Ian also speaks to the challenges of fidelity and witness claims where the official archive is missing and remediated. How can we trust the evidence before our eyes? Indeed, our own journeys through Cathay are bound up with the mechanism for discovering it, because memory is, in a very real sense, media. This is immediately clear from the following provocative statement: without remediation our memory of the original fourth serial ceases to exist.

Memory is not just a facet of new media but also a feature of it. Whereas there has been a decline in the *Doctor Who* historicals, the current boom in historical content means most people experience memories of key historical events through television and social media (Warren 2013, 292). Pam Cook privileges the term memory over history because it has "connotations of subjectivity, individuality, the personal or private" as opposed to history, "with its persistent-popular cultural-connotations of objectivity, collectivity, public and social" (Kilbourn and Ty 2013, 23–24) whereas Kerwin Klein says that memory is sometimes used "as a synonym for history to soften our prose, to humanize it" (Klein 2000, 129). The boom in memory content and studies is a countervailing trend that privileges the aura of the archive object and claims "a sense of time and memory" (Huyssen 1995, 28) while promising to "rework history's boundaries" (Klein 2000, 128) through new conceptual models such as Halbwachs's (1992) notion of collective memory, which emphasizes social processes over personal ones, highlighting the importance of mediation in memory processes. Halbwachs's concept of the cultural mind is premised on memory as a continuous process aided by symbolic artifacts as mediators in creating "communality across both space and time" (Erll and Rigney 2009, 1). In this view, the cultural mind is a medial mind where memory circulates across transmedial and remedial practices shaping our position in the past and present.

The relationship between memory and media is made evident by metaphors that describe memory as media, e.g., photographic memory and computer memory, and therefore present memory as an augmentable reality with a physical integrity. The simple image of Marco writing up his journal promotes the integrity of the memory-mark and conveys the aura of authorship and originality. When Tegana challenges Marco to a mock dual (Lucarotti 1964, 2/70) it is clear that the fight is between the pen and the sword as mnemonic tools (gatekeepers). Marco's pen mediates and remediates, an avatar for history and memory as iterative processes. In his book *History as an Art of Memory* (1993), Patrick Hutton makes the observation that memory is characterized by repetition and recollection, the former engaging the "presence of the past," (Hutton 1993) with the latter engaging "present representations of the past" (Klein 2000, 132–133). Hutton's memorial consciousness raises the issue of presentism as a valuable feature of mediated-memory whereas theorists like Ellis (2007) warn us against presentism and viewing practices which distort the past, arguing that "immanent reading" places a "modern optic" over historical texts. By this view the archive can never be complete because it is always in a process of re-engagement, not exclusively with *the* author but with any user.[15] The Mongol print in the snow is both a reminder and traducer of the simple notion of the archive as an objective historical repository, a memory that can be accessed without the angles of presentism offered by Susan, Barbara and Ian. The print is reworked through media, becoming an inter-medial property, through which the transitive process of seriality reproduces it, not through the "one" pen of Marco, but through "different" pens and iterations, as continued writing.

In attempting to faithfully remediate "Serial D," Derek Handley and *Loose Cannon* approached John Woodcock, whose hand replaces Mark Eden's in the scenes where Marco is writing his journal. Woodcock also made the maps used to visualize progress across the Gobi Desert and over which Marco provides linking narration. Because Woodcock was unable to remember his work, the reconstruction set the memory clock back to the time the story occurs in: "we tried to copy elements from old maps ... and add a 'parchment' effect to the background" (Handley 2005, 32) thereby recalling from stock visual clichés. This shift in approach from authentic memory to mediation is one that makes sense of and is informed by processes that shape memory as an object. As Sielke (2013, 37) points out, a fundamental shift in thinking has been occurring through knowledge production technologies such as the computer and internet and serial practices such as television consumption. Yet seriality is also a feature of pre-modern oral narrative practices where stories are passed along iteratively, audiences remembering and forgetting, blending in what is culturally prescient in *their* moment of adaptation. Seriality links the avatar of Marco and his pen across time to other historical collaborators whose authoring echoes *Doctor Who*'s fundamental principal of repetition-with-variation.

The longevity of *Doctor Who* over several decades marks it as of particular interest in conceptualizing memory. Both its re-emergence in 2005, and its 50th anniversary, serve to sanction television history as *the* view of the past at the same time as radically remediating it. The construction of "milestone moments" of history, such as the origins of William Hartnell's Doctor in "The Day of the Doctor" (2013), validate memory as remediation and history as seriality. This is in stark contrast, of course, to the organizing principal of history in the 1960s stories, famously espoused by Hartnell's Doctor in "The Aztecs" (1964): "You can't rewrite history, not one line." History as seriality is circular and multi-universe, each iteration generative of difference as both the official and unofficial examples of *lieu de mémoire* demonstrate.

The longevity of *Doctor Who* also facilitates us with a memory of viewing practices, a major corrective to the view that television promotes amnesia and the notion that viewing is largely passive. The original context for viewing the program in the 1960s was highly ritualized amongst families and viewers, which helped to establish the BBC as an agent of national culture (Cardiff and Scannell 1987, 160) since the program was aired at a set time and into the conventional space of the family living room. In addition, there was little supplemental information outside of the *Radio Times* blurb (which admittedly sometimes spoiled a major plot twist) and individual episode titles meant the audience would have no way of knowing *a priori* when the serial would finish, a convention "Serial D" plays upon when, at the end of episode five "Rider from Shang-tu," the travelers are set to escape until Tegana unexpectedly grabs Susan. Today, *Doctor Who* stories are told in a "transmedia" setting (i.e., as a seriality that crosses media platforms), and one where information is shared and discussed by fans on social media; the televised program is thus but one manifestation of its media presence. Viewers therefore create their own delayed viewing patterns, access the story in a multitude of formats—some fan-made—watch the serial out of sequence, and in varying contexts. However, there has for some time been an argument that broadcast history should focus on reception, rather than production, not least because viewers have increasing access to viewing choices, deriving independent satisfactions and meanings unintended by the producers of programs (Williams 2004, 3).

Viewing, whether narcotic or vigilant, is never discreet from the matrixed entanglement of media, content and memory. Holdsworth, for example, has talked about television as a "black mirror" through which the viewer not only engages with the aired program, but also sees their own environment and identity reflected back to them as a "layering of space and reflection" (Holdsworth 2011, 26). It is in this context, I alert the reader that I am fortunate to have seen the serial twice—initially upon the original UK transmission (between February and April 1964) and then in Australia (between April and June 1965).The insistence of these memories permits me to recommend the serial as the very best *Doctor Who* story ever. This is a conviction that is hard to shake even when I take account of how my memories of media reflect me back—for example, through my affective investments in the serial as a gateway to other autobiographical childhood scenes—and impossible to disprove. The serial's absence from the archives perhaps only increases the importance of fan-talk which however spins the reputation, if not the reconstructions, of this story. Whereas the TARDIS travelers are quick to forget the print in the snow—not understanding how their interpretations are colored by the presentism they bring—the reconstruction of the archive is one steeped in the media of memory.

The memory-print is inevitably dialogical and performative: what we find at that scene is frequently a reflection of our own agency in remembering or forgetting in the first place. "Serial Z," more familiarly known as "The Gunfighters" (1966), was widely regarded as one of the worst stories from the Hartnell era whereas the missing "The Celestial Toymaker" (a.k.a. "Serial Y" in BBC documentation) (1966) was considered one of the best, yet the recovery of missing material has put these assumptions to the test and challenged our memories as well as our affective and critical judgments. The restoration of memory is always a remediation of it.

Conclusion: "Into the past or the future. Who knows?" (Marco)

In this essay I suggest that remediation is not only concerned with how old media is digitized, but how media shapes content and memory. In the particular case of the fourth serial of *Doctor Who*'s original run, "Marco Polo" (a.k.a. "Serial D")—but also true of *Doctor Who* generally—historical stories have not only been given new televisual form but have then gone on to find new shape through a variety of reconstructing media, ranging from Lucarotti's own novelization to the several bold attempts to restore televisuality to missing episodes through tele-snaps and audio recordings made off air by fans at the time of original transmission. Remediation poses questions about whether the audience sees beyond their immersion into the content, and recognize the media itself through its expressions of style and form. I have considered three reconstructive media, that of print (Lucarotti's camera-scripts and novelization or the story), the "televisual" fan-video and also memory, as themselves remediations and also remediating tools of the earliest *Doctor Who* serial wiped from the archives during the BBC housecleaning in the 1960s and 1970s. While we wait for the original tapes to be "rediscovered," the remediation offers us opportunities for affective televisual entanglements, but also to engage vigilantly as fan-historians and archivists. Remediations are like the Mongol print in the snow inasmuch as they are contaminated by time and the discursive environment in which fans theorize and speculate on the missing episode, remembering it through the very reiterations which new generations will find, marking it, appropriately enough, as *strangely familiar*.

NOTES

1. For the first 25 serials, *Doctor Who* episodes were known by unique titles and only later collectively referred to under a common name (e.g., "Marco Polo" is the collective title for seven episodes). The working title for the fourth serial is "A Journey to Cathay" but, from the outset, the BBC adopted a simple categorization system identifying serials as A, B, C etc., on official documents and scripts. The title of this essay draws attention to the (plural) journeys fans take as they revisit the serial but I will henceforth make reference to "Serial D," which not only seems to capture the flavor of the official archive (from which it is of course absent) but also for clarity, since Marco Polo also designates the historical figure, character and titles of fan reconstructions.

2. It is rather important here to note that I am reliant on camera scripts for many of my observations (not exclusively, but nevertheless heavily). The value of the camera script as an archive is subject to the very same historical cautions I raise throughout this essay and my reliance on it is therefore a constant reminder of the sad loss of the original tapes which, should they eventually be found, would no doubt offer many correctives to my commentary (reader, I will be glad of that eventuality). The camera script identifies intended camera operations, including those where prolonged narrative and point-of-view shots would be shared with the audience, but, as is the case of extant *Doctor Who* episodes, many scenes, lines of dialogue and camera positions would have been changed when put to the test of the studio constraints and director Waris Hussein's commitment to exploring space and camera-

mobility. Whereas the audio soundtrack does provide useful evidence of dialogue changes, unfortunately the handful of tele-photos, off-air shots and floor plans provide limited information in assisting the tracking of camera changes. Yet the likelihood of many variations between camera script and filming is itself evidence of how narrative "travels" between media and is remediated with that new media in mind.

3. Documents at the BBC Written Archives Centre demonstrate the BBC's willingness to promote this commitment to history with one letter from a teacher in Norwich prompting producer Verity Lambert to ask designer Barry Newbery to declare his sources, which included visual research on paintings and architecture as well as descriptions of the journeys through deserts of old Cathay (BBC WAC T5 647/2, April 16, 1964). On the other hand, small budgets fostered a spirit of imaginative compromise and many writers perhaps valued their role as creators more highly than as researchers.

4. It is worth pointing out that this perception is somewhat colored by the reluctance to ask what or whose "history" should remain "pure"; a reluctance that hints at how seriality, adaptation, transmediality and remediation are routes to "difference" rather than singularity in repurposing and therefore subverting "history."

5. BBC Audience research dated over the five weeks ending March 29 1964, of which 64 reports were received, was positive about children's reception of the Daleks, whereas the "Marco Polo" serial was considered to be too discursive. One respondent commented, "Children are very keen on 'Dr. Who,' but they prefer it to take place on other planets!" Another noted that children "prefer this story to look into the future rather than the past" (WAC T5/647/2).

6. From this point, references to the camera script will be in shorthand form, with episode and camera shot appearing each side of forward slash (e.g., Lucarotti, 1964: n/n).

7. The scene is further evidence of Lucarotti's close research of *Marco Polo's Travels*. The Venetian wrote that the sands "fill the air with the sounds of all kinds of musical instruments, and also of drums and the clash of arms" (Polo 2003, 74). Hussein visually augmented the soundscape by using wind-machines, stagehands flicking handfuls of sawdust around and technical experimentation providing "pictorial inference" to the film.

8. Ping-Cho, who is heading to Shang-tu for an arranged marriage with a 75-year-old man, appears alert to contemporary Western values, and the centrality of romantic courtship in marriage. This presentism makes for an unnatural ventriloquism as distorting and disorientating as that of the singing sands.

9. Unfortunately, of course, I cannot point to instances of camera-mobility errors in "Serial D" since the tapes are missing. However, the camera scripts remain a detailed record of the intentions to create a fluid space within which the viewer would be interpolated, using a range of camera equipment including booms, "Mole" cranes and "dolly" adjustments, all of which gave rise to various mobility effects. Clearly the intention was to immerse viewers in a story-space far in excess of the reality of the studio constraints. On the other hand, camera mobility can be used to make audiences conscious of media, and such an example is to be found when the gates to Foreman's Yard are mysteriously opened by the mobile camera, thus breaking the "fourth wall," in "An Unearthly Child" (1963).

10. Off-air color photographs were planned for press and promotions; often referred to in the prelims pages of the camera scripts, they offer unique insights into the studio environment beyond the *mise-en-scène* (defined as those events and objects set before the camera and intended for the viewer's gaze) such as camera operations and lighting rigs.

11. The 444 tele-snaps were taken by John Cura, who chronicled most of *Doctor Who* during Verity Lambert's tenure as producer (Molesworth 2013, 321–327) but was not commissioned for episode 4, directed by John Crockett (also director of "The Aztecs," 1964).

12. Focalization is the term used by Gerard Genette (1972/1982) to identify the perspective through which narrative information is presented.

13. Stephen Cox, animator for *Who Recons* (private correspondence).

14. Although these tweets have since been removed, I made reference to the meme at the time in my essay, "Not One Line: History and Design" (2014) which also includes one version of the fan repurposing: http://www.fbi-spy.com/doctor-who-design-history (accessed December 27, 2016).

15. It is useful to compare the openness of new social media applications like *Vimeo* and *YouTube,* which enable generative, amateur and democratic fan practices, with the authority of the "official" BBC archive, with its restrictions of public access, and ultimate delinquency.

BIBLIOGRAPHY

BBC WAC T5 647/2. 1964. Letter from Verity Lambert to Mr. Ireland, April 16.

BBC WAC T5/649/1. Letters to the BBC.

BBC WAC T5/647/2 Dr. Who General 1964: "Audience Research: Comments on Programme."

Berger, Arthur Asa. 1997. *Narratives in Popular Culture, Media, and Everyday Life.* London: Sage.

Bignell, Jonathan. 2009. "Citing the Classics Constructing British Television Drama History in Publishing and Pedagogy" in *Re-Viewing Television History: Critical Issues in Television Historiography,* Helen Wheatley, ed. London: I.B. Tauris. pp. 27–39.

Bolter, Jay David, and Richard Grusin. 1996. "Remediation." *Configurations* 4 (Fall): 311–358.

Bolter, Jay David, and Richard Grusin. 1999. *Remediation: Understanding New Media.* Cambridge: MIT Press.

Brooks, Peter. 1984. *Reading for the Plot: Design and Intention in Narrative.* New York: Knopf.

Bruner, Jerome. 2003. *Making Stories: Law, Literature, Life.* Cambridge: Harvard University Press.

Cardiff, David, and Paddy Scannell. 1987. "Broadcasting and National Unity" in *Impacts and Influences: Essays on Media Power in the Twentieth Century,* J. Curran, A. Smith, and P. Wingate, eds. London: Methuen. pp. 157–173.

Carr, Edward H. 1961. *What Is History?* Basingstoke: Macmillan.

Caughie, John. 1990. "Playing at Being American: Games and Tactics" in *Logics of Television: Essays in Cultural Criticism,* P. Melencamp, ed. London: BFI.

Caughie, John. 2000. *Television Drama: Realism, Modernism and British Culture.* Oxford: Oxford University Press.

Chapman, James. 2000. "The Avengers: Television and Popular Culture During the High Sixties" in *Windows on the Sixties: Exploring Key Texts of Media and Culture,* Anthony Aldgate, James Chapman and Arthur Marwick, eds. London: I.B. Tauris. pp. 37–69.

Chatman, Seymour. 1990. *Coming to Terms: The Rhetoric of Narrative in Fiction and Film.* Ithaca: Cornell University Press.

Collingwood, R.G. 1993 (1946). *The Idea of History.* Oxford: Oxford University Press.

Cook, Pam. 2005. *Screening the Past: Memory and Nostalgia in Cinema.* London: Routledge.

Cooray Smith, James. 2016. Interview *Radio Free Skaro* podcast #518 "Abbot & Costello." http://www.radiofreeskaro.com/2016/02/28/radio-free-skaro-518-abbot-costello/. Accessed February 28, 2016.

Creeber, G. 2006. "Review: Catherine Johnson and Rob Turnock (eds) ITV Cultures: Independent Television Over Fifty Years." *Screen* 47, no. 2 (Summer): 261–265.

Dancyger, Ken. 2006. *The Technique of Film and Video Editing: History, Theory and Practice.* Oxford: Focal Press.

Darian-Smith, Kate, and Sue Turnbull. 2012. "Remembering and Misremembering Television" in *Remembering Television: Histories, Technologies, Memories,* Kate Darian-Smith and Sue Turnbull, eds. Newcastle upon Tyne: Cambridge Scholars. pp. 1–16.

De Groot, Jerome. 2009. *Consuming History Historians and Heritage in Contemporary Popular Culture.* London: Routledge.

Deleuze, Gilles. 1994. *Difference and Repetition.* New York: Columbia University Press.

Deleuze, Gilles. 2005. *Cinema 2: The Time-Image.* Trans. Hugh Tomlinson and Robert Galeta. London: Continuum.

Derrida, Jacques. 1988. "Signature Event Context." *Limited Inc.* Chicago: Chicago University Press. pp. 1–23.

Ellis, John. 1982. *Visible Fictions.* London: Routledge.

Ellis, John. 1997. *American Sphinx: The Character of Thomas Jefferson.* New York: Knopf.

Ellis, John. 2007. "Is it Possible to Construct a Canon of Television Programmes? Immanent Reading versus Textual-Historicism" in *Re-Viewing Television History: Critical Issues in*

Television Historiography, Helen Wheatley, ed. London: I.B. Tauris. pp. 15–26.

Ellis, John. 2014. "TV and Cinema: What Forms of History Do We Need?" in *Cinema, Television and History: New Approaches*, Laura Mee and Johnny Walker, eds. Newcastle upon Tyne: Cambridge Scholars. pp. 12–24.

Erll, Astrid. 2010. "Literature, Film, and the Mediality of Cultural Memory" in *A Companion to Cultural Memory Studies*, Astrid Erll and Ansgar Nunning, eds. Berlin: Walter De Gruyter.

Erll, Astrid, and Ann Rigney. 2009. "Introduction: Cultural Memory and its Dynamics" in *Mediation, Remediation, and the Dynamics of Cultural Memory*, Astrid Erll and Ann Rigney, eds. Berlin: Walter de Gruyter. pp. 1–14.

Gaunt, Simon. 2013. *Le Devisement du Monde: Narrative Voice, Language and Diversity*. Cambridge: D. S. Brewer.

Genette, Gerard. 1972. *Figures III*. Paris: Editions du Seuil.

Genette, Gerard. 1982. *Nouvea discourse du recit*. Paris: Editions du Seuil.

Gordon, Jason. 2001. "Truth, Memory and 'New World' Theology: In Search of Interpretative Tools" in *Human Rights in El Salvador and Guatemala*, Michael A. Hayes (Chaplain) and David Tombs, eds. Hertfordshire: Gracewing. pp. 240–264.

Haining, Peter. 1986. *The Doctor Who File*. London: W. H. Allen.

Haining, Peter. 1987. *Dr Who The Time Traveller's Guide*. London: W. H. Allen.

Halbwachs, Maurice. 1992. *On Collective Memory*. Chicago: University of Chicago Press.

Handley, Derek. 2005. Carbon Copies. *Nothing at the End of the Lane: The Magazine of Doctor Who Research and Restoration*. pp. 32–35.

Harmes, Marcus K. 2014. *Doctor Who and the Art of Adaptation: Fifty Years of Storytelling*. Lanham, MD: Rowman & Littlefield.

Hartley, John. 1999. *The Uses of Television*. London: Routledge.

Heath, Stephen, and Gillian Skirrow. 1977. "Television, a World in Action." *Screen* 18, no. 2 (Summer): 53–54.

Hegel, Georg Wilhelm Friedrich. 1984 (1975). *Lectures on the Philosophy of World History*. Trans. Hugh Barr Nisbet. Cambridge: Cambridge University Press.

Hendy, David. 2013. *Noise: A Human History of Sound and Listening*. London: Profile.

Hills, Matt. 2008. "The Dispersible Television Text: Theorising Moments in the New *Doctor Who*." *Science Fiction Film and Television* 1, no. 1: 25–44.

Hills, Matt. 2010. *Triumph of a Time Lord: Regenerating Doctor Who in the Twenty-First Century*. London: I.B. Tauris.

Hirsh, Marianne. 2008. "The Generation of Post-Memory." *Poetics Today* 29, no. 1: 102–128.

Holdsworth, Amy. 2011. *Television, Memory and Nostalgia*. Hampshire: Palgrave.

Hoskins, Andrew. 2004. "Television and the Collapse of Memory." *Time & Society* 13, no. 1: 109–127.

Hussein, Waris. 2005. *Myth Makers: Waris Hussein, Director*. Reeltime Pictures.

Hutcheon, Linda. 1988. *A Poetics of Postmodernism*. London: Routledge.

Hutton, Patrick H. 1993. *History as an Art of Memory*. Hanover, NH: University Press of New England.

Huyssen, Andreas. 1995. *Twilight Memories: Making Time in a Culture of Amnesia*. London: Routledge.

Huyssen, Andreas. 2003. *Present Pasts: Urban Palimpsests and the Politics of Memory*. Stanford: Stanford University Press.

Jackson, Shannon. 2004. *Processing Performance: Theatre in the Academy from Philology to Performativity*. Cambridge: Cambridge University Press.

Jacobs, Jason. 2003. *Body Trauma TV: The New Hospital Dramas*. London: BFI.

Jenkins, Henry. 1992. *Textual Poachers: Television Fans and Participatory Culture*. London: Routledge.

Jenkins, Henry. 2006. *Fans, Bloggers, and Gamers: Exploring Participatory Culture*. New York: New York University Press.

Jenkins, K. 1995. *On "What Is History?" From Carr and Elton to Rorty and White*. London: Routledge.

Kilbourn, Russell J.A., and Eleanor Ty. 2013. "Developments in Memory Studies and Twentieth and Twenty-First-Century Literature and Film" in *The Memory Effect: The Reme-diation of Memory in Literature and Film*, Russell J.A. Kilbourn and Eleanor Ty, eds. Ontario: Wilfred Laurier University Press. pp. 3–36.

Klein, Kerwin Lee. 2000. "On the Emergence of Memory in Historical Discourse." *Represen-tations* 69 (Winter): 127–150.

Kompare, Derek. 2002. "'I've seen this one before': The Construction of 'Classic TV' on Cable Television" in *Small Screens Big Idea: Television in the 1950s*, J. Thurmin, ed. London: I.B. Taurus.

Kompare, Derek. 2005. *Rerun Nation* London: Routledge.

Kuhn, Annette. 1995. *Family Secrets: Acts of Memory and Imagination*. London: Verso.

Kuhn, Annette. 2000. "A Journey through Memory" in *Memory and Methodology*, Susannah Radstone, ed. Oxford: Berg.

Kuhn, Annette. 2002. *An Everyday Magic: Cinema and Cultural Memory*. London: I.B. Tau-ris.

Lacey, Stephen. 2006. "Some Thoughts on Television History and Historiography: A British Perspective." *Critical Studies in Television* 1, no. 1: 3–12.

Landsberg, Alison. 1995. "Prosthetic Memory: Total Recall and Blade Runner." *Body Society* 1, no. 3–4 (November): 175–189.

Landsberg, Alison. 2009. "Memory, Empathy, and the Politics of Identification." *International Journal of Politics, Culture, and Society* 22, no. 2: 221–29.

Latham, R.E. 1982 (1958). *The Travels of Marco Polo*. London: Penguin.

Lucarotti, John Vincent. 1955. "The Three Journeys of Marco Polo." *CBC Times Pacific Edition* 2–8 (October).

Lucarotti, John. 1964/1. "*Doctor Who*" Serial 'D' Camera Script. Episode 1: "The Roof of the World." Project No 23/63/0431. BBC Drama Script Library.

Lucarotti, John. 1964/2. "*Doctor Who*" Serial 'D' Camera Script. Episode 2: "The Singing Sands." Project No 23/63/0432. BBC Drama Script Library.

Lucarotti, John. 1964/3. "*Doctor Who*" Serial 'D' Camera Script. Episode 3: "Five Hundred Eyes." Project No 23/63/0433. BBC Drama Script Library.

Lucarotti, John. 1964/4. "*Doctor Who*" Serial 'D' Camera Script. Episode 4: "The Wall of Lies." Project No 23/63/0434. BBC Drama Script Library.

Lucarotti, John. 1964/5. "*Doctor Who*" Serial 'D' Camera Script. Episode 5: "Rider from Shang-tu." Project No 23/63/0435. BBC Drama Script Library.

Lucarotti, John. 1964/6. "*Doctor Who*" Serial 'D' Camera Script. Episode 6: "Mighty Kublai Khan." Project No 23/63/0436. BBC Drama Script Library.

Lucarotti, John. 1964/7. "*Doctor Who*" Serial 'D' Camera Script. Episode 7: "Assassin at Peking." Project No 23/63/0437. BBC Drama Script Library.

Lucarotti, John. 1984. *Doctor Who: Marco Polo*. London: W. H. Allen.

Lucarotti, John. 1990. Archive for the "John Lucarotti" Category. October 20, 2009. https://drwhointerviews.wordpress.com/category/john-lucarotti/. Accessed March 1, 2016.

MacDonald, Myra. 2006. "Performing Memory on Television: Documentary and the 1960s." *Screen* 47, no. 3 (Autumn): 327–345.

MacDonald, Philip. 2004. "Shapes of Things." *Doctor Who Magazine Special Edition: The Complete First Doctor*, pp. 5–9.

McLuhan, Marhsall. 1999 (1964). *Understanding Media: The Extensions of Man*. Cambridge: MIT Press.

McLuhan, Marshall, and Quentin Fiore. 2001 (1967). *The Medium Is the Massage*. Berkely: Gingko Press.

Molesworth, Richard. 2013. *Wiped! Doctor Who's Missing Episodes*. Prestatyn: Telos.

Neisser, U. 1982. *Memory Observed: Remembering in Natural Contexts*. New York: W. H. Free-man.

Newcomb, Horace. 1974. *TV: The Most Popular Art*. New York: Anchor.

Nichols, Bill. 1991. *Representing Reality: Issues and Concepts in Documentary*. Bloomington: Indiana University Press.

October, Dene. 2014a. "Doctor Who? What's He Talking About? Performativity and the First Doctor" in *The Language of Doctor Who: From Shakespeare to Alien Tongues*, Jason Barr and Camille D.G. Mustachio, eds. Science Fiction Television. Lanham, MD: Rowman & Littlefield. pp.1–20.

October, Dene. 2014b. "Not One Line: History and Design" in *Doctor Who by Design*. Fbi-spy.com. http://www.fbi-spy.com/doctor-who-design-history. Accessed October 2015.

October, Dene. 2014c. "Materialising Meaning(s): Fans, Fashions and the Twelfth Doctor," Subverting Fashion: Style Cultures, Fan Culture and the Fashion Industry, July 11, 2014, St Mary's University, Twickenham.

October, Dene. 2014d. "Why Am I Mr Pink? Companions, Character, Culture and Design" in *Doctor Who by Design*. Fbi-spy.com. http://www.fbi-spy.com/doctor-who-design-pink. Accessed May 2016.

October, Dene. 2016. "New Worlds, Terrifying Monsters, Impossible Things: Exploring the Contents and Contexts of Doctor Who." *That's Not Right: Television, History and Education in Doctor Who of the Hartnell Era*. Chicago: PopMatters.

October, Dene. 2017. "Adventures in English Time and Space: Sound as Experience in An Unearthly Child" in *Mad Dogs and Englishness: Popular Music & English Identities*, Lee Brooks, Mark Donnelly, and Richard Mills, eds. London: Bloomsbury.

O'Mahony, Daniel. 2007. "'Now how is that wolf able to impersonate a grandmother?' History, Pseudo-History and Genre in *Doctor Who*" in *Time and Relative Dissertations in Space*, David Butler, ed. Manchester: Manchester University Press. pp. 56–67.

Pixley, Andrew. 1998. Silent Witnesses. *Nothing at the End of the Lane: The Magazine of Doctor Who Research and Restoration*. pp. 28–45.

Plater, Alan. 2000. "The age of Innocence" in *British Television Drama: Past, Present and Future*, J. Bignell, S. Lacey and M. Macmurraugh-Kavanagh, eds. Houndmills: Palgrave Macmillan.

Polo, Marco, and Ronald Latham, notes. 1958. *The Travels*. London: Penguin.

Polo, Marco, and Manuel Komroff, eds. 2003. *The Travels of Marco Polo*. New York: Norton.

Radstone, Susannah. 2000. *Memory and Methodology*. Oxford: Berg.

Radstone, Susannah. 2010. "Cinema and Memory" in *Memory: Histories, Theories and Debates*, Susannah Radstone and Bill Schwartz, eds. New York: Fordham University Press.

Reith, John. 1925. *Memorandum of Information on the Scope and Conduct of the Broadcasting Service*. BBC Written Archive.

Richardson, David. 1990. "Nostalgia: Marco Polo." *Doctor Who Magazine* #162 (July): 22–29.

Richardson, Laurel. 1990. "Narrative and Sociology." *Journal of Contemporary Ethnography* 19: 116–135.

Rigney, Anne. 2010. "The Dynamics of Remembrance: Texts Between Monumentality and Morphing" in *A Companion to Cultural Memory Studies*, Astrid Erll and Ansgar Nunning, eds. Berlin: Walter De Gruyter. pp. 345–353.

Rimmon-Kenan, Shlomith. 1983. *Narrative Fiction: Contemporary Poetics*. London: Methuen.

Robinson, Bruce. 1998. "What's Wrong with the TV? The Pictures Aren't Moving!" *Nothing at the End of the Lane: The Magazine of Doctor Who Research and Restoration*. pp. 16–23.

Russell, Gary. 1986. "Observing History." *Doctor Who Magazine Summer Special*.

Scannell, Paddy. 1990. "Public Service Broadcast: The History of a Concept" in *Understanding Television*, Andrew Goodwin and Garry Whannel, eds. London: Routledge.

Sielke, Sabine. 2013. "'Joy in Repetition'; or, the Significance of Seriality in Processes of Memory and (Re-) Mediation" in *The Memory Effect: The Remediation of Memory in Literature and Film*, Russell J.A. Kilbourn and Eleanor Ty, eds. Ontario: Wilfred Laurier University Press. pp. 37–50.

Sontag, Susan. 1977. *On Photography*. New York: Penguin.

Sorlin, Pierre. 1990. "Historical Films as Tools for Historians" in *Image as Artifact: The Historical Analysis of Film and Television*, John E. O'Connor. Malabarg: Robert E. Krieger. pp. 31–38.

Spigel, Lynn. 2001. *Welcome to the Dreamhouse*. Durham: Duke University Press.

Spigel, Lynn. 2004. "Introduction" in *Television After TV: Essays on a Medium in Transition*, L. Spigel and J. Olsson, eds. Durham: Dale University Press. pp.1–36.

Spigel, Lynn. 2005. "Out TV Heritage: Television, the Archive and the Reasons for Preservation" in *A Companion to Television*, J. Wasko, ed. London: Blackwell.

Spilsbury, Tom. 2015. *Re-Writing History!* Doctor Who Magazine #490 (October). Panini Magazines.

Stam, Robert. 2000. "Beyond Fidelity: The Dialogics of Adaptation" in *Film Adaptation*, James Naremore, ed. New Brunswick: Rutgers University Press, pp. 54–76.

Stearn, Tom. 2005. "What's Wrong with Television?" *History Today* 52, no. 12 (December): 26–27.

Todorov, Tzvetan. 1975. *The Fantastic: A Structural Approach to a Literary Genre*. Ithaca: Cornell University Press.

Tulloch, John. 1990. *Television Drama. Agency, Audience and Myth*. London: Routledge.

Turnock, Rob. 2007. *Television and Consumer Culture: Britain and the Transformation of Modernity*. London. I.B. Taurus.

Warren, Kate. 2013. "Creative Re-Enactment in the Films and Videos of Omer Fast" in *The Memory Effect: The Remediation of Memory in Literature and Film*, Russell J.A. Kilbourn and Eleanor Ty, eds. Ontario: Wilfred Laurier University Press.

Watts, Halina. 2013. "Seven Lost Episodes of Doctor Who 1964 Series Marco Polo Filmed by Fan to Be Unveiled Next Month." *Daily Mirror* 22 November. http://www.mirror.co.uk/tv/tv-news/doctor-who-missing-episodes-seven-2839102. Accessed July 2015.

Wheatley, Helen. 2007. "Introduction: Re-Viewing Television Histories" in *Re-Viewing Television History: Critical Issues in Television Historiography*, Helen Wheatley, ed. London: I.B. Tauris. pp. 1–14.

White, Hayden. 1975. *Metahistory: The Historical Imagination in Nineteenth-Century Europe*. Baltimore: John Hopkins University Press.

White, Hayden. 1987. *The Content of Form: Narrative Discourse and Historical Representation*. Baltimore: John Hopkins University Press.

Williams, Jack. 2004. *Entertaining the Nation: A Social History of British Television*. Stroud: Sutton.

FILMOGRAPHY

"Marco Polo" 2002. Loose Cannon Productions.

"Marco Polo" 2013. Loose Cannon Productions.

"Marco Polo" 2015. Whoflix.

"Marco Polo" 2015. Who Recons.

"Marco Polo" Reconstruction. 2006. "Doctor Who: The Beginning."

"O tempora, o mores"

Class(ics) and Education in Doctor Who

AVEN MCMASTER *and* MARK SUNDARAM

"Sing of them as better than they were," says a character in "The Wrath of the Iceni" (2012) audio adventure, urging her children to learn from her and to keep the memory of the past alive in a glorified form.[1] The past, in this case, is the struggle of Boudica against the Romans in AD 60/61, and it is of course the Doctor whose memory the singer most wants to celebrate. This connection between teaching, historical accuracy, idealizing the past, and British self-definition reappears in various forms throughout the world of *Doctor Who*, but can be particularly striking in the context of the show's engagement with classics. The representation of classical material and themes in *Doctor Who* reflects the changing place of classical education in British schooling and its connection to class, and the transformation in British attitudes towards Latin and Greek, imperialism, and history. After giving a brief overview of the trends in classics education in British schools over the course of the second half of the 20th century, and an even briefer sketch of some relevant aspects of classics scholarship over the same period, we examine specific instances of classical material in *Doctor Who*. These range from entire serials set in the ancient world to allusions and adaptations of classical history, myth, and language. We focus mainly on the television show, but also discuss some novelizations of serials and a Big Finish audio adventure. The program's relationship to specifically classical references demonstrates its role in exposing and contributing to the modern scholarly and popular understanding of the contested and constructed nature of historical narrative, especially in the area of classical history, with its strong classist and imperial connotations.

"Veni, vidi, vici"

We begin with a general outline of the development of the teaching of classics in schools and universities in England and Wales over the run of *Doctor Who*. (The general trends in Scotland were similar, though the details of the educational system differ.) Before 1960, Latin was standard in both state-funded grammar schools and privately run "public" schools, taught with a focus on grammar and the language itself, with great emphasis on composition (that is, writing passages in Latin or translating passages from English to Latin). Public schools often taught Greek at higher levels (with the same approach as with Latin), while only some grammar schools did; preparatory schools (i.e., fee-paying primary schools) started teaching Latin as early as age seven, but no other primary schools did, while most other types of secondary schooling, such as secondary moderns and technical schools, did not teach Latin at all. Cambridge and Oxford required proficiency in Latin for all entering students, regardless of program; other universities did not. Therefore knowledge of the Latin language, and even more so of Greek, was a class marker, part of what defined a British gentleman; those who were middle-class and above would have some Latin, and the higher up the class scale the more Latin they would have, the earlier they would have learned it, and the better they would be at the grammar. In general, the most upper-class people would have knowledge of Greek (as a default expectation) regardless of their profession. There was also a gender divide: fewer girls would routinely learn Latin, and very few would learn Greek, at least until university; this was less true the higher a person's class, so that the gender divide was more dramatic in the middle class than the upper class.

In spite of the relatively widespread teaching of Latin, however, there was at the same time little direct emphasis on classical culture, other than what was acquired through reading passages from classical authors (which were themselves usually studied only for their grammatical and rhetorical features). So those who were not taught Latin or Greek would learn very little Roman or Greek history (beyond some basics in their history classes) or culture or mythology.

After compulsory Latin was dropped from the Oxford and Cambridge entrance requirements in 1960, and with the reorganization of secondary education, the end of the secondary moderns, and the expansion of comprehensive secondary schools, the teaching of Latin became much less widespread in the state-funded system, even in grammar schools, and tended to start later in the student's career if they chose to study it. It continued mostly unchanged in the fee-paying public schools and prep schools, however. Teaching of the subject also changed, in part in order to attract more students now that there were fewer incentives for students to take it, in part in response to general developments in pedagogy. The *Cambridge Latin Course* (a series of Latin textbooks aimed at ages 11 and up) was introduced in 1970, and along with *Ecce Romani* (a similar series developed in Wales), became widespread in schools, though many public schools and prep schools continued to use more traditional textbooks. These new textbooks emphasized developing reading proficiency, rather than in-depth formal grammatical knowledge, and they incorporated substantial amounts of Roman culture and history, while also making the subject more approachable with entertaining stories about a fictional family's activities and copious illustrations.[2] One effect of this change was to associate Latin language learning with these fictional characters and story rather than directly with Roman authors in the minds of many students. At the same time, curricular elements focusing on Classical Civilization (that did not require or include language training) were being developed, starting in the mid–1970s, and were becoming popular in comprehensive schools as well as, eventually, the universities, where Classical Civilization became an accepted area of study. This movement toward Classical Civilization programs was part of a conscious effort by universities and teachers to make the ancient world more accessible to a wider group of students, including those without language training, both in order to "democratize" the subject and to attract more enrolment as other subjects gained prestige.

Over this same period the discipline of classics itself (as taught in universities and studied by scholars) was also changing, on similar lines. From its origins in philology it gradually expanded into a broader approach, taking in history and archaeology, and then social history, economics, and other related fields, and then, belatedly, encompassing and grappling with various types of literary theory. For the purposes of this essay, two developments are particularly relevant: the growing attention to theoretical approaches to mythology from the 1970s onward, including the concept of the "monomyth" and the study of comparative mythology begun in the 19th century but greatly expanded over the 20th century; and, especially in the 1990s and later, the problematizing of "history" as a concept, with theoretical approaches such as postmodernism, post-colonialism, feminism, and others that challenged the idea of a fixed "truth" about the ancient world that could be recovered.

"A classical education"

When the First Doctor (William Hartnell) and his companions are staying at an ancient Roman villa in "The Romans" (1965), Ian Chesterton (William Russell) shows his pleasure at being in this well-known time period, enjoying the grandeur that was Rome, by quoting a brief Latin tag ("*O tempora, o mores*" from Cicero), without translating it, and the opening lines of Mark Antony's speech from Shakespeare's *Julius Caesar*. These are clearly the things he, an educated man (a school teacher) who is not a specialist, knows about Rome: the type of phrase learned by schoolboys and dropped into conversation as a marker of "classical education," and one of the most quoted passages from Shakespeare. This fits with the general portrayal of the Roman world in this serial, which reflects the *idea* of Rome that was standard at the time in British schools and on the screen (notably in *Quo Vadis* [1951] and the *Carry On* series): an Imperial Rome, expanding into "barbaric" Britain but inhabited by characters familiar from British comedy; a Rome of over-the-top luxuries, slaves, and cruelty; and a Rome filled with the cultural tags and well-known episodes that populated the textbooks and writing exercises of schoolchildren (Chapman 2006, 36). By contrast, no Greek is quoted in the somewhat similar "The Myth Makers" (1965). In the 1960s, Latin was still widespread enough that it could be used as a throwaway line in a family show, but although there was a popular awareness of Greek myth at the time, helped by the success of *Jason and the Argonauts* (1963), the Greek language was not. Both of these serials, by using times and stories familiar to the audience, are in line with one of the guiding principles of the show's early historical episodes. As Chapman (2006, 32) says, "Historical *Doctor Who* tended to focus on periods of the past that were taught in schools and would, therefore, be familiar to children, but the series did not exclusively privilege British history." Though it is sometimes stated that the historical stories were less popular, leading to them being phased out, Chapman (2006) points out that there is no evidence for this. And in the correspondence of Donald Wilson, Head of Serials, we see evidence that the educational context at the time was a consideration in the choice of historical topics; he says that children are as interested in the historical stories as in the alien stories, perhaps because "the past subjects do have some bearing on lessons that the children are having to do" (Chapman 2006, 31).

Ian's use of the Latin tag in "The Romans," then, helps to situate his character in British society, suggesting his class and educational background. We can see the knowledge of classical languages being used in a more pointed way to delineate character and class in two serials from the following decade. In "The Daemons" (1971), the Master (Roger Delgado) turns up as a vicar named "Mr. Magister," and at one point the Doctor chides Jo Grant (Katy Manning) for missing this obvious clue due to her lack of knowledge of Latin—"*magister*" means "master." Similarly, in "The Time Monster" (1972) the Master turns up again, this time with the alias "Prof. Thascalos," and the Doctor chides Brigadier Lethbridge-Stewart (Nicholas Courtney) for missing this clue (that "*thascalos*" is Greek for "Master") with the words "Perhaps a classical education would have helped you, Brigadier."[3] In both these stories, by pointing out the lack of a "classical education" in his companions, the Doctor is being rather condescending—as he often is—but not insulting. Pertwee's Doctor (who has been described as "an implacable ultra–English hero in the Bulldog Drummond mold" with a touch of Sherlock Holmes (Chapman 2006, 78) can scold the upper-middle-class Jo Grant and Brigadier for their educational lack without great insult; but if one imagines him saying the same line to Sergeant Benton (John Levene), the class implications of the comment become clear. The fact that the Doctor and the Master share an understanding of these classical clues that excludes the other characters is also in line with the portrayals by their respective actors, who play them as upper-class gentlemen whose interactions with those around them are often marked by condescension and, in the case of the Master, explicit snobbery.

There are some notable points about these aliases, though. As Tony Keen (2008a) points out, both *"magister"* and *"thascalos"* mean "Master" in the sense of *school*master, unlike, e.g., *"dominus,"* master of slaves, even though "the Master," as a villain, is clearly trying to become "Lord and Master" by enslaving worlds, not by teaching. While this may well be, as Keen suggests, a joke by the writers, it also points, at least in the case of Magister, to the schoolboy Latin that would be most familiar to *Doctor Who*'s audience; this makes it even more notable that Jo, in spite of her reasonably posh background (her uncle is a Cabinet Minister), doesn't recognize the word—perhaps Latin wasn't taught to girls in her school. In the case of *"thascalos,"* however, there is another twist; although the Doctor's reference to "a classical education" suggests that the word is ancient Greek, it is actually modern Greek—the classical word is *"didaskalos."* While this could be intended as an extra layer to the joke, it is likely that the writers (Robert Sloman and Barry Letts) knew Latin but not ancient Greek and were not themselves aware of the difference. This error makes it clear that the use of Greek here is a shibboleth, marking the Doctor as part of an exclusive group; since neither the writers nor the audience are part of that group, it doesn't matter whether the word is indeed ancient Greek or not.

The implied invocation of the class and educational distinctions signaled by the knowledge of Latin and Greek in these Third Doctor stories is made more evident when compared to the attitude toward Latin in "The Fires of Pompeii" (2008), when the Tenth Doctor (David Tennant) and Donna Noble (Catherine Tate) visit Pompeii (thinking it is Rome). The Tenth Doctor does not mock Donna for not having learned Latin, and if one imagines the Third Doctor's line about "a classical education" being addressed to her, one can see how unacceptably rude it would be in this context. Donna comes from a working-class background and would almost certainly have never had the chance to learn Latin or seen any value in doing so; but at the same time she knows enough about Rome to know that it has "seven hills, not one." She is of the generation whose state schooling may well have included a fair amount of classical civilization, without being "a classical education." Her excitement at being in Rome comes in part from the unexpectedness of someone like her being there: "It's so *Roman*! ... Donna Noble, in *Rome*!" When she wonders why everyone sounds like they're speaking English and is told that it's the TARDIS affecting her, so that she's actually speaking and hearing Latin, she's amazed: "Seriously? ... I just said 'seriously?!' in Latin!" Then she asks "What would happen if I said something in Latin? ... Like, *veni, vidi, vici*. My dad said that when he came back from football." Her Latin is explicitly not learned at school, nor is this famous tag a signal of an upper-class "classical education," but of working-class football culture. The whole opening scene plays humorously with the contrast between the "classy" image of Rome and its "common" reality, and Donna's words to the Doctor a little later "Don't get clever in Latin!" seem to sum up this rejection of the old-fashioned, scholarly notions of Rome (which may recall "The Romans"; in fact, there is an explicit reference to that earlier serial at the beginning of the episode).

There is another signal of the changing place of Latin in the British consciousness in this story. The names of the Pompeian family that the Doctor and Donna meet are those of the main characters in the *Cambridge Latin Course*, with the addition of the daughter Evelina, though little else about the family, other than their presence in Pompeii, matches those characters (Hobden 2009). The writer of this episode, James Moran, has said that these names were used on the instructions of show runner Russell T. Davies, who (according to Moran) "did that course. He just loved it, and they all did, because it was a real family. Because at the end of each lesson you got a slice of life about how they lived. It was great. And they all got killed—it was really horrible. So he wanted to do a little tribute to them" (Brew 2016). This is a very different kind of reference, however, from the "*O tempora, o mores*" of "The Romans." The introduction of the *Cambridge Latin Course (CLC) was* an attempt to make learning Latin fun and accessible to students who were interested as much in the culture or history of the period as in the language; Davies' affection for it, which is shared by many students who have learned from it, comes from the aspects of the course that most distinguish it from the traditional "classical education" of grammatical forms and Latin composition: the informal domestic storylines, the inclusion of cultural information, and the (both intentional and unintentional) humor. Latin, as taught via the *CLC*, was no longer elitist and exclusive, but everyday and approachable; it was also a vector for learning about the Roman world more generally. Many children probably first learned about Pompeii and Vesuvius through the stories of the *CLC* (in which Quintus is the only member of the family to escape the eruption). Davies himself attended a comprehensive school, and his use of the trappings of a Latin course is an in-joke for those who also learned from it. Unlike Ian's Latin tag or Prof. Thascalos' name, however, it is not drawing class-specific distinctions.

This transition from the idea of classics as part of a gentleman's education to that of an education that teaches about the classics, can be seen even more clearly in "The Pandorica Opens" (2010) in connection with Amy Pond's (Karen Gillan) schoolgirl exposure to Roman history and Greek myth. These episodes are discussed in more detail below, but for now it is sufficient to point out that Amy clearly studied the Roman invasion of Britain ("My favorite topic at school: Invasion of the Hot Italians!") and has read the myth of Pandora ("Pandora's Box—with all the worst things in the world in it. My favorite story when I was a kid") but shows no sign of having learned Latin or Greek. Here is classical civilization and history learned on its own, without the languages, in what seems to be a middle-class to upper-middle-class education.

"We are our stories, you and I"

Mythology has always been an element of the study of classics, both in school and by scholars, but as a field it has been growing in importance since the 1950s. Study of myth has gone, in the 20th century, from a positivist, philological and historicist approach to constructivism and a deep engagement with literary critical theory. Earlier approaches to myth (in the 19th century) focused largely on seeing myth as either a primitive analogue to science or studying it for its historical value, as for instance trying to uncover the historical reality of Troy which lies behind Homeric epic. Gradually more theoretical approaches began to be taken up over the course of the 20th century, from anthropological focus on ritual, to psychological (as the field developed from the work of Freud and Jung), to the literary and structuralist, with the ground-breaking work of Levi-Strauss. In a parallel manner, earlier serials in *Doctor Who* tended to be fairly conservative in their treatment of mythical (and historical) material. "The Romans" and "The Myth Makers" both assume a detailed knowledge of mythology as literature and of history, and they are thus playfully allusive in their references, in both cases humorously hinting at the "true" history that lies behind the well-known stories of Nero setting fire to Rome and "fiddling" while it burned, and the myth of the Trojan horse: "The viewer's pleasure arises from the script's knowing and playful deconstruction of the classics" (Chapman 2006). In each case it turns out that the Doctor either accidentally or reluctantly was the cause of these events (though he often professes that he is not allowed or able to influence the course of history). The serial "The Time Monster" makes reference to archaeological theories about the historical "fact" behind the Atlantis myths, with the theory that it was the destruction of the Minoan settlement in Thera (modern-day

Santorini) that inspired the Atlantis story—though Mike Yates (Richard Franklin) queries, "Isn't that all just a myth?" As it turns out, the destruction was the result of the ongoing conflict between the Doctor and the Master, and again, the Doctor is revealed to have played a role in the "true" history behind the myth. This is in contrast to the treatment of Atlantis in the 1967 story "The Underwater Menace," in which the setting is a very different version of Atlantis, one that has nothing in common with the myths except the name, and that is completely ahistorical; at that time it seemed the writers expected that their audience would know little about Atlantis but its name. There is a fair amount of exposition about Atlantis and its (possible) history at the beginning of "The Time Monster," which suggests the writers weren't sure how much their audience knew, but the change in the treatment of the classical material may also reflect the growing emphasis on archaeology and classical civilization in schools in the 1970s.

Around the middle of the 20th century, Joseph Campbell introduced the notion of the "monomyth," a pattern underlying all myth, and shortly after a revised edition was issued in the late 1960s we see the notion entering the popular conception and influencing popular culture, most famously in the film *Star Wars* (1977) which had numerous influences on *Doctor Who*. *Star Wars* put into practice Campbell's monomyth in developing its archetypal pattern and storylines but within a science fiction setting. Perhaps unsurprisingly it is just shortly after this ground-breaking film that we see two serials that feature Greek mythical storylines translated into a modern futuristic setting, "Underworld" (1978) and "The Horns of Nimon" (1979). Both are retellings or adaptations of Greek myth, the first of Jason and the Argonauts, the second of Theseus and the Minotaur. Anthony Read was script editor on the first and writer on the second, and the mythological inspiration was his. Both serials are filled with subtle and not-so-subtle references to various Greek figures, as well as 19th- and 20th-century artists and thinkers who themselves engaged with Greek culture and myth (Sullivan 2016); notably, names of the main characters are versions or anagrams of the Greek characters (e.g., Jackson for Jason, Seth for Theseus, Nimon for Minotaur), and the main plot lines echo the original myths, with Jackson and his crew searching for a golden treasure, and Seth and his companions being sent as tribute to a bull-headed monster. Neither story depends on the viewer's previous knowledge of the original myths, and in both the Doctor makes the connection pretty explicit at the end. In "Underworld" he calls Jackson "Jason" and says, "Jason was another captain on a long quest…. He was looking for the golden fleece. Perhaps these myths are not just old stories of the past, but prophesies of the future, maybe." Similarly, in "The Horns of Nimon" he says, in a subtler reference to the tragic end of the Theseus story, "I'm glad this time I reminded them to paint their ship white. Last time anything like this happened I completely forgot, caused quite a hoohah…. Other times, other places." In both of these stories, however, knowing the myths—both their plots and their cultural and symbolic values—enhances the viewer's appreciation to some degree. These mythological storylines would have been at least generally known to audiences through popular sources such as movies, as with Ray Harryhausen's famous film adaptation of *Jason and the Argonauts* (1963), and through the increasing attention to classical civilization and culture in school curricula over the 1970s. And in both instances, in case the implicit parallels between the myths and the stories weren't clear to the audience, the Fourth Doctor (Tom Baker) alludes to the fact that he was present at the actual mythical events, and that the monomythic patterns repeat themselves in the distant future.[4] Once again the Doctor is revealed to have taken part in the "historical" events of classical myth.

By the 21st century we see the impact of modern critical theory making its way into the series with writers influenced by the teaching of literary criticism in the university classroom. As discussed above, "The Fires of Pompeii" makes in-joke references to the storyline of the *Cambridge Latin Course*; in a sense, these people are in Pompeii because Davies was taught his Pompeian history through their (fictional) story. History now is a product of our education—how history is taught affects how history happened, and in this instance we see that time can be rewritten, as can the storyline from the *CLC* with the Tenth Doctor rescuing the entire family from the eruption of Pompeii, instead of only Quintus making it out, as in the books. There is a tension between the popular conception of history, which continues to follow the older intellectual notions of a "real truth" that can be discovered if (for instance) one has a time machine to go back to Pompeii to find out why the volcano "really" erupted, and the modern scholarly approach to history as a fragmented series of different pieces of evidence, "the product of diverse literary and pictorial narratives, which changes as the narratives, shaped by their production contexts, shift and combine in different ways" (Hobden 2009, 162–163). This is even clearer if one examines the material on the BBC website that surrounded the airing of the episode, as Hobden does in detail. A mock documentary about evidence of "monsters" in the ruins of Pompeii and the discovery of the plaque showing the family gods of the Caecilius family (which includes a depiction of the TARDIS) joins mini featurettes about the behind-the-scenes production work and the attempts at historical authenticity. Also included is a visit by David Tennant to the actual site of Pompeii which makes evident how little the sets (borrowed from the series "Rome") resemble the layout of the historical city of Pompeii (Hobden 2009, 158–159). This postmodern approach to history, very much a product of late 20th-century trends in scholarship, can be seen even more clearly in the later episode "The Pandorica Opens."

In this episode, a very complicated culmination of the season's various plot arcs, the Eleventh Doctor (Matt Smith) and Amy Pond find themselves in Roman Britain, AD 102. But almost immediately it becomes clear that there are unhistorical aspects to the scene: the Doctor is greeted as "Caesar" and brought to meet "Cleopatra" (who turns out to be River Song (Alex Kingston). Eventually the Doctor and River realize that this encampment, Roman legion, and entire situation has been created (by aliens, as a trap) out of Amy's memories of Romans from her childhood, specifically drawing from one of her picture books about Roman Britain. Here we see history literally constructed by a person's experience of the narratives and images about that history; one of the centurions even turns out to be Amy's dead fiancé Rory Williams (Arthur Darvill), recreated in plastic because of her memories of him. The elements—invading Romans, Caesar, Cleopatra, Stonehenge—are drawn from "real" history, but the particular conditions of Amy's life shape how they combine to produce a narrative, one that may also fit into the expectation of the average viewer of the show, whose schooling is likely to have been not dissimilar to Amy's. There may be no more postmodern history than one that is created to match the perspective of a single person, in order to be plausible enough to convince one other person (the Doctor, so as to entrap him).

As a final illustration of the impact of changing approaches to classical studies on *Doctor Who* storytelling, we return to the Big Finish audio "The Wrath of the Iceni." The writer, John Dorney, says he was given the brief "Romans in Britain" for a story with the Fourth Doctor and Leela (Louise Jameson), and immediately thought of having Leela meet Boudica; the story is a pure historical, and Dorney says he read a number of children's reference books on the period for background, as well as a more extensive book about Boudica (Big Finish website). His concern for accurate historical detail ("There's a few historical inaccuracies in there that I know of already, but they're all consciously chosen to help make the story work. Hopefully the only mistakes are ones I chose to make, in other words" [Big Finish website]) suggests a standard positivist attitude toward classical history, but other developments in classical studies are reflected in his script. The focus on Boudica is unsurprising for a British audience, since she has always been a figure of national importance and her story is taught in school. But the choice to tell the story from her perspective, and to focus on the relationship between her and Leela, mirrors recent trends in classical scholarship to reevaluate the sources about women in the ancient world and to reassess critically both the restrictions placed upon them and their resistance, as opposed to the earlier model of classical historians who accepted the perspectives and priorities of the aristocratic male authors who provide the literary sources for Roman history.

This story as a whole shows an explicit concern for the question of how history is made, who makes it, and how it is altered by telling and retelling; this is essentially a postmodern approach to history, which had finally made its way into classics by the end of the 20th century. The first episode begins with a meditation on the importance of storytelling as the genesis of history and as a form of idealizing self-creation for a cultural group. Throughout the story the issue of whose version of history can or should be believed is raised repeatedly, and the Doctor is several times pressured to use his knowledge of the "real" history to influence events; in the end, however, he uses a falsified version of history (which is understood by Boudica as prophecy) to ensure that things turn out as the audience knows they "actually" did, thereby in a way setting up a paradoxical relationship between historical truth and fiction.

Another important shift in scholarship that can be seen in this story is postcolonialism; the Doctor is presented in many ways as a paternalistic, colonialist voice, dismissing pre–Roman Britain as "a savage land" and, while decrying Roman atrocities in the treatment of the Iceni, declaring that this moment of Boudica's loss to the Romans is the beginning of "history, culture, civilization." Leela, whose character is both descended from colonists and portrayed as a type of "indigenous" figure whose tribe was oppressed by technocratic imperialists, argues against the Doctor's unwillingness to help the Iceni and ends up breaking with him and joining Boudica to try to help her fight against the oppressive Romans. But this anti-imperialist narrative is itself disrupted by the complicated portrayal of Boudica. Instead of being depicted as the noble British folk-hero who has often been used as a potent national symbol, she is shown as power-hungry, driven by pride, and focused on glorious conquest rather than justice; in other words, she's just like the Romans. This, then, is doubly post-colonial; the story starts out as a narrative of driving out the invaders, but ends by complicating one of the national myths that has underpinned British imperialism itself.

"The stories live on"

This examination of the presence of classics in *Doctor Who* reveals the usefulness of classical material in constructing identity: in terms of class, education, national character, and even selfhood (e.g., Rory remade as a centurion). Identity has always been a major theme in *Doctor Who*—for instance how his companions are changed by their travels with him and how he himself changes—and the show's use of classics is an important thread in this ongoing discussion. *Doctor Who's* changing engagement with classics reflects the transformations of British identity itself and its relationship to the classical world, both shaping and being shaped by the culture that both creates and consumes it.

NOTES

1. We would like to thank everyone on Twitter who helped us figure out the intricacies of the British school system, as well as those who clarified the nuances of class distinctions among the companions. Special thanks to Liz Gloyn and Mary Cooper for their generous help. Any continuing confusion is of course our own fault.

2. The CLC, for instance, centered on a family living in Pompeii: father Caecilius, mother Metella, son Quintus, and their household slaves Grumio, Clemens, and Melissa. At the end of the first book the family dies in the eruption of Mt. Vesuvius, except for Quintus and Clemens, who end up in Britain in the following books.

3. In the novelization of the serial by Terrance Dicks the line is given as "A more classical education might have helped, Brigadier." As often in the novelizations, it is hard to know if this is what was originally in the script or if Dicks made the change, but in either case this version does fit better with the portrayal of the Brigadier. As played by Nicholas Courtney, he surely *did* have a "classical education" but one that apparently only covered Latin, not Greek. So it was not classical *enough* to help him here.

4. This point is emphasized in the novelization of the "Horns of Nimon," in which the author Terrance Dicks inserts into the Doctor's final speech the line from "Underworld" about myth as prophecy, making the connection between the stories explicit.

BIBLIOGRAPHY

Brew, Simon. 2016. "James Moran Interview: Writing *Doctor Who*, Torchwood, Severance, Primeval & More!" *Den of Geek*. http://www.denofgeek.us/tv/spooks/19488/james-moran-interview-writing-doctor-who-torchwood-severance-primeval-more. Accessed May 1, 2016.

Campbell, Flann. 1968. "Latin and the Elite Tradition in Education." *The British Journal of Sociology* 19, no. 3: 308–25.

Chapman, James. 2006. *Inside the TARDIS: The Worlds of Doctor Who. A Cultural History.* London: I.B. Tauris.

Forrest, Martin. 2003. "The Abolition of Compulsory Latin and Its Consequences." *Greece & Rome* 50: 42–66.

Hardwick, Lorna, and Christopher Stray. 2011. *A Companion to Classical Receptions.* Hoboken: John Wiley & Sons.

Hobden, Fiona. 2009. "History Meets Fiction in 'Doctor Who,' the 'Fires of Pompeii': A BBC Reception of Ancient Rome on Screen and Online." *Greece & Rome* 56, no. 2: 147–63.

Keen, Tony. 2008a. "Memorabilia Antonina: *Doctor Who*, 'The Fires of Pompeii.'" http://tonykeen.blogspot.com/2008/04/doctor-who-fires-of-pompeii.html. Accessed April 30, 2016.

Keen, Tony. 2008b. "Memorabilia Antonina: What's in an Alias? (A Post about *Doctor Who*)." http://tonykeen.blogspot.com/2008/03/whats-in-alias-post-about-doctor-who.html. Accessed April 30, 2016.

Lambert, G. R. 1971. "The Cambridge School Classics Project in Great Britain." *The Classical Journal* 66, no. 4: 338–46.

"1.03. The Wrath of the Iceni—*Doctor Who*—Fourth Doctor Adventures—Big Finish." https://www.bigfinish.com/releases/v/the-wrath-of-the-iceni-656/behind_the_scenes. Accessed May 1, 2016.

Rogers, Brett M., and Benjamin Eldon Stevens. 2015. *Classical Traditions in Science Fiction.* Oxford: Oxford University Press.

Stray, Christopher. 1998. *Classics Transformed: Schools, Universities, and Society in England, 1830–1960.* Oxford: Clarendon Press.

Sullivan, Shannon. 2016. "A Brief History of Time (Travel): Underworld." http://www.shannon sullivan.com/drwho/serials/4y.html. Accessed May 1, 2016.

Remixing the Imperial Past
Doctor Who, *British Slavery* and the *White Savior's Burden*

Susana Loza

> Science fiction often talks about race by not talking about race, makes real aliens, has hidden race dialogues. Even though it is a literature that talks a lot about underclasses or oppressed classes, it does so from a privileged if somewhat generic white space.
> —Isiah Lavender, III, *Race in American Science Fiction*

John Rieder once pronounced that colonialism is not "science fiction's hidden truth" but rather "part of the genre's texture, a persistent, important component of its displaced references to history, its engagement in ideological production, and its construction of the possible and imaginable" (2008, 15). In many ways, science fiction is the literature of colonization. The genre emerged at the height of European imperialism and many of its early narratives center on the colonial encounter. For example, in *The War of the Worlds*, H.G. Wells compares the Martian invasion of Earth to the European conquest of Tasmania, thus encouraging British readers to imagine themselves as the Martian colonizers. The anti-imperial potential of this tale, and other stories premised on reverse colonization, are undone when the alien Other is represented as a hostile savage in need of human civilization and, if that fails, annihilation. Such constructions not only justified invasion, colonization, and, extermination, but reinforced the racial hierarchies erected by European imperialism. One hundred years after its emergence, science fiction remains an immensely popular genre and a "key site where the ideological dreamwork of imperialism unfolds" (Higgins 2011, 331). But one must ask: do contemporary science fiction narratives such as the television program *Doctor Who* question, critique, or move beyond the colonizing impulse? Or have they just technologically modernized the plots, scenes, and tropes of imperialism (Grewell 2001, 26)?

Born in 1963 amidst the turmoil of decolonial struggles in Africa, South Asia, and the Caribbean, *Doctor Who* is "a product of those dying days of empire" (Charles 2007, 115). As Lindy Orthia elaborates in the introduction to *Doctor Who & Race*, the show "emerged from and continues to dwell in the post-empire period of British history, a time when formerly colonized people were migrating to Britain in larger numbers than ever before as well as reclaiming their cultural heritage and political independence elsewhere in the world, transforming conceptions of Britishness, the meaning of 'race' on the global stage, and the ways in which the western media understand and deal with racism" (2013, 4). From its inception, *Doctor Who* has envisioned itself as an anti-imperialist, postcolonial, and multicultural antidote to entrenched British ethnocentrism. Scholars of *Doctor Who*, such as Orthia (2010), Charles (2007), Firefly (2013) and Clark (2013), maintain the serial's ontological and ideological perspective is more accurately described as liberal humanist and colorblind universalist. This perspective is embodied by the show's protagonist, "the Doctor," a sardonic white male alien who could easily be mistaken for a traditional Western hero.

Doctor Who centers on the galactic misadventures of the Doctor, a Time Lord who journeys through space and time in a ship called the TARDIS. One or more Earthlings typically accompany him on these jaunts. The Doctor looks suspiciously like a human but he has two hearts and his body is able to regenerate if fatally injured. This plot device has allowed the show to continue for over half a century with different actors playing the lead role, thus far all of them have been straight white men (Orthia 2010, 209). Although the Doctor is ostensibly an alien, he behaves like a quintessentially British dandy; he adores tea, the European aristocracy, and fashion. His costumes—Edwardian frock-coats, Victorian vests, smoking jackets, cricket whites, and Bohemian garb—visually "recall the period of the height of British imperial power" (Charles 2007, 117). In terms of political disposition, the Doctor epitomizes colonial liberalism. He is an objective, emotionally detached, savior-explorer who thirsts for knowledge and technical mastery (Charles 2007, 117). The Doctor eagerly embraces the "imperialist Enlightenment ideal of objectivity" (Fly 2013, 19). As Lindy Orthia, the editor of *Doctor Who & Race*, wryly comments, the Doctor "possesses near-omniscience and near-omnipotence that scientists and imperialists can only aspire to, but like them his tools are Western science and Western morality" (Orthia 2010, 217–218). Phenderson Djèlí Clark, an Afro-Caribbean speculative fiction writer and critic, suggests that the Doctor epitomizes "triumphant western humanism, with all its arrogance, self-proclaimed superiority and blindness" (Clark 2013).

One might say the Doctor possesses a colonial gaze, a gaze that "distributes knowledge and power to the subject who looks, while denying or minimizing access to power for its object, the one looked at" (Rieder 2008, 7). In this essay, I suggest that the liberal humanist whiteness of *Doctor Who* is revealed in the latest regeneration of the series, in particular in episodes that thematize the sins of European imperialism: slavery, genocide, and dispossession. It is in such episodes that it becomes evident that the show is framed and filtered through the Doctor's cosmopolitan, colonial, and colorblind gaze and thus tells stories "from an uncontested White British viewpoint," not from the perspective of the subjugated and enslaved (Malik 2002, 146).

Since the program's return in 2005, the most sustained engagement with slavery occurs in "The Impossible Planet" (2006), "The Satan Pit" (2006), and "Planet of the Ood" (2008), the three episodes that feature the Ood, an alien species described as "born to serve." Utilizing an interdisciplinary amalgam of critical ethnic studies, media studies, cultural studies, and postcolonial theory, this essay examines how the reboot of *Doctor Who* utilizes deracialized and decontextualized slavery allegories to absolve white guilt over the Transatlantic Slave Trade; express and contain xenophobic anxieties about post-colonial British multiculture; reinforce black racial stereotypes, and bolster white privilege by demanding viewers adopt the series colorblind liberal humanist standpoint. In *The Racial Contract*, Charles Mills asserts that "white misunderstanding, misrepresentation, evasion, and self-deception on matters related to race are among the most pervasive mental phenomena of the past few hundred years, a cognitive and moral economy psychically required for conquest, colonization, and enslavement" (1999, 19). The strategic white ignorance threaded throughout *Doctor Who*'s slavery episodes remind us that film and television "do not simply retell history from an apolitical and ideologically neutral place but subtly rewrite historical events so that white colonizers, paternalistic controllers, and meddling interlopers seem necessary, relevant, and moral" (Hughey 2014, 65). By closely examining the historical fictions and post-racial slavery parables of *Doctor Who*, I illuminate the program's "structural opacities," how its colorblind universalism sustains and nourishes the boundaries of contemporary whiteness and colonial consciousness, and the fraught place of race in multicultural and ostensibly postcolonial Britain.

Savage and Servile: The Ood as Natural Slave Race

> The West created the dangerous savages against which it set itself.—Preeti Nijhar, *Law and Imperialism*

Although "The Impossible Planet" and "The Satan Pit" allude to the existence of natural slave races "born to serve," this popular colonial theory—which justified the subjugation and enslavement of Africans and indigenous New World peoples—is the central theme of "Planet of the Ood." In this episode, the historical horrors of British imperialism are transposed onto Cthulhu-like cephalopods and projected into the year 4126, the era known as the Second Great and Bountiful Human Empire. "The Planet of the Ood" opens with a brief commercial that establishes the servile nature of the aliens. As glimmering galaxies glide by, the narrator's voice informs us that the Ood came from a distant world with one purpose: to serve. In the advertisement's closing shot, the camera zooms in on a cheerful Ood expectantly holding a teapot aloft and asking if you take your tea with milk and sugar. Tea and sugar are, of course, products suffused with colonial import. These freighted commodities symbolize the apex of British mercantilism. Tea invokes The East India Company and its role in growing and maintaining the British Empire in the Indian subcontinent. Sugar recalls the Caribbean plantations in which Caribbean Indians and then Africans toiled and died to sweeten the coffers of British slaveholders. This short scene suggests that the Ood are surrogates for the South Asians, Caribbean Indians, and Africans colonized by the British. In the future, space ships may have replaced slave ships but European imperialism churns on. The parallels between Ood oppression and African enslavement intensify as the episode unfolds.

Like the Africans enslaved by the British, the captured Ood are treated like mere livestock. They are chained, whipped, bred, branded, imported, and exported. Like the Africans whose bodies were broken through a brutal process called "seasoning," the Ood are maimed and rendered mute through "processing." Much like the Africans forced into chattel slavery, the Ood are dehumanized and animalized, a process Aimé Césaire called "thingification" (1972). Thingification is fundamental to the workings of colonialism (Mavhunga 2011, 154). It is how colonialism creates unequal classes, how it cements racial hierarchy, how it decides which beings can be sacrificed and subjugated. The edifice of colonialism is erected upon relations of domination and submission. It requires thingification. It thrives on zombification. The lobotomized Ood "represents the ultimate imperialist dream—a slave laborer that is truly a thing, unthinking, un-aspiring, and non-threatening" (Bishop 2010, 71). And just as the bloody slave revolts throughout the Americas exposed the docile laborer as a self-serving fiction of exploitative Europeans, the rebellion of the Ood suggests that slaves are not "born to serve" but ideologically manufactured for imperial purposes. Let us consider a few examples of how slavery and conquest are discursively produced in "Planet of the Ood."

In "The Ood as Slave Race: Colonial Continuity in the Second Great and Bountiful Human Empire," Eric Foss emphasizes how *Doctor Who* reiterates previous justifications for imperial conquest. "Just as the public records of early European explorers and conquerors emphasized the importance of 'civilizing mission' and described native populations as natural-born slaves" (Foss 2013, 112), Klineman Halpen (Tim McInnerny), the industrious CEO of Ood Operations, plays up the naturalness of having Ood servants and claims that they "rescued" the Ood from a life of savagery and aimlessly roaming the ice. Halpen's mapping of species characteristics onto biological differences, the conversion of savagery and civilization into permanent and fixed conditions, clearly echoes how Westerners used science to cement a racial hierarchy. In this white supremacist worldview, rationality is reserved for the West and the "dangerous irrational non–Western and the colonial savages and heathens could therefore be excluded. They were primitives, children of a lesser god, requiring management and control, and in some cases, outright extinction" (Nijhar 2015, 75). The same imperial logic animates Halpen's racist dismissal of the Ood as lowly beasts. His insistence that the Ood are a natural laboring class, suited only for performing the dirty work of civilization, expresses "a nostalgia for lost authority and for a pliable, completely subordinate proletariat that is one of the central fantasies of imperialism" (Brantlinger 1985, 181). Halpen clearly sees the Ood as primitive beings, chattel to be corralled, savages to be domesticated. As Francis Jennings notes in *The Invasion of America: Indians, Colonialism, and the Cant of Conquest*, the British devised the term 'savage' to indelibly mark the inferiority of non–Westerners: "The savage was prey, cattle, pet, or vermin—he was never citizen" (1976, 59). This inherent inferiority meant that there could be no justification for resistance to European invasion. By labeling the Ood as animals roaming the ice, Halpen not only justifies the enslavement of the Ood but the conquest of their planet as well.

Halpen's virulent racism toward to the Ood can be contrasted with the benevolent, yet equally lethal, racism of his chief marketing officer, Solana Mercurio (played by South Asian actress Ayesha Dharker). During her sales pitch to the young, male, and multi-racial gathering of would-be slave-owners, Mercurio repeatedly emphasizes how well the Ood are treated. According to Mercurio, Ood Operations doesn't just breed and sell the Ood, it makes them better by keeping them healthy, safe, happy, and educated. In effect, by having a South Asian woman perform the role of the British slave dealer, the series forces the formerly subjugated to symbolically defend their colonization as natural and necessary, thus implicitly shoring up imperial racism while seeming to break with these supposedly defunct racial formations. Ood Operations thus cunningly neutralizes the prospective buyer's guilt by suggesting that slavery is beneficial for the Ood because they lack the mental capacity to properly care for themselves. The aliens are offered as proof that Aristotle was right when he proclaimed: "From the hour of their birth, some are marked out for subjection, others for rule" (as cited in Davis 2006, 55). Ood Operations' professed desire to better the Ood through breeding and education replicates the white supremacist logic of scientific racism, the Western discourse that self-servingly carved up the world into enlightened Europeans and dangerous Others that must be remolded in their image, by force if necessary (Nijhar 2015, 75). The naturalistic and scientific arguments that Halpen and Mercurio "make about slavery, suggest that far from overcoming the problems of the past, the Second Great and Bountiful Human Empire has simply outsourced them" (Foss 2013, 112).

The Tenth Doctor (David Tennant) and his human companion Donna Noble (Catherine Tate) do not see the Ood as dangerous Others that must be reformed but rather as harmless and benign creatures. Towards the end of "Planet of the Ood," Donna angrily confronts Halpen for lobotomizing the aliens. Donna reminds Halpen that the Ood are born with hindbrains in their hands. For Donna, this biological quirk makes the aliens simultaneously peaceful, trusting, and vulnerable to attack. Donna's depiction of the Ood as docile amicable beings invokes the specter of the "noble savage." The term, which can be traced to 17th-century French literature, personified "European discontent with modernity. As European colonialism gained momentum, Africans and indigenous New World peoples were said to possess the noble qualities of harmony with nature, generosity, childlike complicity, happiness under duress, and a natural innate moral compass" (Hughey 2014, 64). Donna's impassioned defense of the Ood recycles similar stereotypes and is as patronizing and unintentionally derogatory as the imperialist rhetoric deployed by Halpen and Mercurio (Brantlinger 1985, 170). The humans are united in their belief that the aliens are savages and need saving. The only difference is the Halpen and Mercurio seek to rescue the Ood from themselves and Donna seeks to rescue them from her fellow humans. Saviorism is a powerful imperial fiction woven through "Planet of the Ood," and one that I will further unravel in the next section.

Innocence, Ignorance and Imperialism: The White Savior's Burden

> The white savior film is an important cultural device and artifact because it helps repair the myth of white supremacy and paternalism in an unsettled and racially charged time. The white savior film perpetuates, in subtle and friendly terms, the archaic paradigm of manifest destiny, the white man's burden, and the great white hope.
> —Matthew Hughey, *The White Savior Film: Content, Critics, and Consumption*

In "The Impossible Planet," the South Asian ethics officer Danny Bartock (Ronny Jhutti) blithely explains to blonde and fair Rose Tyler (Billie Piper) that the Ood are a basic slave race born to serve. Rose, the Tenth Doctor's human companion before Donna, is young, white, and working-class. She hails from 21st-century London and simply cannot believe that humans in the 42nd century have slaves. She self-righteously demands: "Since when do humans need slaves?" This brief exchange, which implicitly positions white working-class Rose as a defender of the subjugated Ood and Bartock, a descendant of those colonized by the British, as an amoral and avaricious imperialist, testifies to Britain's historical amnesia about the nasty racial realities of slavery and conquest. As French historian Ernest Renan reminds us, "forgetting is a crucial factor in the creation of the nation" (1990, 11). "The nation must disremember the fact of its violent beginning to fashion its national identity," suggests postcolonial literary scholar Ali Behdad (2000, 148). Historical amnesia and white ignorance are thus indispensable weapons in the imperialist arsenal. Critical whiteness scholars define white ignorance as a form of "seeing wrongly, resulting from the habit of erasing, dismissing, distorting, and forgetting about the lives, cultures, and histories of peoples whites have colonized" (Bailey 2007, 85). It brutally suppresses minority knowledge and aggressively produces knowledge that serves the social and political purposes of the racial elite (Sullivan 2007, 154). In *The Racial Contract*, Charles Mills opines that whiteness itself is anchored in white ignorance: "Part of what it means to be constructed as 'white,' … part of what it required to achieve Whiteness, successfully to become a white person … is a cognitive model that precludes self-transparency and genuine understanding of social realities" (1999, 18). When *Doctor Who* constructs Rose, the white woman, as the savior of the enslaved and the South Asian man as the callous colonizer, it not only post-racializes imperialism but actively suppresses the actual histories of the subjugated, thus absolving contemporary white British subjects for the sins of their colonial ancestors. As this exchange between Rose and Bartock indicates, imperial ignorance and white liberal humanist saviorism lurk beneath the surface of "The Impossible Planet" and "The Satan Pit." The disastrous intertwining of white innocence with colonial benevolence is more clearly manifested in "Planet of the Ood," when the Doctor and Donna "save" the extraterrestrials from exploitation.

Donna's reaction to the second great and bountiful empire's intergalactic slave trade is particularly telling. When the Doctor and Donna chance upon shipping containers crammed with hundreds of Ood awaiting export to the three galaxies, Donna realizes with horror that future Britain is an empire built on slavery. The Doctor wryly opines that it's not so different from the 20th century, the historical period from which Donna originates. Clearly affronted, Donna exclaims: "Oi. I haven't got slaves!" To which, the Doctor acerbically responds: "Who do you think made your clothes?" Much like Rose, Donna seamlessly fuses white innocence and strategic historical amnesia. Her aggrieved reaction to the Doctor's suggestion that she materially benefits from slavery echoes the defensive rhetoric of contemporary whites when confronted with the persistence of systemic racism or, worse, asked to pay reparations for the lives and labor stolen by their ancestors. While the existence of sweatshops, sex trafficking, and other forms of racialized global capitalist exploitation testify to the longevity of slavery, the Doctor's neat suturing of past bondage to the slavery of the neoliberal present effectively erases the British imperialism that laid down the colonial circuits upon which the transnational corporations of today trade. *Doctor Who*'s timeshifting of slavery into the present and the distant future deracializes an institution that was built on white supremacy and European colonialism and thus relieves whites of their historical guilt for African chattel slavery. Reanimating bondage in a different time and space also creates an opportunity for *Doctor Who*'s white protagonists to "perform their antiracist outrage" (Ahmed 2004) by valiantly saving the oppressed aliens from the true menace: "evil, ignorant, and overtly racist whites" (Hughey 2014, 170).

Like the white savior narratives meticulously chronicled in Matthew Hughey's *The White Savior Film: Content, Critics, and Consumption*, "Planet of the Ood" juxtaposes the heroic actions of good whites (the Doctor and Donna) with the unscrupulous deeds of bad whites (Halpen, Ood Operations' ruthless CEO and proud slave-owner). The moral differences between these two camps are starkly revealed when the time-travellers confront Halpen over his corporation's reprehensible decision to capture, lobotomize, and sell the Ood as servants. The Doctor and Donna chastise Halpen for exploiting the "peaceful" and trusting Ood but they do not question the aliens' status as subhuman 'creatures' or their need to be saved by superior beings. Castigating Halpen for overt acts of white supremacy allows the Doctor and Donna to preserve "white dominance through subtle forms of racial paternalism" (Hughey 2014, 171). Their dogged focus on Halpen as the source of evil also allows "audiences to ignore the deep systems, institutions, and resources that resulted in and now reproduce contemporary structures of inequality" (Hughey 2014, 167). Blaming Halpen for the enslavement of the Ood, "rather than a system of symbolic and material violence," absolves the future British Empire for propagating and profiting from bondage (Hughey 2014, 167).

During this confrontation with the Doctor and Donna, Halpen casually refers to a system that's "worked for two hundred years." Ironically, it is this fleeting reference that reminds the audience that the episode also operates as a futuristic allegory for the horrors of African chattel slavery. "Planet of the Ood" does not "recreate a verisimilitude of the past, but rather reveals how this long history of slavery and oppression constitutes an integral part" of the present and future (Joo 2011, 291). In "Victorians and Africans: The Genealogy of the Myth of the Dark Continent," Patrick Brantlinger suggests that "nothing points more uncannily to the processes of projection and displacement of guilt for the slave trade, guilt for empire, guilt for one's own savage and shadowy impulses than those moments" when good whites confront bad whites in conquered lands (1985, 196). Seeing "Planet of the Ood" as a white savior fantasy about the transatlantic slave trade reveals that the confrontation between the Doctor, Donna, and Halpen is less about the need for alien liberation than a way for well-meaning whites to absolve themselves from their lingering guilt for their European ancestors' imperialist annexation of foreign lands and bodies. Viewing the Doctor, Donna, and Halpen, not as adversaries, but rather beneficiaries and agents of British imperialism illuminates how all three are afflicted with the most colonial of maladies: the white (wo)man's burden.

The Doctor and Donna's status as benevolent sufferers of the white (wo)man's burden is manifested in a variety of ways. The most painful and personal misery is endured by the Doctor who can telepathically hear the "song of captivity," which the unprocessed Ood sing before they are lobotomized and shipped off. In "'Sociopathetic Abscess' or 'Yawning Chasm'? The Absent Postcolonial Transition in *Doctor Who*," Lindy Orthia reflects upon how the episode constructs the empathetic Doctor and Donna as Christ-like saviors: "The Doctor and Donna resemble the colonizers (who are human) and merely stand in solidarity with the Ood as they revolt; yet the Ood almost worship them. The Doctor asks for the privilege of pulling the switch that effects the Ood's liberation and his wish is granted, thus depriving the colonized of their own symbolic moment. At the end of the serial, the Doctor and Donna are given a glorious send-off with their very own hymn-like Ood song and as they climb, Christ-like, into the TARDIS for literal ascension into the heavens, they are told their input will never be forgotten" (2010, 212).

The deification of the Doctor and Donna simultaneously emphasizes their role in the Ood's liberation and obscures the complicity of humans in alien enslavement. The episode also emphasizes the critical role played by white abolitionists in securing the freedom of the racialized aliens by having Dr. Ryder (Adrian Rawlins), a member of the "Friends of the Ood," infiltrate Ood Operations and lower the telepathic forcefield that makes it physically impossible for the Ood to revolt. Liberation from bondage, which should be a moment that commemorates the agency of the colonized, becomes yet another "moment to celebrate whiteness, to see white civilization as benevolence" (Leonard 2015). Instead of challenging self-serving imperialist narratives, "Planet of the Ood" remixes "long-standing tradition of whites saving the racial other unable to save him/herself" (Leonard 2015). But what is truly saved is the lethal fiction of White innocence. The strategic white ignorance threaded throughout *Doctor Who*'s Ood episodes remind us that film and television "do not simply retell history from an apolitical and ideologically neutral place but subtly rewrite historical events so that white colonizers, paternalistic controllers, and meddling interlopers seem necessary, relevant, and moral" (Hughey 2014, 65). But, the rare moments of rupture in "Planet of the Ood," when the specters of slavery swirl and rise before us, prove that you cannot "erase the indelible" (Rodriguez 2008). For the "social and economic system that rests on the subjection of Africans as racial chattel is not a compartmentalized or reconcilable event" in the white racial destiny of the West, but is the foundation of what critical race scholar Cheryl Harris has called the "ongoing legal consolidation of whiteness as property, a consolidation that can only occur at the expense of those who are dispossessed and/or actually owned" by the white state (as cited in Rodriguez 2008).

Reconciliation or Reparation? The Ood, Meta-Slavery and the Return of the Repressed

> Television, far from being "free" and independent, actively racially organizes, constructs a reality and "neutrality" of its own, and always makes active choices and judgments about who, what and how to represent.
> —Sarita Malik, *Representing Black Britain: Black and Asian Images on Television*

Britain's development as an imperial nation-state, the industrialization of its economy, and its current standing as a super power on the global stage was "founded upon a crime against humanity in the form of racial chattel enslavement of African bodies and the global trafficking of millions of these bodies for three hundred years" (Beckles 2013, 23). Although it was the largest slave-trading nation and "extracted more wealth from enchained and enslaved Africans than any other European nation," modern-day Britain prefers not to dwell on its colonial excesses and capitalist successes (Beckles 2013, 82). It prefers to celebrate having banned the slave trade in 1807, to commemorate the heroics of white abolitionists like William Wilberforce (Mohanram 2007, xviii). Two hundred years after abolishing chattel slavery, Prime Minister Tony Blair expressed regret for the "unbearable suffering" caused by Britain's role in slavery but made no mention of financial compensation.

In fact, the British government has repeatedly stated that paying reparations for slavery is the wrong way to address "an historical problem" (Leonard and Tomlinson 2013). While Britain refuses to reckon with the evils of bondage, the subject is frequently allegorized in science fiction and fantasy television series, typically through encounters with alien slave races. Speculative fiction scholar Isiah Lavender, III, suggests that meta-slavery narratives "take us into a space where the interplay of past, present, and future allows [viewers] to experience slavery and examine the painful social divisions it has created" (2011, 60). Meta-slavery narratives do not just make the past present; they remind us that the past is not past. Slavery lives on and we must grapple with its horrific legacies if we hope to heal the weeping wounds of racism.[1]

Doctor Who allows us to replay—and reconsider—what occurs when a "great big empire of slavery" violently implodes. What happens after the slaves secure their freedom, when the subjugated become citizens? For *Doctor Who*, the solution is to repatriate the aliens, to ship them back to their home planet. The series thus actualizes the preferred solution of 19th-century whites to the "slavery problem": shipping Africans back to Africa. And much like former Prime Minister Tony Blair, *Doctor Who* studiously avoids the subject of reparations. The notion that the Ood—subjugated, sold, and exported throughout the Tri-Galactic—have a right to remain where they are after liberation, that they are an integral part of the Second Great and Bountiful Human Empire, is never considered. Their labor—in factories, homes, and the military—built future Britain. Are they not deserving of remuneration for being tortured, mutilated, and robbed of their freedom?

As my readings of the Ood episodes suggest, the latest regeneration of *Doctor Who* seems more concerned with justifying the sins of British colonialism than making reparations for slavery. Instead of unmasking the evils of empire, these episodes demonstrate the tenacity of white innocence, the durability of racial stereotypes, and the suppleness of white supremacy. The Ood episodes illustrate how deeply ingrained race and racism are in the "political imaginaries, structures and practices of 'the West'" (Lentin and Titley 2011, 49). In an era of racial backlash, "in which increasing numbers of people (including nonwhites) believe racism and racial inequality are things of the past," *Doctor Who*'s liberal humanist white savior narrative promotes a watered-down retelling of British imperial history (Hughey 2014, 66). It reengineers the colonial past to fit within Britain's contemporary moment of conservative racial politics. The story of the Ood's liberation from enslavement becomes yet another romantic tale about the brave Doctor rather than a much-needed examination of the "actual legal, political, and social structures that reproduced racial inequality and oppression in the face of good intentions and individual heroic deeds" (Hughey 2014, 66).

Recovering from the trauma of transatlantic slavery requires acknowledging the racism of the imperial past in the present and refusing to imagine future worlds that replicate such colonial hierarchies. It requires letting go of imperial fictions and post-racial fantasies. In *Re-Forming the Past: History, The Fantastic, and The Postmodern Slave Narrative*, A. Timothy Spaulding argues that we need new narratives about slavery, speculative narratives that "reveal the complexities embedded within the slave experience and obscured by traditional historical accounts" (2005, 4). Fantastic fictions "designed to reshape our view of slavery and its impact on our cultural condition" (Spaulding 2005, 4). Fictions "designed to intrude upon history as a means to re-form it" (Spaulding 2005, 4). Although *Doctor Who* claims to be anti-imperialist, postcolonial, and multicultural, the long-running serial often operates as "a paradigm of ideological and ontological conservatism" (Charles 2007, 120–121). Thus, while the series may intend to re-form the imperialist past; currently, it reifies it. David Higgins once observed that science fiction's emergence from—and ongoing entanglement with—imperialism means that it not only performs the dreamwork of empire but also produces rich imaginative possibilities for empire's antithesis" (2011, 333). While the Ood episodes testify to how *Doctor Who* performs the dreamwork of multiracial white supremacist neoliberal empire, I hold out hope that a popular science fiction television program about "retrospectivity and prospectivity, legacy and latency, pasts as horizons of futures," might someday reshape how we remember British imperialism and perhaps even remind us why there can be no racial reconciliation without reparations (Goldberg 2009, vii).

NOTE

1. In 2013, Britain, Holland and France were sued by 14 Caribbean countries for the lingering legacies of the transatlantic slave trade. Caricom, a group composed of 12 former British colonies together with the former French colony Haiti and the Dutch-held Suriname, have brought the lawsuit. A reparations committee, led by Barbados historian Sir Hilary Beckles, has been set up to work out how much the European governments should pay for the theft of Caribbean life and labor. Sir Beckles says they are focusing on the UK because "the British made the most money out of slavery and the slave trade—they got the lion's share. And, importantly, they knew how to convert slave profits into industrial profits" (Sir Hilary Beckles as cited in Tom Leonard and Simon Tomlinson, "14 Caribbean Nations Sue Britain, Holland and France for Slavery Reparations That Could Cost Hundreds of Billions of Pounds," *The Daily Mail*, http://www.dailymail.co.uk/news/article-2451891/14-Caribbean-nations-sue-Britain-Holland-France-slavery-reparations.html).

BIBLIOGRAPHY

Ahmed, Sara. 2004. "Declarations of Whiteness: The Non-Performativity of Anti-Racism." *borderlands* 3, no. 2. http://www.borderlands.net.au/vol3no2_2004/ahmed_declarations. htm. Accessed June 21 2016.
Bailey, Alison. 2007. "Strategic Ignorance." In *Race and Epistemologies of Ignorance*, edited by Shannon Sullivan and Nancy Tuana. Albany: State University of New York Press. pp. 77–94.
Beckles, Hilary McD. 2013. *Britain's Black Debt: Reparations for Slavery and Native Genocide*. Kingston: University of the West Indies Press.
Behdad, Ali. 2000. "Founding Myths of the Nation, or What Jefferson and Hamilton Forgot about Immigration." *Aztlan: A Journal of Chicano Studies* 25, no. 2: 143–149.

Bishop, Kyle William. 2010. *American Zombie Gothic: The Rise and Fall (and Rise) of the Walking Dead in Popular Culture.* Jefferson, NC: McFarland.

Brantlinger, Patrick. 1985. "Victorians and Africans: The Genealogy of the Myth of the Dark Continent." *Critical Inquiry* 12, no. 1): 166–203.

Césaire, Aimé. 1972. *Discourse on Colonialism.* New York: Monthly Review Press.

Charles, Alec. 2007. "The Ideology of Anachronism: Television, History, and the Nature of Time" in *Time and Relative Dissertations in Space: Critical Perspectives on "Doctor Who,"* edited by David Butler. Manchester: Manchester University Press. pp. 108–22.

Clark, Phenderson Djèlí. 2013. "Doctor Who(?)-Racey-Wacey-Timey-Wimey." *The Musings of a Disgruntled Haradrim.* https://pdjeliclark.wordpress.com/2013/06/03/doctor-who-racey-wacey-timey-wimey/. Accessed June 3, 2016.

Davis, David Brion. 2006. *Inhuman Bondage: The Rise and Fall of Slavery in the New World.* Oxford: Oxford University Press.

Firefly. 2013. "The White Doctor" in *Doctor Who & Race*, edited by Lindy Orthia. Bristol: Intellect. 15–20.

Foss, Eric. 2013. "The Ood as a Slave Race: Colonial Continuity in the Second Great and Bountiful Human Empire" in *Doctor Who & Race*, edited by Lindy Orthia. Bristol: Intellect. pp. 109–21.

Goldberg, David Theo. 2009. *The Threat of Race: Reflections on Racial Neoliberalism.* Malden, MA: Blackwell.

Grewell, Greg. 2001. "Colonizing the Universe: Science Fictions Then, Now, and in the (Imagined) Future." *Rocky Mountain Review of Language and Literature* 55, no. 2: 25–47.

Harper, Graeme. 2008. "Planet of the Ood." *Doctor Who.* BBC One.

Higgins, David M. 2011. "Toward a Cosmopolitan Science Fiction." *American Literature* 88, no. 2): 331–54.

Hughey, Matthew. 2014. *The White Savior Film: Content, Critics, and Consumption.* Philadelphia: Temple University Press.

Jennings, Francis. 1976. *The Invasion of America: Indians, Colonialism, and the Cant of Conquest.* New York: W.W. Norton.

Joo, Hee-Jung Serenity. 2011. "Old and New Slavery, Old and New Racisms: Strategies of Science Fiction in Octavia Butler's 'Parables' Series." *Extrapolation* 52, no. 3: 279–99.

Lavender, Isiah, III. 2011. *Race in American Science Fiction.* Bloomington: Indiana University Press.

Lentin, Alana, and Gavan Titley. 2011. *The Crises of Multiculturalism: Racism in a Neoliberal Age.* London: Zed Books.

Leonard, David. 2015. "Remixing the Burden: Kony 2012 and the Wages of Whiteness." *Australian Critical Race and Whiteness Studies Association* 11, no. 1. http://www.acrawsa.org.au/files/ejournalfiles/251Leonard2015111.pdf. Accessed June 5, 2016.

Leonard, Tom, and Simon Tomlinson. 2013. "14 Caribbean Nations Sue Britain, Holland and France for Slavery Reparations." News. *Daily Mail Online.* October 11. http://www.dailymail.co.uk/news/article-2451891/14-Caribbean-nations-sue-Britain-Holland-France-slavery-reparations.html. Accessed June 19, 2016.

Malik, Sarita. 2002. *Representing Black Britain: A History of Black and Asian Images on British Television.* London: Sage.

Mavhunga, Clapperton Chakanetsa. 2011. "Vermin Beings, On Pestiferous Animals and Human Game." *Social Text* 29, no. 1: 151–76.

Mills, Charles. 1999. *The Racial Contract.* Ithaca: Cornell University Press.

Mohanram, Radhika. 2007. *Imperial White: Race, Diaspora, and the British Empire.* Minneapolis: University of Minnesota Press.

Nijhar, Preeti. 2015. *Law and Imperialism: Criminality and Constitution in Colonial India and Victorian England.* London: Routledge.

Orthia, Lindy. 2010. "'Sociopathetic Abscess' or 'Yawning Chasm'? The Absent Postcolonial Transition in Doctor Who." *The Journal of Commonwealth Literature* 45, no. 2: 207–25.

Orthia, Lindy. 2013. "Introduction" in *Doctor Who & Race*, edited by Lindy Orthia. Bristol: Intellect. pp. 1–11.

Renan, Ernest. 1990. "What Is a Nation?" in *Nation and Narration*, edited by Homi Bhabha. New York: Routledge. pp. 8–22.

Rieder, John. 2008. *Colonialism and the Emergence of Science Fiction*. Middletown, CT: Wesleyan University Press.

Rodríguez, Dylan. 2008. "Inaugurating Multiculturalist White Supremacy." *Colorlines*. http://www.colorlines.com/articles/dreadful-genius-obama-moment. Accessed June 18, 2016.

Spaulding, Timothy A. 2005. *Re-Forming the Past: History, The Fantastic, and The Postmodern Slave Narrative*. Columbus: Ohio State University Press.

Strong, James. 2006a. "The Impossible Planet." *Doctor Who*. BBC One.

Strong, James. 2006b. "The Satan Pit." *Doctor Who*. BBC One.

Sullivan, Shannon. 2007. "White Ignorance and Colonial Oppression Or, Why I Know So Little About Puerto Rico" in *Race and Epistemologies of Ignorance*, edited by Shannon Sullivan and Nancy Tuana. Albany: State University of New York Press. pp. 153–172.

Doctor, Go Roman
"The Romans," Emperor Nero
and Historical Comedy in Doctor Who

CAREY FLEINER

Introduction[1]

BBC production files on *Doctor Who* indicate that a Roman-era drama had been a given from the days of *Doctor Who*'s earliest conception,[2] and the Doctor has encountered Romans at least seven times in his 1000-plus years, in televised serials, audio plays, and printed novels and stories (Parkin 2007, 51–53). Although the Doctor (William Hartnell) tells Vicki (Maureen O'Brien) that he's been to Rome before, "The Romans" (1965) was the Doctor's first televised visit to Rome. Since then, he has met various Romans in 1969's "The War Games" and "The Fires of Pompeii" (2008); companion Rory Williams (Arthur Darvill) was "Romanized"—erased in time in "Cold Blood" (2010), he reappears as a centurion when the Doctor travels to Stonehenge circa AD 100 in "The Pandorica Opens" (2011).[3]

Despite its small budget, "The Romans" delivers audience expectations from any big budget "HollyRome"[4] extravaganza: director Christopher Barry, writer Dennis Spooner, and production designer Ray Cusick put all of the classical signposts in place including references to an aqueduct, grapes and wine.[5] There is a villa, palace, and dinner party[6]; a market, slaves, and galley; gladiators, lions,[7] and Christians; and Nero (Derek Francis), a fiddle and the fire.[8] Sure, there are only two gladiators and one Christian, Ian (William Russell) faces unmatched stock footage of wild beasts, and Rome afire is a cardboard cutout, but Barbara (Jacqueline Hill), who has been captured by slave-traders, is worth a whopping 10,000 sesterces, Ian sports a toga, and the Doctor shows off his skills on the lyre—or, rather, obfuscates his lack thereof.

Doctor Who was conceived as an educational, family program, and history lessons were part of that directive. What is particularly interesting about "The Romans," however, is its strong comedic bent, a first for the program, especially that it is played against the darker plot of slave trading, gladiatorial combat, and the brutality of the Julio-Claudian household. Nero himself, who is frequently the default comedy emperor onscreen, veers here between extreme cruelty and impish humor. This chapter then takes into consideration the contemporary context of "The Romans," audience expectations and response to the serial, and comedy and the Romans, especially the portrayal of Nero, in early 1960s pop culture.

The story of *Doctor Who*'s development is well-documented. Amongst his initial travelling companions are a pair of comprehensive schoolteachers, science instructor Ian Chesterton and history teacher Barbara Wright. Producers Sydney Newman and Verity Lambert's vision for the show was that it educate as it entertained, and early efforts at teaching history were earnest. The production crew expected writers and script-editors to do their homework (Tulloch and Alvarado 1983, 39–40),[9] even in comedies. Several of *Doctor Who*'s writers have had degrees or a background in history, including John Lucarotti ("Marco Polo," 1964) and Louis Marks ("Masque of Mandragora," 1976), who had a Ph.D. from Oxford.[10] Examples of extracurricular research are found within "The Romans'" production notes: Christopher Barry wrote to Professor A. M. Collini of the Museo Della Civilita Romana for postcards of Rome and models to be used as reference material on the serial[11] (*ibid.*, 29 October 1964). Lack of formal education did not preclude historical knowledge among the writers, however, and reflects, too, what could be appreciated by the audience: Dennis Spooner, who left school at a young age, was praised by David Whitaker for the depth of treatment in his initial draft-script for the program, "The Reign of Terror" (1964).[12] His follow-up script of "The Romans" hit all the marks required in a screen-version of Rome and assumes the audience is conversant in the general history of the period.[13] The BBC received positive feedback from schoolteachers at the time of the early serials (Tulloch and Alvarado 1983, 39); for example, Antony Ireland, a schoolteacher, contacted Verity Lambert praising "Marco Polo"; he also asked Barry Newman if he could borrow plans or costumes from the serial to use in lessons.[14] There were, nevertheless, complaints of liberties and frivolity in the storytelling.[15] Presenting history to the masses, however, has always been a tricky business, as Tacitus himself complained, in the preface of his *History*, that one's audience prefers to hear (and to believe) scandal and crime and distrusts the historian who "curries favor."[16]

"The Romans" may have been classified as an "adventure—historical,"[17] but producer Verity Lambert suggested that the serial be written as a farce.[18]

"The Romans" consequently romps through its paces especially in Part 3, when Nero appears and fulfills the expectations of an audience accustomed to cinematic Rome.[19] The black humor and farce of "The Romans" had some precedence for *Doctor Who* viewers; for example, "The Reign of Terror," an otherwise grim and sober serial, had moments of light comic relief. Spooner, who was friends with *Carry On Cleo* (1964) film star Jim Dale, apparently attended rehearsals of the film and took inspiration from it (Tulloch and Alvarado 1983, 46–47; Wood and Miles 2006, 126). "The Romans'" close connection to *Carry On Cleo* would have also made its style of humor familiar to *Doctor Who*'s audience: the *Carry On* films were a successful institution by 1965, and William Hartnell's role as eponymous character in *Carry On, Sergeant* was still familiar. *Cleo* is noteworthy in particular for not only for its humor, but its target: the overblown and over-budget spectacle of the 1963 Lizpatra vehicle *Cleopatra*—on whose abandoned British sets it was filmed.[20]

Usually when events of the Roman era have been dramatized for popular consumption, they fall into two general categories: one is the deadly serious spectacle depicting the extravagance of the era if not the struggles of the early Christians against the decadence of the pagans. Such films tend to be based on popular novels rather than academic historiography,[21] and even if based on novels by academics and didacts, tend to reflect current popular culture and events. So while such films may be touted for their historical accuracy, and most cinematic and television depictions of the Roman era show their scholarship, much of the humor in modern-day visions of Rome comes at the expense of the solemnity of the epic, and not just the production: historical humor succeeds as it subverts its subject as it references and mocks well-known schoolboy facts, deflates pretention, or mocks modern authority figures even as it dresses them up in togas and spangles.[22]

Anachronism and self-reference also contribute to the comedic elements of "The Romans." For example, as they relax at the villa, Barbara sends Ian to a non-existent fridge for ice, a joke Ian revisits on his friend at the end of the serial. The Target novelization goes full-blown *Carry On* and expands its anachronism to modern awareness, for example, comparing "New Rome" to Milton Keynes and other British New Towns. Elsewhere in the novelization, Nero remarks, "People seem to imagine that I do simply nothing all day, but sit around writing songs, and persecuting Christians, and organizing orgies, and all that ... but there's a lot more to being an Emperor than you might suppose" (Cotton 1987, 112). Finally, the Doctor wants to visit Rome because he believes that Nero has been treated unfairly by the history books and wants to see for himself the actual events (17).

How Much History Did the Audience Know?

In the case of "The Romans," erudition about the Roman era does not necessarily depend on one's conversance with the historiography: most, if not all, plot points and sign posts present in historicals are drawn from popular culture rather than textbooks[23]—19th-century artist Jean-Léon Gérôme had a great influence on popular perception of Roman grandeur with his 1859's *Ave Caesar, Morituri Te Salutant* and 1872's *Pollice Verso.* The latter depicts a gladiator who considers the "thumbs down" signs from the emperor and his box seat neighbors—"HollyRome" films have got more mileage from this fiercely debated hand gesture (Vance 1989, 48–49)[24] and a one-off line from Suetonius's *Life of Claudius*[25] than they have from the past 150 years' worth of Classical scholarship—but everyone knows that gladiators who are about to die salute the emperor, and everyone knows that if the crowd gives the fallen gladiator a thumbs down, his day is about to get much worse. Indeed, in the novelization of "The Romans," poor Ian writes a series of letters to his future headmaster in order to explain his predicament, and he admits that he is depending on his knowledge of *films* (specifically *Spartacus*), rather than the history books, to plan his strategy against his gladiatorial opponent (Cotton 1987, 90). Compare that to Barbara in "The Aztecs" (1964), who mentions that she specialized in Aztec culture as part of her teacher training—and she plans to use that knowledge to try to pose as a reincarnation of High Priest Yetaxa and convince the Aztecs to cease their practice of human sacrifice—earning a reprimand from the Doctor on the perils of changing the course of history (Wood and Miles 2006, 66, 68; Howe, Stammers, and Walker 1994, 26).

Why Is Nero the Funny Emperor, Anyway?

Everyone knows a few things about Nero: he murdered his mother; and he fiddled while Rome burned; he tortured Christians by feeding them to the lions.

Interpretation of Nero's behavior has a complex history; his reputation is currently changing from "zero to hero" among some academics.[26] Well-educated, and an aspiring musician, artist, and poet, he was a politically inexperienced boy of 16 when he became emperor. Despite the sensational claims by the historians that his own his mother murdered rivals—including her husband and Nero's stepfather, the emperor Claudius—to secure Nero's succession,[27] he was, in fact, publicly sanctioned, supported, and promoted as the official heir by Claudius. And he *was* actually very popular. The young emperor may have scandalized conservative Romans with his predilection for acting, music and athletics,[28] but he was popular in the Greek east where such pursuits were an acceptable part of an aristocrat's education (Mratschek 2013, 45–62), and the lower classes in Rome loved him for the lavish spectacles and entertainments he put on for them. After his death, flowers were regularly left on his grave for years, and during the reign of the subsequent dynasty, no less than three false Neros showed up in the year after his death (AD 68).[29]

Whence comes the scandalous reputation? The most easily accessible Roman sources on Nero—the works of Suetonius, Tacitus, and Dio Cassius— saddle Nero with bad press. If Nero's inclinations towards art and music offended the conservative sensibilities of the Roman court and the secular authors who described him, his behavior towards the Christians cement his legacy as a villain of Western entertainment. Christian historians of Late Antiquity through to the Middle Ages present him as if not the Anti-Christ, then his accomplice (Champlin 2003, 16–24, no. 3, 4). These authors together provide us with the best known stories (or at least the best known gossip) about Nero, and they tend to be read uncritically by non-scholars. Sensational stories told by contemporaries to illustrate a moral point or to vilify what they perceived as the excesses of the aristocracy are presented in film and on television as indisputable, factual events[30]—and these works are usually the extent of background research by screenwriters and novelists. Thus derives the popular image of Nero: a fat, spoiled, bearded,[31] man-child who shirks his responsibilities towards his office and the state and who treats cruelly anyone who might threaten his authority, his mother, wives, or Christians.

Portrayals of Nero On-Screen

After Caligula, Nero is probably the most recognized Roman emperor in popular culture, but Nero becomes the sinister buffoon while Caligula is the sex-depraved madman (even if Peter Ustinov's Nero gets one of Caligula's best lines in *Quo Vadis*).[32] Italian director Enrico Guazzoni made a number of Rome-era films in the silent era including *Agrippina* (1911)[33] which, although a tragedy, features a scenery-chewing Nero; his 1912 *Quo Vadis* includes vicious scenes of Nero at the arena, watching Christians viciously attacked and killed by lions.[34] Before Ustinov, character actor Emil Jannings played Nero in the 1925 version of *Quo Vadis*, another larger-than-life performance. So even in even "serious" silent films, Nero is the go-to comic villain; an early dedicated Neronic comedy is Universal's 1925 silent *Nero* touted as an "hysterical historical comedy" (Solomon 2001, 287–94). He shows up as a figure of mocked excess in deliberate farce: a 1975 episode of *The Goodies* called "The Rome Antics," Nero appears twice: clips from an elaborately produced silent film feature at the start of the episodes showing a well-accessorized, orgiastic banquet scene featuring a very recognizable Nero; in the show itself, Nero (Roy Kinnear) is depicted feeding Christians to the lions when not chasing the boys around the palace. He is readily familiar in a children's cartoon: the animated emperor in the Bugs Bunny cartoon *Roman Legion-Hare* (1955) orders lions to chow down on Christians in the anachronistic Coliseum—he is not addressed by name, but recognizable as a caricature of William Laughton's 1932 Nero (*The Sign of the Cross*). Even in more recent, serious drama, he's shown as a spoiled, dangerous twit: Christopher Biggins plays Nero as a giggly, murderous mama's boy in the BBC's *I, Claudius* (1976); Anthony Andrews relishes his role of the Christian-killing Caesar in *A.D.* (1985). It is useless to reinvent Nero as a sympathetic character: the least appealing celluloid Nero is the most recent, Hans Matheson, who plays a skinny, clean-shaven emo Nero in *Imperium: Nero* (2004). Most dramatic (and comedic) treatments of Nero include the matricide and the burning of Rome, but this version has Nero sent into slavery at a young age. He grows up to be a reluctant emperor who just wants to write sensitive poetry, and he kills himself by the side of a pretty river after he's been declared an outlaw by the Senate.

Derek Francis and Nero

Derek Francis requested a role in *Doctor Who*, the first famous name to do so and an unusual if not unique request at the time (Wood and Miles 2006, 129)—although he had to be persuaded to take the specific role of Nero by Jacqueline Hill (Howe, Stammers, Walker 1994, 89). He was 45 to real-Nero's 34, but he leapt into the role of a man who had never heard the word "no" in his life with great aplomb and made his Nero an "innocent psycho" (Wood and Miles 2006, 125). Appearing fresh from the baths at the end of episode 2, Francis's emperor sports a laurel wreath as he belches and gnaws on a joint of meat, then fussily wipes his hands on a servant. He lusts immediately for Barbara, pursuing her through the corridors and ambushing her in his wife's bedroom, yet at the same time cowers before his imperious spouse. Francis captures Nero's moodiness and temper tantrums well with ghastly black humor: for example, following an homage to *The Court Jester*, when the Doctor saves Nero from a poisoned cup of wine, the emperor thanks him very kindly, then hands the cup to his servant. The man obediently downs the wine and dies. Shrugs Nero, "[The Doctor] was right." Just another day in the imperial palace, where, according to poisoner Locusta (Anne Tirard),[35] "[it's] almost a tradition … that the family of Caesar want to murder each other." Indeed, in real life, in addition to his mother, Nero murdered his step-brother Britannicus,[36] and then went on to murder two wives (Octavia and Poppaea) and a potential third (Antonia)[37] when she rejected his proposal—in rejecting him, Barbara was, to coin a phrase, playing with fire. Another example of Nero's whimsical cruelty comes when he orders Barbara to accompany him to the gladiatorial school and asks her, "Have you ever seen a fight?" She says no; he replies, "Then I will arrange one while we're there…. I feel like seeing someone hurt myself tonight."

A final example of black humor hinges on the main plot point of the music competition between Nero and Maximus Pettullian (Bart Allison), an expert musician. The real Pettullian had been murdered on Nero's orders, so the emperor is shocked when the musician, that is, the Doctor, appears. Caesar is aggravated as he assumes Pettullian can outplay him—in fact, we hear Nero strike only a bad chord (which the Doctor attempts even more badly to imitate). The emperor fumes when the Doctor plays the "silent" lyre piece that the audience admires ("It's the Emperor's new clothes, my dear! I gave the idea to Hans Anderson [sic]!") knowing full well he is being mocked. Ever the showman, Nero decides the best way to enhance the Doctor's/Pettullian's performance is to set lions on the man in the middle of a command performance. Rightfully so, the Doctor suspects Nero's choice of venue and asks, "You want me to play in the arena? … Then I shall try to make it a roaring success … something they can really sink their teeth into, hmmm?"

The real-life Nero did take his musical prowess seriously even if he did not feed his rivals to the lions (Champlin 2003, 54–83): the sources tell us that he practiced diligently,[38] and that he had images made of himself in the guise of a cithara-player displayed throughout the palace and struck on coinage.[39] While he might have organized his own music competitions (for example, the *Neronia*)[40] and used imperial prerogative to move one festival to a more convenient time for his schedule, he insisted on being judged by the same standards as the other musicians (*ibid.*). Out of self-preservation, the other musicians allegedly played more badly than usual deliberately to lose to him—if Nero did not bribe them outright to lose[41]—and Nero also planted supportive claques, rather similar to living applause-o-meters, in the audience.[42]

Francis plays these scenes and these lines with the same farcical humor one finds not only in *Carry On, Cleo* but also in the performance given by Zero Mostel as Pseudolous the Slave in *A Funny Thing Happened on the Way to the Forum* (which ran in the West End in 1963 and so may have influenced Francis's performance). Such scenes of horror, fear, and murder may seem an odd choice for easy laughs—but Nero was a default boogeyman among the early Christians; if Nero is "every-emperor" for us, he was as well for Christian writers through to the Middle Ages when it came to the suffering of its practitioners, as the worst of the horrors of the persecutions under the pagan emperors were attributed to him—reinforced by Pope Gregory the Great's dramatic presentation of blood squeezed from a handful of sand taken from the Circus of Gaius (Caligula) and Nero.[43] This sports facility, the actual site of their blood-thirsty spectacles and execution of criminals, eventually became part of the papal complex, and it was transmogrified in cinema to the more recognizable Coliseum (which was built after Nero's death in 68, and finished in 79; the Flavians deliberately had it set on the property where Nero's Golden House and lake were located). Nero's persecution of Christians as scapegoats after the fire was small in comparison to later pogroms especially of the late second and into the third centuries, but it was horrific enough to catch the attention of the historian Tacitus, neither a Christian nor Christian sympathizer, regarding them as a disreputable if not criminal element of society. Nevertheless, the historian reports the horror and pity felt even by pagan Romans that Nero had Christians crucified, and those who did not die right away were covered in pitch and set alight as human torches to line the walkways of his palace[44] (a scenario played for laughs in Cotton's novelization [1987, 81–82]).

With "The Romans" we, the audience, feel safe laughing despite the real-life consequences of these situations: angry both that Barbara prefers a gladiator (namely Ian) over the emperor and that Ian has escaped, Nero grabs Barbara and demands a sword from his guard; instead of killing the terrified woman, he turns the sword on his guard: "He didn't fight hard enough!" We laugh in relief, but also because despite Barbara's terror, viewers were confident that nothing could or would happen to the principle characters (at least not yet; *Doctor Who* would shock viewers a few serials later by killing a companion). Strangers die in *Doctor Who*; those who die in "The Romans" are frequently unnamed, and, as with the so-called "Red Shirts" in *Star Trek*, anonymous ensigns who were frequently cannon fodder on that television series, we have no investment with the unnamed characters who perish in *Doctor Who* episodes—they are expendables that break to advance the plot, much like the vase with which Barbara accidently hits Ian at the villa, leading to their capture.

Did Nero Have a Sense of Humor?

Considering the mockery made of the emperor for the past two millennia, one wonders: did Nero himself have a sense of humor? It was not unusual in Antiquity to depict authority figures or cruel people as silly fools and lunatics; Roman street plays and pantomimes frequently mocked the goings-on among the aristocrats and civic leaders. In "The Romans," Nero is surrounded by fawning yes-men, a survival skill that is also attested to in the sources. Nero himself did have a cruel sense of humor, and accounts of his jokes emphasize his predilection of betraying and humiliating of others.

One can find, for example, a number of black jokes and pranks attributed to him that he alone would have found amusing. Much as his uncle Gaius, Nero had a twisted sense of humor, albeit again, one must be critical in reading sensational stories, especially as authors such as Suetonius wrote with an eye to scandalize, and Tacitus had an agenda against the Julio-Claudians. Nevertheless, the sources remark on Nero's quip about mushrooms being the food of the gods, his step-father Claudius was allegedly fatally poisoned with a mushroom dish.[45] On another occasion, when Nero's step-brother and rival Britannicus lay convulsing and dying in front of a horrified dinner-party (including Nero's mother and Britannicus's sister), Nero brushed off the sight by remarking that the boy was simply having another one of his funny turns.[46] The sources also record that after his mother's murder, Nero man-handled Agrippina's corpse and quipped about her beauty.[47] According to Dio Cassius, Nero made public jokes about the misfortunes of his relatives—usually the ones he had just had executed: on being brought the severed head of his cousin Plautus, he supposedly made a joke about the size of the man's nose.[48] As for Nero "fiddling" while Rome burnt, there is at least some evidence that he regarded the event with grim humor: upon hearing of the conflagration (Nero was in Antium, not Rome), he picked up his cithara and sang sadly a song about the destruction of Troy.[49] Perhaps not the most tactful of jokes, but then again, this is the same person who said, allegedly on the completion of his new palace of gold, "At last I can live like a human being!"[50]

Perhaps even more interesting than Nero's black humor, however, is Nero's reaction to jokes told by others about himself. For example, Nero was lampooned shortly after his mother's murder, with graffiti, popular songs, and stand-up comics all making reference to and openly jeering Caesar's hand in the murder—some in front of the emperor on stage, and at other times whilst passing Nero in the street. He made no move to arrest the comedians or even to have them punished, and he instead appeared amused by the quips.[51] Allegedly he even received letters congratulating him on finally killing her, and again, did not order that the senders be hunted down and punished. Vandals placed a leather bag over the head of one of Nero's statues in Rome—a reference to the punishment meted out to parricides, who were sewn up into a leather bag with vicious animals and thrown into the sea. No response from Nero. It was thought by Tacitus that this would simply confirm Nero's role in his mother's murder—to hunt down the graffiti artists and vandals would be a sure sign of his guilt. Finally, Nero himself continued enthusiastically to perform in public after 59, and his favorite role was that of Orestes—famed in myth for killing his mother—as a rather ghastly acknowledgment of his popular image.

So How Does the Humor Hold Up?

It is one thing for Donna Noble (Catherine Tate) to try out her rusty Latin at the local Marcus and Spensius in the "Fires of Pompeii" (2008), but some of the humor found in "The Romans" has had its critics. Some modern critics argue that if "The Romans" fell flat on its original transmission, perhaps it was because episode 3, which featured the strongest points of farce, was transmitted the day of Winston Churchill's funeral and marred an otherwise somber occasion (Wood and Miles, 2006, 129). Contemporary reaction and audience research, however, does not mention Churchill's funeral at all; a surviving audience poll from the time reveals mixed reception (those polled were in a "carping mood" according to the researcher): some complained that the serial was a "bore" and "too violent" and "lacking in realism"; what had started as a promising story had "declined to a farcical and pathetic anti-climax."[52] The complaints, however, stem more from a general dissatisfaction with *Doctor Who* historicals and not necessarily because of a comedic script; children polled on their opinion of the previous year's "Marco Polo" found it "boring" and "too long drawn out"—maps and charts could not compete with the Daleks.[53] Modern fans have also found the mix of violence and humor off-putting (Howe and Walker 1988, 46–47; Tulloch and Alvarado 1983, 154–56). Most offensive recently is Nero's lusty pursuit of Barbara, criticized as "sexual harassment" and "a rape plot." For example, in his online blog (now a published book), *The Tardis Eruditorum*, Philip Sandifer finds Nero's interest in Barbara "distasteful" (Sandifer 2011).

Some British comedies of the '60s and '70s that based their humor on innuendo and lust have not aged well; recent revelations and allegations of sexual abuse and harassment in the British entertainment industry, too, has certainly put a damper on appreciating the humor in its contemporary context. While Nero's pursuit of Barbara may strike some now as harassment, contemporary viewers would have identified Francis's Nero as "the most feared tyrant in classical history [acting] like the boss at the office Christmas party" (Wood and Miles 2006, 126). Modern viewers, too, certainly recognize the outrageous comedy for its intention: episode 3 was screened (2013) for a group of History Society students at the University of Winchester in the UK, and the moment Nero appeared, someone laughed, "Oh, geez, he's that drunk uncle who shows up at Christmas and all the weddings, isn't he?"

The Romans themselves would have found the serial cracking good humor as the situational comedy was something they invented: Two seminal influences on modern comedy, Plautus (the "sit-com") and Terence (the "rom-com") frequently included as their main plot point the kidnap of a high-born maiden which results in her rape; in real life when such things happened, the marriage value if not social status of the young woman would be compromised. Fortunately, however, such plots resolve themselves happily as we find out that the young man rapist is her real-life fiancé on a boys-night-out: a double standard, but accepted in Roman society was the expectation that young aristocratic men would wantonly sow their oats even when affianced to proper young ladies. For example, in Terence's *Hecyra*, the young man in question seizes and rapes a young girl without seeing her face (it is nighttime); the next thing he knows, his fiancée refuses to see him, and she hides herself away in disgrace because she is pregnant. The happy ending comes when he puts two and two together and realizes that he himself is the father, the young woman has not been defiled, and they can get married happily ever after.[54]

In "The Romans," one must not look at Nero's infatuation as a "rape plot." There is no denying that the murders and enslavement in "The Romans" are morally reprehensible, and that the fate that awaited slaves in Ian and Barbara's position could be horrible. But the key thing to remember is that the episode is played as farce, and it was promoted as such in official contemporary BBC literature: Christopher Barry specifically requested in a letter to fight choreographer that the fight between the Doctor and Ascanius be "humorously staged"[55] to contrast with the later life or death combat between Ian and his fellow gladiator; the synopsis sent out by the Serials Department describes Nero's "playful advances" towards Barbara.[56] The Romans themselves lampooned and played out as slapstick scenes in contemporary comedies that would be horrifying in real life. But how can one reconcile the popular image of Nero as a murdering monster with the farcical character in a television program aimed at children?

Three possible explanations come from surviving BBC audience research polls of 1964. First, these polls, conducted mainly by women, asked children about their viewing preferences. The children preferred to watch the splashier programming offered by the BBC's rival, commercially-sponsored ITV which had the money to afford then-current American sit-coms. The questioners noted that "comedy shows [are] very popular with young children."[57] The children frequently mention such comedies as their favorites, and several pollsters noted that, because "an hour is all that many children are allowed, so not to be cheated, they watch ITV" instead of an hour of "quality" on the BBC, and therefore "many children are unaware of what the BBC has to offer."[58] Second, the two research polls were conducted during the transmission of the Doctor Who serial "Marco Polo"—which followed closely on the heels of a Dalek serial. Dalekmania was in full swing in early to mid–1964, and many children complained that *Doctor Who* was not as exciting without the Daleks, and that they found the historical "Marco Polo" full of "boring detail of maps and charts."[59] Finally, a number of the children remarked on how much they loved watching wrestling[60]—a pseudo-sport beloved by grannies and filled with pantomime villains who, despite their despicable personas, always got their comeuppance by the goodies.

It is probably no coincidence, then, that Verity Lambert requested that the Romans go out as a deliberate farce: Roman-style comedies were a hot commodity at the time with *Funny Thing* and *Carry On, Cleo*; Lambert wanted to add comedic punch to *Doctor Who* to capture the audience who enjoyed the sitcoms transmitted over on ITV. More interestingly, in BBC promotional material, Nero is referred to as "The Mad Emperor"[61]—surely a sort of wrestling name if there ever was one. This last certainly indicates to the audience that this Nero is the sort of comic villain one might find in the ring on Saturday mornings: over-the-top, dangerous, and cruel, but ultimately thwarted by the good Barbara and undermined by the intellect of the Doctor. As indicated in the polls, the children interviewed could distinguish between the goodies and the baddies in *Doctor Who* and knew that the goodies would always win; as one mother who wrote in to the BBC requested on behalf of her children, "Keep the baddies as vile as possible, as her children loved to see them defeated."[62]

Conclusions

And so it goes—the TARDIS crew escapes Nero's palace and rendezvous back at their villa hideaway, and prepare for their next adventure ("The Web Planet," 1965); the next time the Doctor would encounter any Romans, he would be Patrick Troughton in "The War Games," and those Romans were unwitting participants whisked away from Rome into a battlefield created by the War Chief, a renegade Time Lord, who planned to use them as part of a super army. At the end of the day, "The Romans" was an enjoyable romp through an ancient Rome familiar to its audience through school-lessons and popular culture drawn from literary sources, tradition, and contemporary theatre.

It contains all of the signifiers of Ancient Rome, but does the story educate as it entertains? Does it have to, really? Hobden notes in her recent article on the *Doctor Who* episode "The Fires of Pompeii," even if we had time machines, we could not actually travel back to "Ancient Rome" (Hobden 2009, 149–52)—not only do new finds and new interpretation of old sources constantly affect how scholars define and interpret what Rome and *Romanitas* actually means (both to us, and to the Romans themselves), but popular engagement with the ancient world—whether through museum exhibition, film and television, re-enactment and role-playing games—will always reflect our own current culture and affect our expectations. The difficulty comes when we see things that might look familiar (how tempting it is, for example, to apply Freudian psychology onto the relationship between Nero and his mother), but because they are meant to be "long ago and far away" applying too much of ourselves can be jarring—a case in point being the too-modern attitudes and ways of speaking used by Caecilius's son in "Fires." "The Romans" succeeds because it straddles that line between audience expectation (fire, fiddling, and feasting) with knowing winks and anachronism from the future.

NOTES

1. The origins of this essay are twofold, both from events from 1975. The first was finding my mother avidly watching *I, Claudius*. The second came when my dad stumbled across a strange program on our local PBS station (WHYY, Wilmington [DE]–Philadelphia) which featured a mad Englishman wearing a long knitted scarf running around a spaceship; Dad said, "What in the hell is *this*?" (answer: "Ark in Space," 1975). I am grateful to Louise North at the BBC Written Archives, who let me run rampant through their *Doctor Who* files. All references to the program and character as "Dr Who" [sic] are as written on and in the BBC files and documents which I consulted.

2. An early memo from David Whitaker lists a commissioned story on Roman Britain by Malcolm Hulke (BBC Written Archives Centre [afterward WAC] T5/647/1 Dr Who General 1963, n. d.), and a memo was put forth on 14 April 1964 from David Whitaker to Verity Lambert that projected at least four historical serials including a Roman story (WAC T5/647/2 Dr Who General 1964, 14 April 1964). On 26 February, John Crockett supplied David Whitaker with another long list of history topics (op. cit., 26 February 1964) including a story on either the Roman invasion of Britain or the decline of the Romans in Britain, and one on Boudicca.

3. He's actually a plastic Auton in a Roman Auton legion; the Romans always did assimilate other cultures into their military. For a thorough catalogue of the Doctor's encounters with the Romans, see Parkin 2007.

4. I.e., in the style of a Hollywood spectacle, in which style and audience expectation takes precedent over historical accuracy.

5. The props list notes that this was originally Ribena, itself replaced with blackcurrant cordial (WAC, T5/1, 234/1 Dr Who [sic] Serial M, Episode 1, TX 65.01.16, 8 December 1964).

6. Historian Mary Beard's "dormouse test" posits that the sooner dormice appear at a cinematic banquet, the quicker we know how seriously (or not) the filmmakers will take their subject (Blanshard and Shahabudin 2011, 1–14; 183–86; Cull, 2001, 162–65). The props list for "The Romans," episode 3, calls for "non prac[tical] food, but it must be very exotic looking, i.e., peacock, boars [sic] head, etc.," presumably the request of Christopher Barry (WAC, T5/1, 236/1 DR WHO Serial M, Episode 3 (B/e 30.1.65), 4 January 1964).

7. Director Christopher Barry sent several requests to M. Cooper requesting stock film shots of lions, including one that specifies close-ups of "angry lions" (WAC, T5/1, 234/1 Dr Who Serial M, Episode 1, TX 65.01.16, 15 October 1964).

8. Cusick admitted that he had no time for extensive research –and even if he had had the time, there was no budget; thus he relied on stock architecture such as columns (qtd. in Howe, Stammers, and Walker 1994, 90). The floor plan for the serial shows how little space there was for what appeared a spacious villa and palace set onscreen (Plans for "The Romans" as drawn up by Cusick are included in the BBC written archives files for Episodes 1 and 2, WAC, T5/1, 234/1 Dr Who [sic] Serial M, Episode 1, TX 65.01.16 and WAC, T5/1, 235/1 DR WHO [sic, and so forth] Serial M, Episode 2 (B/e 23.1.65)

9. Wood and Miles call the exposition in such episodes as "the educational info-dump … considered normal practice at this point [transmission of "The Aztecs" in 1964]" (2006, 72). Newman and Lambert's stress on well-researched historicals for *Doctor Who* follows similar lines found in the custom of Hollywood spectacles emphasizing the research behind the scripts; a good example of this is the 1954 production *Quo Vadis*, following advice by an

Oxford-educated researcher, Hugh Gray. For examples of the research behind "HollyRome" films, see Blanshard and Shabudin 2011, 36–57 (*Quo Vadis*) and 216–38 (*Gladiator*).

10. On Lucarotti, history, and "Marco Polo," see Wood and Miles 2006, 49–56, especially 54–55.

11. WAC, T5/1, 234/1 Dr Who Serial M, Episode 1, TX 65.01.16, 29 October 2964.

12. WAC T48/542/1 Spooner Dennis, 31 August 1964.

13. For discussion on Classics, class status, and classroom instruction in Britain through the 1960s, see for example, Cull 2001, 171–75; Blanshard and Shahadubin 2011, 177–79; 186–89. Wood and Miles note that if Dennis Spooner, who left school as a child, knew the references, it was a safe bet that the majority of the audience did as well (2006, 127).

14. WAT T5/647/2 Dr Who General 1964, 5 April 1964. Although the early fight between the Doctor and Ascanius was meant deliberately to be slapstick (the fight "is to be treated humorously so that Dr Who [sic] by his wits and not by his strength gets the better of Ascanius" [WAT 1T5/1,234/1 Dr Who TX 65.01.16 Series M, 11 November 1964]), director Christopher Barry requested that skilled stage fighters—at the cost of 28 guineas each—be engaged to act as the Roman guards in episode 4 (WAT T5/1, 237/1 Dr Who Serial M, Episode 4 [B/e 6.2.65)]. See Tulloch and Alvarado (1983, 54–56) and Howe, Stammers, Walker (1992, 32); both sources discuss Verity Lambert's insistence that the show not talk down to its audience, something she emphasized especially to ensure that the program would not be regarded as simply a "children's show" by the BBC.

15. See Howe and Walker (1988) for a selection of comments from contemporary viewers and '80s and '90s fans on the farcical nature of "The Romans," 46–47. Spooner himself later commented that he felt the humor in the serial did not work as well as it could have (qtd. in Howe, Stammers, and Walker 1994, 89); on the other hand, director Christopher Barry was pleased with the result (89–90). On the complications of historical accuracy and *Doctor Who*, see O'Mahony (2007).

16. Tac., *Hist.* 1.

17. WAC T48/542/1 SpoonerDennis, 31 August 1964.

18. An undated BBC in-house history of *Doctor Who* refers to the Romans as a serial with an "accent on comedy" (WAC T5/647/1 Dr Who General 1963, "A History of *Doctor Who*" addressed to John Wiles and Donald Tosh). See also Howe, Stammers, and Walker 1992, 46 and Tulloch and Alvarado, 1983, 156–57.

19. On cinematic signposts to denote Rome, see, for example, Blanshard and Shahabudin 2011, 1–14 and 183–86; Cull 2001, 162–65. See Wyke 1997 who provides background to the appeal and use of Rome as a film setting (1–13). On the role of the historical consultant, see Coleman 2005, 45–52.

20. On humor and the Romans in the cinema and television, see, for example, Cull 2001, 162–90; Blanshard and Shanabudin 2011, 172–93; Solomon 2011, 283–306 and Cyrino 2005, 159–206.

21. See note 27, above.

22. See, for example, Cull's discussion of epic, and class and authority as mocked by *Cleo* (168–73); Banshard and Shahabudin 2011 on *Life of Brian*, 179–82.

23. Two novels which influenced the look and expectations of "Ancient Rome" in popular culture were Henryk Sienkiewicz's 1895 *Quo Vadis* and Lew Wallace's 1880 *Ben Hur: A Tale of the Christ*. On the cultural impact of these works on cinema and popular reception of Nero and the Roman empire, see Cyrino 2005, 7–34 (*Quo Vadis*) and 59–88 (*Ben Hur*); Blanshard and Shahabudin 2011, 36–57 (*Quo Vadis*).

24. As for the gesture, Juvenal references it, but it is still not exactly clear what, precisely, the gesture may have been and which gesture signified what (Juv. 3.36).

25. Suet., *Claud.* 21.6. This is the only recorded instance of this greeting, and Suetonius includes it only to note Claudius's sarcastic response to the fighters—the gladiators then refused to fight, and the emperor had to threaten them with "fire and sword" to make them put on the very expensive show for which he had paid.

26. For a recent survey on Nero's re-evaluation in current scholarship, see Griffin 1987, 467–480 and Champlin 2003, 9–35.

27. Tac., *Ann.* 12.4, 8, 22, 44–45, 47, 49; 13.1.

28. Tac., *Hist*. 4. Champlin discusses the problem of Suetonius and Tacitus's bias in *Nero* (2003, 34–39) as well as positive contemporary response (24–34).

29. See Tuplin 1989, 364–404 and Champlin 2003, 10–24.

30. For recent discussion and evaluation of Neronian sources, see Champlin 2003, 1–52, 84–92 and Griffin 1987. On the Neronian era, see Buckley et al. 2013.

31. Nero seems depicted as the original neckbeard; he probably didn't wear one, as Roman aristos did not in the first century AD, but he is depicted with one as a symbol of his love of all things Greek. See Mratschek 2013 for a recent discussion.

32. On depictions of Nero in cinema at least through to the end of the 1990s, see Wyke 1997, 110–46.

33. *Agrippina* can be found on YouTube (with Dutch title cards) in its entirety at http://www.youtube.com/watch?v=MaJfY9XBzfo (accessed 27 August 2013).

34. As clips from the persecution scenes show on YouTube, http://www.youtube.com/watch?v=Kgf-KNtRti4 (accessed 27 August 2013), Guazzoni seems inspired by Jean-Léon Gérôme's paintings, especially, for example, his 1883 *The Christian Martyrs' Last Prayer*, to create his tableaux.

35. Locusta is based on a real person, but she was not officially employed as imperial poisoner; allegedly Agrippina engaged a woman called Locusta to create the poison daubed on Claudius's mushrooms (Tac., *Ann*. 66); she seems to have been the go-to for ridding the household of unwanted rivals, as she was also contracted to mix the poison that killed Britannicus (Suet., *Ner*. 47). She was executed by the emperor Galba in AD 68 (Dio Cass., 63.3.4).

36. Tac., *Ann*. 13.15.

37. Both wives are discussed by Suetonius in his *Life of Ner*. 34. 4–5.

38. Suet., *Ner*. 20.1.

39. *Ibid*., 23.3.

40. *Ibid*., 12.3.

41. *Ibid*., 23.3.

42. *Ibid*., 20.3.

43. For a recent survey on Nero's portrayal in Jewish and Christian culture, see Maier 2013, 385–404.

44. Suetonius mentions only that Nero punished the Christians, a class of men "given to a new and mischievous superstition" (*superstitionis novae ac maleficae*—*maleficio* has connotations of witchcraft or magic) as part of a general program to curb abuses extant during his reign (Suet., *Ner*. 26.2); Tacitus is more detailed in the specific horror inflicted upon those Christians persecuted for the fire (Tac., *Ann*. 44), and that, despite finding the sect a ridiculous superstition himself, he notes that those who saw the tortures were moved to pity.

45. Dio Cassius reports Agrippina's hand in the murder of Claudius (Dio Cass. 61.34.1), but Aveline, aptly defends his objections to the veracity of this rumor (2004, 453–475). Other scholars (Osgood 2011, 242–45; Barrett 1996, 141) are on the fence on whether she killed Claudius or not. Someone poisoned Claudius with mushrooms, and Nero and his detractors joked about it: Nero's joke that mushrooms were the "food of the gods" (Claudius was deified after his death) (Dio Cass. 61. *Preface* 4); a popular comic who mimicked Nero would perform a routine in which he sang, "Goodbye mother, goodbye father" while miming swimming (Nero tried to drown Agrippina, Tac., *Ann*. 14.3–4) and miming drinking (Suet., *Ner*. 39).

46. Tac., *Ann*. 13.15.

47. Tac., *Ann*. 14.9; Dio Cass., 62.14.3

48. Tac., *Ann*. 14.9; Dio Cass., 62. 14.1.

49. Dio Cass. 62.18.1; Tac., *Ann*. 15.39; Dio Cass. 62. 16–18.1.

50. Suet., *Ner*. 31.2.

51. Suet., *Ner*. 39; Dio Cass. 62.16.1–4.

52. WAC, T5/1, 237/1 Dr Who Serial M, Episode 4 (B/e 6.2.65), Week 6 audience research poll on *Doctor Who* in general, typed up on 2 March 1965.

53. WAC T5/647/2 Dr Who General 1964, Audience research report at five weeks ending on 29 March 1964. It was not only children dissatisfied with the grandeur of "Marco Polo"; two adults described as "professional class fathers" in the same report thought that the serial was "bad and pernicious."

54. On *Hecrya*, see Knorr 2013, 295–317.
55. WAC, T5/1, 234/1 Dr Who Serial M, Episode 1, TX 65.01.16, in letter from director Christopher Barry to fight choreographer Peter Diamond dated 11 November 1964
56. An undated memo from the BBC sent to, among others, director Christopher Barry (WAC, T5/1, 234/1 Dr Who Serial M, Episode 1, TX 65.01.16).
57. WAC T5/647/2 Dr Who General 1964, Audience research polls of five weeks ending on 29 March 1964, 1.
58. *Ibid.*, 2 ("an hour of quality") and 4 ("allowed only one hour")
59. *Ibid.*, 3.
60. *Ibid.*, 4.
61. WAC, T5/1, 234/1 Dr Who Serial M, Episode 1, TX 65.01.16, undated memo (the same memo which describes Nero's "playful advances" toward Barbara).
62. WAC T5/647/2 Dr Who General 1964, 7 December 1964: Mrs R. Taylor wrote to the BBC urging them on behalf of her children not to water down the program, and how children always know that good triumphs over bad on television—and that the understanding that the baddies get their comeuppance in *Doctor Who* is certainly comparable to the violence in her generation's appreciation and enjoyment of the *Dan Dare* comic.

BIBLIOGRAPHY

Primary

BBC Written Archives Centre T5/647/1 Dr Who [sic] General 1963.
BBC Written Archives Centre T5/647/2 Dr Who General 1964.
BBC Written Archives Centre T5/1, 234/1 Dr Who, Serial M, Episode 1, TX 65.01.16.
BBC Written Archives Centre T5/1, 235/1 DR WHO [sic] serial M, Episode 2 (B/e 23.1.65).
BBC Written Archives Centre T5/1, 236/1 DR WHO [sic] serial M, Episode 3 (B/e 30.1.65).
BBC Written Archives Centre T5/1, 237/1 Dr Who Serial M, Episode 4 (B/e 6.2.65).
Dio Cassius, *Roman History*. Translated by Earnest Cary. Loeb Classical Library 176 & 177. Cambridge, MA, 1925 & 1927.
Suetonius, *Lives of the Caesars, Volume II*. Translated by J. C. Rolfe. Loeb Classical Library 38. Cambridge, MA, 1914.
Tacitus, *The Annals*. Translated by Clifford H. Moore. Loeb Classical Library 249. Cambridge, MA, 1931.
Tacitus, *The Histories*. Translated by Clifford H. Moore. Loeb Classical Library 111. Cambridge, MA, 1925.

Secondary

Aveline, John. 2004. "The Death of Claudius." *Historia* 53.4: 453–475.
Alastair, J. L., and Kim Shahabudin. 2011. *Classics On Screen: Ancient Greece and Rome on Film*. Bristol: Bristol Classics Press.
Barrett, Anthony. 1996. *Agrippina: Mother of Nero*. London: B.T. Batsford.
Champlin, Edward. 2003. *Nero*. Cambridge: Harvard University Press.
Coleman, Kathleen M. 2005. "The Pedant Goes to Hollywood: The Role of the Academic Consultant." In *Gladiator: Film and History*, edited by Martin M. Winkler. London: Routledge. pp. 45–52.
Cotton, Donald. 1987. *The Romans*. London: Target Books.
Cull, Nicholas J. 2001. "'Infamy! Infamy! They've All Got it in For Me!' *Carry On, Cleo* and the British Camp Comedies of Ancient Rome." In *Imperial Projections: Ancient Rome in Modern Popular Culture*, edited by Maria Wyke. Baltimore: Johns Hopkins University Press. pp. 162–65.
Cyrino, Monica Silveira. 2005. *Big Screen Rome*. Oxford: Blackwell.
Danes, Frank. 2013. *Fifty Years in Time and Space: A Short History of Doctor Who*. Pavenham: St. Mark's Press.
Dinter, Martin T., and Emma Buckley, eds. 2013. *A Companion to the Neronian Age*. Oxford: Blackwell.

Griffin, Miriam T. 1987. *Nero: The End of a Dynasty*. London: Routledge.

Griffith, Miriam, T. 2013. "*Nachwort*: Nero from Zero to Hero." In *A Companion to the Neronian Age*. Edited by E. Buckley. Oxford: Blackwell. pp. 467–480.

Hobden, Fiona. 2009. "History Meets Fiction in *Doctor Who*, 'The Fires of Pompeii': A BBC Reception of Ancient Rome on Screen and Online." *Greece and Rome* 56, no. 2: 147–63.

Howe, David J., Mark Stammers, and Stephen James Walker. 1992. *Doctor Who: The Sixties*. London: Virgin.

Howe, David J., Mark Stammers, and Stephen James Walker. 1994. *Doctor Who the Handbook: The First Doctor*. London: Virgin.

Howe, David, and Stephen James Walker. 1988. *Doctor Who: The Television Companion: The Official BBC Guide to Every TV Story*. London: BBC World Wide.

Knorr, Ortwin. 2013. *Hecyra*. In *A Companion to Terence*. Edited by A. Augoustakis. Oxford: Blackwell. pp. 295–317.

Maier, Harry O. 2013. "Nero in Jewish and Christian Tradition from the First Century to the Reformation." In *A Companion to the Neronian Age*. Edited by Emma Buckley and Martin T. Dinter. Oxford: Wiley-Blackwell. pp. 385–404.

Mratschek, Sigrid. 2013. "Nero the Imperial Misfit: Philhellenism in a Rich Man's World." In *A Companion to the Neronian Age*. Edited by Emma Buckley and Martin T. Dinter. Oxford: Blackwell. pp. 45–63.

O'Mahony, Daniel. 2007. "'Now How Is That Wolf Able to Impersonate a Grandmother': History, Pseudo-History, and Genre in *Doctor Who*." In *Time and Relative Dissertations in Space: Critical Perspectives on Doctor Who*. Edited by David Butler. Manchester: University of Manchester Press. pp. 56–67.

Osgood, Josiah. 2011. *Claudius Caesar: Image and Power in the Early Roman Empire*. Cambridge: Cambridge University Press.

Parkin, Lance. 2007. *A History: The Unauthorised History of the Doctor Who Universe*, 2nd ed. Des Moines: Mad Norwegian Press.

Sandifer, Philip. 2011. "Like You Do When You're Young: *The Romans*," *The Tardis Eruditorium* (blog). http://www.philipsandifer.com/2011/02/like-you-do-when-ure-young-romans.html. Accessed 8-12-2016).

Solomon, Jon. 2001. *The Ancient World in the Cinema*, Rev. ed. New Haven: Yale University Press.

Tulloch, John, and Manuel Alvarado. 1983. *Doctor Who: The Unfolding Text*. New York: St. Martin's Press.

Tuplin, C. 1989. "The False Neros of the First Century," *Studies in Latin Literature and History* 5: 364–404.

Wood, Tat, and Lawrence Miles. 2006. *About Time: The Unauthorized Guide to Doctor Who: 1963–1966, Seasons 1 to 3*. Des Moines: Mad Norwegian Press.

Wyke, Maria. 1997. *Projecting the Past: Ancient Rome, Cinema and History*. New York: Routledge.

History as Genre, Aesthetic and Context in "The Gunfighters"

RAMIE TATEISHI

"The Gunfighters," a *Doctor Who* serial from 1966 that finds the time-traveling hero caught up in the gunfight at the O.K. Corral in the American West of 1881, has long been the subject of scorn among devotees of the program. Having first risen to widespread infamy in fandom through a scathing overview in the 1983 book *Doctor Who: A Celebration*, the serial went on to consistently rank among the least favorite stories in fan surveys conducted in publications such as *Doctor Who Magazine*, becoming known primarily as the story directly responsible for putting an end to the historical *Doctor Who* adventure after its poor reception upon its original airing. In light of more favorable contemporary reappraisal of the serial,[1] however, it is useful to consider other approaches to looking at "The Gunfighters." Its unique status as the only (1963–1989 series) example of a *Doctor Who* Western makes it a fascinating focal point for a variety of issues broadly related to the theme of "history," from the visual and narrative techniques used to depict the American West of the 1800s to the cultural discourse about the presence of U.S. Western television programs in Britain during the time of the serial's original airing.

By examining how the trope of "history" functions as genre, aesthetic, and context in the production and reception of "The Gunfighters," the material effects of these different "histories" can be better understood as they influence and shape this British-made Western.

History as Genre

"The Gunfighters" came about in the mid–1960s at a point when the idea of the *Doctor Who* historical was being reconstituted, with a foothold in the previous production team's adherence to some notion of historical "realism" and a move toward exploring and pushing at those very same boundaries. Within this lineage of different notions of *history as genre* came "The Gunfighters," a story brought into existence by a production team that wanted to move the series in new, experimental directions while still valuing the emphasis on historical accuracy held by their predecessors, and ultimately realized by a production team with an antipathy toward the historical serials.

The unanticipated success of the first Dalek serial shortly after the series premiere in late 1963 would eventually shift the program more toward stories featuring monsters and aliens, and a corresponding change in the perception of the generic criteria that constituted the historical. By the third season in 1965, the series had a completely new production team, with John Wiles replacing Verity Lambert as producer, and Donald Tosh stepping in as the show's third script editor. The Wiles era typically tends to be characterized as more "experimental" in nature, with storylines that began to deviate from the original series format. In an interview, Wiles (1983, 9) remarked how "we were fairly keen to find our way around this whole business of doing historical stories. Should the Doctor actually get involved with the main characters? I was more interested in testing the temperature of the water to see what we could do, and how far we could take the format." The first serial to be commissioned and produced by the team of Wiles and Tosh was "The Myth Makers" (1965), a historical that featured sophisticated approaches to the execution and realization of its material (with the cast being drawn from BBC Radio's *Third Programme*, which was considered to be the elite drama broadcaster of its time) as well as literate, wit-based humor (such as a dialogue exchange playing upon the "woe"/"whoa" homonym).

It was Tosh's appreciation of "The Myth Makers," with its different, less-straightforward approach to the historical, that led him to commission "The Gunfighters" from writer Donald Cotton in November 1965. The turnover in production teams, however, meant that it was Wiles' successor, Innes Lloyd, who would end up producing the Western serial from March to April 1966, along with his new script editor Gerry Davis. Lloyd was interested in emphasizing present-day science-based stories, and his negative perception of the historicals affected the production of "The Gunfighters," with a push toward broader comedy in an attempt to compensate for the serial's perceived shortcomings.[2] Reflecting on the historicals, Lloyd commented in an interview: "We did find that the historical stories weren't popular! The problem, I thought, was that we had too many very good costume dramas on the BBC, especially at that family viewing slot. So we were really stepping into somebody else's territory" (1983, 13). The effects of the material conditions of production upon the constitution of *history as genre* can be seen in Lloyd's quote, in that concerns over internal departmental divisions and programming/scheduling logistics informed his perspective on the historical stories.

The desire to experiment with the possibilities of the program's format and to expand the boundaries of genre reflects what Daniel O'Mahoney describes as the "slippage away from a conception of pure history and towards popular storytelling styles" (2007, 60), which can be understood as part of the evolution of the historical as a genre. Despite this, Tosh still maintained the same perspective on history as his predecessors, commenting in an interview that "historical accuracy was hugely important. You must not change the facts of history as far as they are reported because if you do you're in danger of misleading the next generation about what happened back then. That is unforgivable. The programme was still educational insofar as it was possible to establish historical accuracy" (2010, 43). While carefully avoiding the notion of an "authentic" historical accuracy, Tosh referred to both the "realism" factor (the "facts of history as far as they reported") and the original educational component in assessing his tenure on the program.

In defining the concept of genre, Steve Neale notes how these "systems of expectation and hypothesis involve a knowledge of, indeed they partly embody, various regimes of verisimilitude—various systems of form and plausibility, motivation and belief" (2000, 32). In the earliest days of the series, plotlines that fell under the "historical" category would be shaped by the outcomes allowed by the circumstances of historical fact, nested within a framework based on some notion of real-world "authentic" that would influence and motivate the characters' actions. This framework contributed to the type of story in which the Doctor and his companions would become involved in historical events, but would not be permitted to alter them, such as Barbara's (Jacqueline Hill) desire and ultimate inability to turn the Aztec civilization away from human sacrifice in "The Aztecs" (1964). By the program's third season, this foundational notion of generic verisimilitude as reflected in Tosh's quote was in flux, with the integration of comedy and the Wiles/Tosh experimental elements co-existing in tension with the idea of historical accuracy.

"The Gunfighters" can be seen as a product of this flexible quality of genre, by which the adaptable nature of its core qualities allows production teams to shape it in response to historical and cultural trends. Along these lines, Rick Altman reframes the notion of genre as an evolving category rather than as a fixed entity by asking, "What if genre were not the permanent product of a singular origin, but the temporary byproduct of an ongoing process?"

(2000, 54). The outward move toward different storytelling styles described by O'Mahoney, combined with the multiple perspectives on the series' approach to historicals, formed the basis for this process of genre reformulation and the conditions which gave rise to "The Gunfighters."

History as Aesthetic

While the notion of *history as genre* gave rise to the conditions in which "The Gunfighters" came about, a different application of some of these aspects of genre theory can provide us with another history-related lens through which this serial can be viewed. The narrative and visual elements that identify the serial as one set in the past can be seen as signs of *history as aesthetic*—the cues which are deployed in the presentation of the historical. As a sense of the period is conveyed through the costumes, set designs, and other diegetic and non-diegetic signs, the aesthetics used to convey *history as genre* become an important consideration. Thomas Schatz defines "iconography" as "*narrative and visual coding*," noting that all encoded objects "serve a specific symbolic function within the narrative system" (1981, 22). It is through this iconography that the historical transmits key information about its setting, and the degree to which this iconography is aestheticized can further shape the viewer's conception of the period in question.

The visual realization and narrative presentation of "The Gunfighters" relies heavily on the iconography developed by the Hollywood Western film genre, most notably in the 1957 John Sturges film *Gunfight at the O.K. Corral*, which members of the production team (including director Rex Tucker) viewed in preparation for making the serial. The use of these symbolic markers further complicates this example of a *Doctor Who* historical, which retells the tale of an already-mythologized past rather than presenting an attempt at an "authentic" tale within the actual historical timeframe of Tombstone, Arizona, in 1881. "The Gunfighters" calls attention to its own status as a reproduction of a reproduction of history through the excess and self-reflexivity of its iconography and coding practices in visual and narrative components such as costuming, set design, cinematography, the performance of "Western" accents, and the use of a Western-style song as a storytelling device.

The period of American history in which "The Gunfighters" takes place has been heavily depicted in film and television, to the point where the line between fiction and reality has been blurred in the recounting of the most famous historical episodes from that period.[3] In addition to the ways in which history provided the material for film and television, the media representations affected some aspects of real life, creating a reciprocal relationship between the fiction and the reality of the American West. For example, Holly

George-Warren describes how cinematic cowboy costuming in the early 20th century influenced and changed actual Western apparel (2002, 113). Gaines and Herzog further comment on this relationship by noting how "the image supplants the reality as the one fills out what is missing or unknown about the other," with "authenticity" as a confluence of ideas and images of questionable origin (1998, 173).

Clothing is linked to identity in various ways throughout the serial, from Seth's confidence that he can identify Doc Holliday by his "black buck's back coat" and "gambler's fancy vest" to the Clanton Gang's belief that the Doctor is Doc Holliday based on his gun belt. Through these scenes referencing and involving Western apparel, most notably dealing with the wardrobe-related antics of companion Steven (Peter Purves), "The Gunfighters" comments on its own presentation of history as a mingling of "authentic" and fictive/mythic. In analyzing the signifying practices associated with fashion in cinema, Sarah Street writes about "the ability of film costume to support or transcend the demands of film narrative: to what extent can film costume be said to articulate a language of its own, capable of offering alternative interpretations from the main thrust of the plot and characterization?" (2001, 5). Related to "The Gunfighters," the superficial outer layer of Western clothing provides one such counter-narrative to the main story.

The serial begins to toy with the notion of Western costuming when Steven and fellow companion Dodo (Jackie Lane) first realize that they have landed in the "Wild West" period of American history. Excited by the prospect of exploring this time period, with Steven exclaiming how he has always wanted to be a cowboy, the duo race back into the TARDIS for the purpose of donning Western garb, establishing a link between clothing and identity. When Dodo emerges in a cowgirl outfit, she asks the Doctor (William Hartnell) for his opinion, and he introduces the issue of the pragmatism/utility of clothing versus its fanciful/ornamental properties with his reply of "Oh, good gracious! Absolutely absurd!" The value that the Doctor places on the practical use of clothing is developed further when he asks Steven, "Why can't you wear inconspicuous clothes like I do?" The contrast between the Doctor's Victorian dress and Dodo and Steven's garish outfits is further highlighted in a shot framing the three main cast members so that the Doctor is in the foreground nursing a toothache, while behind him, Dodo and Steven beam with pride at their newly-acquired look, with the playful and subtle suggestion that the pair's clothing is exacerbating the Doctor's toothache. The only alteration to the Doctor's clothing in this early part of the story is the cowboy hat that Dodo places on his head, which he deems "most suitable" as "at least it'll keep the rain off," again asserting how his pragmatic viewpoint extends to his choices and thoughts on wardrobe accessories. The scene pits these different perspectives on clothing against each other in a way that plays up the outlandishness of the Western outfits by juxtaposing them against the Doctor's perspective on clothing.

Steven's outfit in particular is a glaring, gaudy sight, consisting of a set of spurs attached to his boots, a six-gun belt strapped to his waist, and a shiny satin shirt laced with fringe and an embroidered design pattern of flowers and vines. The Doctor comments on the outfit by telling Steven, "Why you've got to dress yourself up like Tom Mix, I can't imagine," and the reference to the Hollywood Western film star serves as a reflection on the process of transforming history into myth through aesthetics. Tom Mix, the first major Hollywood Western film star in the earliest days of the 20th century, constructed his celebrity persona by conflating aspects of his actual ranch work and his stint as a sheriff with elements of showmanship and imagery, as chronicled by William E. Tydeman III (1998). As a mythic popular culture icon constructed of elements both true and fictional, Tom Mix is a fascinating image for Steven to adopt as his "Western" look, adding yet another layer of complication to this presentation of history. As the story of "The Gunfighters" retells a culturally mythical account of an actual historical event, one of the characters in "The Gunfighters" adopts a guise that will ostensibly help him to fit in with his surroundings, but that guise is based on yet another popularized image with its basis in an indeterminate mixture of fiction and historical fact.

Through Steven's fumbled attempts at engaging with the accouterments of his attire, his "true" self conflicts with this superficial outer layer, unable to completely and comfortably adopt this guise. When Steven first emerges from the TARDIS in his Tom Mix outfit, the camera frames his boots, so that the focus is on his feet as one of his spurs causes him to trip. His attempts at drawing his gun end with him dropping the gun, as well as twirling and catching it so that the weapon is pointed at himself. A later instance where Steven's outfit leads to negative consequences is at the Last Chance Saloon, where his assumed occupation as an entertainer is betrayed by his gun belt, with Clanton brother Billy (David Cole) commenting to the gang, "Now any of you boys ever seen a singer carry six-guns 'afore?" Through these examples, the Western attire seems to actively work against Steven's best attempts to utilize it in the reshaping of his identity, emphasizing the conflict between the "authentic" and the "inauthentic" through this focus on period clothing.

Another marker of the Western aesthetic is the period accent used by characters when they speak, a dialect referred to as Western American English which is stereotypically identified by its "twang" and "drawl" features that emphasize a more "nasal" tone and longer, slower, drawn-out vowel sounds. Rather than further establishing a sense of legitimacy and authenticity to the proceedings, the adoption and use of this accent by the actors/characters in "The Gunfighters" instead ends up commenting indirectly on the status of this serial's use of history as aesthetic. Although the degree of accuracy of the accents adopted by the British cast members portraying the populace of Tombstone is perhaps debatable, it can be taken as a generalization that the realization of these accents is less authentic than more, with the four episodes exhibiting various instances of the actors' own British accents emerging periodically. Indeed, Andrew Pixley notes how the cast members' own acknowledgment of their poor ability to emulate the Western accent was a source of humor during production (1995, 27). The incongruous nature of the Western accents brings to the forefront the performed nature of this historical drama, and along with this awareness comes a heightened degree of attention to the artifice of the other aesthetics of "the Western" as genre. In writing about the consistency of the verisimilitude of the historical film, Pam Cook notes how "the symbolic carriers of period detail—costume, hair, décor—are notoriously slippery and anachronistic. They are intertextual sign systems with their own logic which constantly threatens to disrupt the concerns of narrative and dialogue" (1996, 17). In relation to this claim, the accents could be seen to create a separate level of extra-diegetic performativity that makes the O.K. Corral characters seem more like performers in a historical play, akin to how the aforementioned examples of Steven and his Western costuming make him out to be "playing cowboy." A heightened awareness of this level of performance marks "The Gunfighters" as a performance of history, rather than a straightforward depiction of historical events.

The early scenes in which Steven puts on a "Western" persona build upon this level of awareness, as in addition to the examples of his costuming, he also attempts to speak in this stereotypical voice. The inclusion of these scenes, taking place on the diegetic level featuring a person with a British accent doing a poor imitation of a Western accent, are an interesting corollary to the aforementioned scenes where this sort of performance takes place on the extradiegetic level, creating another level on which questions about authenticity and performativity arise. Steven first attempts this accent as he steps out of the TARDIS in his Western garb, intent on not merely looking like a character from a Western film, but acting like one as well. Immediately after drawing and dropping his gun, Steven exclaims that "I was just a-practicin' mah quick draw!" to an appreciative Dodo and an unimpressed Doctor, and in this first Western utterance, his words align with the exterior marker of identity by describing his actions in this exaggeration of the "expected" sort of voice that a gunfighter would use. Steven refers to himself as "Dead-Eye Steve, the fastest, meanest gun in the West," reinforcing the construction of this adopted persona through his affected vocalization of his new moniker. When Tombstone marshal Wyatt Earp (John Alderson) comes across the trio and decides to take them to the Sheriff's office "so as you can identify yourselves in decent, law-abidin' manner," Steven immediately reasserts his identity via his true voice by saying, "I'm not really a gunman," distancing himself from the "Dead-Eye Steve" persona/accent through another example of the link between voice and identity.

"The Ballad of the Last Chance Saloon," the song used throughout the serial to describe general setting and to narrate specific events, is an example of a storytelling device taken directly from *Gunfight at the O.K. Corral.* The use of songs in Western films was popularized in the "singing cowboy" sub-genre of the 1930s and 1940s, and also in such dramatic Westerns as *Rancho Notorious* (1952) and *High Noon* (1952). As originally written by Donald Cotton, the ballad consisted of verses that set an overall, general sense of tone and mood that could be used sparingly throughout the serial. Director Rex Tucker, however, wrote additional verses that conveyed information about specific plot points such as the murder of bartender Charlie (David Graham), and the past relationship between outlaw Johnny Ringo (Laurence Payne) and saloon singer Kate (Sheena Marshe). The different functions of these two types of verses are the same as those in the song from the Sturges film, in which some portions focused on establishing the tense and portentous tone, while others accompanied the action in specific moments (such as the "Boot Hill, Boot Hill, so cold, so still" verse heard as Wyatt Earp and Doc Holliday advance toward the cemetery).

Unlike the song in the Sturges film, however, "The Ballad of the Last Chance Saloon" is heard as both non-diegetic soundtrack and diegetic entertainment in "The Gunfighters." While the song serves its soundtrack function as it plays over the beginnings and endings of scenes, it is also performed by Steven and Dodo as part of their assumed cover as a singer and a pianist. Forced to sing the song repeatedly by the Clanton gang, an exasperated Steven exclaims, "I've sung this song four times already!" This comment could be interpreted as a joking reference to the frequent non-diegetic use of the song throughout the entirety of the serial, but on another level, it reinforces how much the serial relies upon this particular aesthetic of the Western film, emulating this cinematic rendering of the O.K. Corral story more so than attempting to convey the actual historical event.

The depiction of the landscape and the setting of the Western film is a key characteristic that visually defines this genre. The attention to the environment as realized through the properties of cinematography has been commented on extensively, with scholars attributing the significance of this generic quality to themes such as Marcia Landy's point about the construction of "natural obstacles to be overcome" (2012, 29) and Philip French's examination of how "this contrast between open land and the town, between the illusion of freedom and the necessity of compromise, between a relaxed association with nature and a tense accommodation to society, lies at the roots of the genre" (1977, 107). Whatever the theme associated with the visual aesthetic, the aesthetic itself is primarily one of visual *depth*, utilizing the tools of cinematography to emphasize the openness of space. This aesthetic is also used in "The Gunfighters," where the camerawork and the set design work together to impart a greater sense of depth to the setting of Tombstone, helping the serial to replicate this visual aesthetic associated with the Western.

Designer Barry Newbery based the exteriors (such as the building facades, signs, and the corral) primarily on photographs of the American West in the 1800s that the BBC Library obtained from Yale University. However, when it came to the interiors, Newbery notes that "I did pay heed to the conventions of the Western and made sure they had all the features you'd expect" (2013, 62). The conflation of myth and reality can thus be seen again on the level of set design, as the environment itself consists of elements drawn from actual historical example, as well as from images perpetuated through film and television. The physical construction of the sets and the conditions of production allowed for different shooting practices, as an additional camera was placed atop a 10-foot tower in the center of the studio floor, giving director Rex Tucker the ability to create high-angle shots looking down upon the action (Pixley 1995, 28).

The high-angle camera, with its "bird's-eye view" of Tombstone, enabled Tucker to capture the size of the mob gathered to hang Steven, with shots looking down at the crowd of people, in addition to shots recorded with the regular mounted cameras, in which the number of people is more difficult to discern as a result of those in the foreground obscuring those in the background. In addition to displaying a large number of people to impart a grander sense of scope, Tucker employed other techniques to visually echo the feel of the Western, as in the first two shots of the scene that introduces Tombstone sheriff Bat Masterson (Richard Beale). We first see Masterson close to the extreme left of frame, and the camera follows as he walks away from the camera, crossing the street to meet the Clanton Gang's enemy Doc Holliday (Anthony Jacobs) and Kate. The focus on Masterson in relation to the painted backdrop at the end of this set furthest from the camera creates a forced perspective shot that gives a greater sense of dimension to the street. This is followed by a high-angle shot of Masterson meeting Doc Holliday and Kate in the middle of the street, framing the three characters in relative long shot and constructing a point of view that makes the street appear larger, before reverting to the typical shot-reverse-shot medium close-ups in which it becomes more difficult to discern a sense of scale among the actors and their surroundings. Ironically, the physical limitations of the studio-bound setting meant that the climactic gunfight was actually closer to the real-life scenario than its typical Hollywood depiction, due to the relatively small space in which the action took place, although the implications of this are undercut by the staging of the event (in which the Clanton Gang repeatedly fires and misses at close range).

An unusual aesthetic seen in varying degrees in the first half of the serial is the use of comedy, which on one hand appears to be an incongruous addition, but on the other hand, aligns "The Gunfighters" with the small, esoteric category of British-made Western films which emphasize humor. In his overview of British-made Westerns, Edward Buscombe identifies the majority of these films as parodies of the Hollywood Western (1993, 77), and the uses of humor in "The Gunfighters" parallel the best-known examples of these films. The use of the giant tooth in front of Doc Holliday's office, as well as the quips and one-liners scattered throughout Cotton's script, echo the type of humor seen in the film *Carry On Cowboy*, released just one year prior to the 1966 *Doctor Who* Western. The broad prop-based humor of the giant tooth that leads the Doctor to comment on Holliday's lack of a "subtle form of advertising" is similar to the oversized magnifying glass used by Sheriff Earp (played by future *Doctor Who* star Jon Pertwee) in *Carry On Cowboy*, while the Doctor's remark "Good thing I didn't have to have my tonsils out," delivered almost as an aside to the camera, is reminiscent of the delivery of one-liners, as in the opening scene where the outlaw Rumpo Kid (Sid James) guns down three strangers before remarking "I wonder what they wanted?" The humor derived from Steven's perceptions of the West is similar to how humor is generated by the informed-yet-misinformed perspective of the main character of *The Sheriff of Fractured Jaw* (1958), a British gunsmith who travels to the American West in an attempt to boost his sales, based on the understanding that the violent territory would be an ideal marketplace for his product. The most notable humor parallel deals with the confusion of identity resulting from characters' names, as the Doctor is mistaken for "Doc" (Holliday), just as a character named Marshall (Jim Dale) in *Carry on Cowboy* is thought to be an actual marshal. In addition, the *Carry On* film and the *Doctor Who* serial use the same joke involving the name Earp, with the *Carry On* characters substituting the word "twerp" and the Doctor referring to Wyatt as "Mister Werp," evoking the word "twerp" through the utterance of the name. As with the examples of costuming, props, set design, cinematography, and song, the use of humor aligns "The Gunfighters" more closely to its cinematic lineage than the real-life historical events from which its narrative is drawn.

History as Context

One more form of "history" that comes into play when assessing "The Gunfighters" is the historical context of the discourses about television at the time of the serial's transmission. By the mid–1960s, ITV had firmly established its presence on the television landscape, consolidating fears about the influence of commercial television and the encroachment of American television into a singular threat. As an example of a British-made Western produced as an installment of a BBC program, "The Gunfighters" iconically embodies this tension between Reithian values and commercial concerns. The serial's low Audience Reaction Index and its negative Audience Research Report were perhaps symptomatic of *history as context*, with the dual anti-commercial and anti–Americanization biases of the period affecting audience perception of the genre and aesthetic of "The Gunfighters."

The concern over American television on British screens in the 1960s was the culmination of a lineage of such debates over the implications of U.S. media. David Lusted catalogs the various steps in this series of debates, starting with American film in the 1920, through American comics in the 1940s, and into ITV's screening of American television programs beginning in the 1950s, describing it as a "long history in Britain of moral panics" (1998, 178). This progression shows how American popular culture crossed a variety of media, from print to radio, creating a pervasive U.S. media presence by the 1960s. In terms of television specifically, the advent of commercial network ITV in 1955 in response to the monopoly held by public service BBC led to both a battle for audience viewing figures, as well as the need to fill air time. American television programs, shot on film and produced over longer periods of time (thus generating more hours of content), provided an ideal solution to the latter issue, although they gave rise to an entirely new problem.

The ensuing perception of American television that Lusted characterizes as a "moral panic" has been analyzed in terms of its corporate connotations (Rixon 2006, 140), its pandering to the lowest common denominator (Crisell 1997, 103), and its emphasis on gaudy, distasteful escapism (Higson 1986, 74). The multitude of anxieties embodied in the notion of "Americanization" are summarized by John Ellis, who notes that the U.S. stood "for the extensive modernization of society; for the abolition of older social relationships in favour of market relationships; for a liberal attitude to sexual and family relations; for a democratic style of life; for a society in which gun ownership was legal and violent crime a fact of urban life; for a standard of living that was simply unattainable by many of the world's regions and economies" (2000, 53–54). It was the Western, arguably perceived as the most uniquely "American" genre of foreign television programs being screened in Britain, that could most easily become the target of these criticisms.

Although the Western was generally associated with ITV, with its screenings of *Wagon Train* (1957–1965) and *Gun Law* (a re-titled version of *Gunsmoke*) (1955–1975) among the top 20 rated programs throughout the 1950s and into the 1960s, the BBC also ran programs such as *The Lone Ranger*

(1949–1957) and *Bronco* (1958–1962) during the same period. Notably, during the mid–1960s, the BBC ran a program block on Saturday nights called *The Western*, which would feature a Hollywood Western film—meaning that the original Saturday night airings of the four episodes of "The Gunfighters" throughout April and May of 1966 were followed by a Hollywood Western later in the evening. The screenings of American Western films and television programs on the BBC underscore a certain contradiction in the company, whereby the public service network is obligated to compete for viewers in order to justify its license fee, which it could do by airing popular programs that directly compete with the commercial network (such as the ITV Western in the 1950s and 1960s).[4]

Placing "The Gunfighters" in the context of these circumstances can illuminate one possible reason for its poor reception, as contemporary criticisms of this British-made Western can be seen to reflect elements of the negative bias against American television programs. The average audience for the four episodes of the serial was 6.25 million viewers, which was the lowest figure that the 1965–1966 season had seen up to that point. However, the average audiences for the two serials that followed it ("The Savages" and "The War Machines") fell to even lower figures of 4.975 million and 5.225 million, respectively. Viewing figures typically fall off as the season approaches the summer months, so the conclusion of "The Gunfighters" toward the end of May 1966 and the airing of the subsequent two serials throughout June and July of 1966 could be seen to be in keeping with this general trend. The main cause for concern was the Reaction Index for the *Doctor Who* Western, which was the lowest in the program's history up to that point.

The BBC Audience Research Report, compiled by the BBC Audience Research Department, summarizes and breaks down the results of surveys administered to members of a viewing panel who had watched the program in question. The surveys ask the viewers to rank the program on a letter-grade scale, the results of which are averaged into a "Reaction Index" percentage. The survey also asks for open-ended comments on the program, which the Audience Research Report cites in their findings on how the program was received. In the Audience Research Report on "The Gunfighters" issued on June 13, 1966, the responses from some of the viewing panel members resonate with the issues and concerns about U.S. programs on British airwaves, providing interesting insights into how perception of the serial may have been influenced by the general discourse about American television at the time. For example, one viewer condemned "all that shooting for such ridiculously trifling misdemeanours" (Hearn 1995, 9), pointing out the level of violence and the conversely low level of meaningful import associated with it. Another viewer commented on the dramatic quality of the production, noting that it was "insincerely acted," as though it was "put on by the local Sunday school" (*ibid.*), which could possibly be read a perception of the affected Western accent and its impact upon the entirety of the actors' performance. Most telling was a criticism that the serial "appeared crude even beside the worst that reaches us from America" (*ibid.*), connecting "crude" specifically with American television programs in an observation that reflects and reinforces the notion of the poor quality of U.S. television, brought into clear focus through this attempt at a British Western.

When viewed together, connections can be made between the specific viewer criticisms of "The Gunfighters" and the greater television landscape at the time of transmission. As a BBC serial specifically dramatizing the American West, "The Gunfighters" is a unique production in the history of *Doctor Who*—and in British television in general—that provides entry points into discussions about how different conceptions of history can influence the life cycle and legacy of a television program.

NOTES

1. See Wood and Miles 2010.
2. See Pixley 1995.
3. See Coyne 1997 and 1990 and Maynard 1974.
4. See Ellis 2000 and Buckingham 1987.

BIBLIOGRAPHY

Altman, Rick. 2000. *Film/Genre*. London: BFI.
BBC Audience Research Report on "The Gunfighters" quoted in Hearn, Marcus. 1995. "Vox Pops." *Doctor Who Magazine* 229: 8–10.
Buckingham, David. 1987. *Public Secrets: EastEnders and Its Audience*. London: BFI.
Buscombe, Edward. 1993. *The BFI Companion to the Western*. London: Deutsch/BFI.
Cook, Pam. 1996. *Fashioning the Nation: Costume and Identity in British Cinema*. London: BFI.
Coyne, Michael. 1997. *The Crowded Prairie: American National Identity in the Hollywood Western*. London: I.B. Tauris.
Crisell, Andrew. 1997. *An Introductory History of British Broadcasting*. London: Routledge.
Ellis, John. 2000. *Seeing Things: Television in an Age of Uncertainty*. London: I.B. Tauris.
French, Philip. 1977. *Westerns: Aspects of a Movie Genre*. London: BFI.
Gaines, Jane Marie, and Charlotte Herzog. 1998. "The Fantasy of Authenticity in Western Costume" in *Back in the Saddle Again: New Essays on the Western*. Edited by Edward Buscombe and Roberta Pearson. London: BFI. pp. 172–181.
George-Warren, Holly. 2002. *How Hollywood Invented the Old West*. New York: The Ivy Press.
Higson, Andrew. 1986. "'Britain's Outstanding Contribution to the Film': The Documentary-Realist Tradition" in *All Our Yesterdays: 90 Years of British Cinema*. Edited by Charles Barr. London: BFI. pp. 72–97.
Hitt, Jim. 1990. *The American West from Fiction (1823–1976) into Film (1909–1986)*. Jefferson, NC: McFarland.
Landy, Marcia. 2012. "The Hollywood Western, the Movement-Image, and Making History" in *Hollywood and the American Historical Film*. Edited by J.E. Smyth. New York: Palgrave Macmillan. pp. 26–48.
Lloyd, Innes. 1983. Interview. *Doctor Who Magazine Winter Special*. 11–13.
Lusted, David. 1998. "The Popular Culture Debate and Light Entertainment on Television"

in *The Television Studies Book*. Edited by Christine Geraghty and David Lusted. London: Arnold. pp. 175–190.

Maynard, Richard A. 1974. *The American West on Film: Myth and Reality*. Rochelle Park, NJ: Hayden Book Company.

Mittell, Jason. 2004. *Genre and Television. From Cop Shows to Cartoons in American Culture*. New York: Routledge.

Neale, Steve. 2000. *Genre and Hollywood*. London: Routledge.

Newbery, Barry. 2013: *The Barry Newbery Signature Collection*. Kent: Telos.

O'Mahoney, Daniel. 2007. "'Now how is that wolf able to impersonate a grandmother?' History, Pseudo-History, and Genre in Doctor Who" in *Time and Relative Dissertations in Space: Critical Perspectives on Doctor Who*. Edited by David Butler. Manchester: Manchester University Press. pp. 56–67.

Pixley, Andrew. 1995. "Doctor Who Archive Feature: Serial Z: The Gunfighters." *Doctor Who Magazine* 221: 23–30.

Rixon, Paul. 2006. *American Television on British Screens: A Story of Cultural Interaction*. Basingstoke: Palgrave Macmillan.

Schatz, Thomas. 1981. *Hollywood Genres: Formulas, Filmmaking, and the Studio System*. Philadelphia: Temple University Press.

Street, Sarah. 2001. *Costume and Cinema. Dress Codes in Popular Film*. London: Wallflower.

Tydeman, William E. 1998. "Tom Mix: King of the Hollywood Cowboys" in *Back in the Saddle: Essays on Western Film and Television Actors*. Edited by Gary A. Yoggy. Jefferson, NC: McFarland. pp. 25–42.

Wiles, John. 1983. Interview. *Doctor Who Magazine Winter Special*: 8–9.

FILMOGRAPHY

"The Aztecs." May 23, 1964–June 13, 1964. *Doctor Who*. BBC.

Carry On Cowboy. 1965. Directed by Gerald Thomas.

Gunfight at the O.K. Corral. 1957. Directed by John Sturges.

"The Gunfighters." April 30, 1966–May 21, 1966. *Doctor Who*. BBC.

"The Myth Makers." October 16, 1965–November 6, 1965. *Doctor Who*. BBC.

The Sheriff of Fractured Jaw. 1958. Directed by Raoul Walsh.

A Rude Awakening

Metafiction in Eric Pringle's
"The Awakening"[1]

Andrew O'Day

From its outset in the 1960s, *Doctor Who* moved very quickly from stories set in history where the only science-fictional elements were the Doctor and the TARDIS to stories set in Earth's past featuring aliens and monsters. This essay focuses on Eric Pringle's *Doctor Who* narrative "The Awakening" (1984), produced after the program had been on-air for 20 years, and will argue that it is an example of metafiction reflecting on the mixing of science fiction with history in the program as a whole both for educational and entertainment purposes. Although Kate Brown notes in the fan publication *In-Vision* that what is presented is a "play within a play" (Brown 1997, 72), she does not point out how the narrative, which sees the Doctor (Peter Davison), Tegan (Janet Fielding) and Turlough (Mark Strickson) arrive in the village of Little Hodcombe, reflects on the merging of history and science fiction in the wider series, as this essay does. The essay then turns to examine the way the narrative pastiches texts in a post-modernist historical fashion, also pointing to its constructed quality.

Genre, Metafiction and Role-Play
in Doctor Who

Genres consist of series of conventions which are repeated across texts; texts are therefore highly constructed. Daniel O'Mahony has written about history in 1960s *Doctor Who* and argues that even the earliest "classical historicals" are constructed. O'Mahony, for example, comments that "History is not simply what is past but the way knowledge about that past is arranged" and that "History is a construct of the present" (O'Mahony 2007, 56–67). These are points that had previously been raised by historians such as E.H. Carr (2001), Arthur Marwick (1989), and John Tosh (2002) and by media critics such as Pierre Sorlin (1990) and Patricia Ann-Lee (1990). Carr writes that history involves "an unending dialogue between the present and the past" (Carr 2001, 62) Marwick, meanwhile, states that history "gives insights … into the preoccupations of the age in which it was actually written" (Marwick 1989, 20). Tosh, too, observes that history rests on principles such as "*difference* … a recognition of the gulf which separates our own age from all previous ages" (Tosh 2002, 9). Sorlin states that "it should immediately occur to viewers … that the historical scene had to be interpreted by someone in order to be represented before the cameras" (Sorlin 1990, 32). Commenting on the documentary, Sorlin notes that "the presence of a narrator's voice … would certainly remind viewers that somebody is telling this story, and telling it in a certain way" and this is so even where there is not an explicit narrator (*ibid.*).

However, the *Doctor Who* pseudo-historical, which mixes science fiction and history, and meaning "not genuine history," is more apparently constructed than the "classical historical" since we automatically *know* it did not happen in the way being presented. The science fiction element is so obviously invented. This is the case with all such narratives and is reflected upon in "The Awakening" where Sir George Hutchinson (Denis Lill) recreates history, the English Civil War at Little Hodcombe, to awaken the alien Malus. Brown is at a loss to place "The Awakening"; she correctly points out that it is not a "pure" historical, or a typical "pseudo-historical" (Brown 1992, 13). What it is, in fact, is a metafiction or meta-drama as it involves characters acting out a drama.

"The Awakening" fits in with a string of *Doctor Who* metafictions. Patricia Waugh (1984) and Mark Currie (1995) define metafictions as narratives reflecting on their own construction or reception as fiction. These are more than brief moments such as Morgus (John Normington) turning and making asides to the camera in a Shakespearean villainous fashion in "The Caves of Androzani" (1984) and Sil (Nabil Shaban) commenting that he must maintain continuity from "Vengeance on Varos" (1985) in "The Trial of a Time Lord" parts 5 to 8 (1986). For example, "The Mind Robber" (1968) reflects on the way many viewers of the program become absorbed in fiction (O'Day 2016a), "Carnival of Monsters" (1973) on the program's playful nature (O'Day 2016c), "The Five Doctors" (1983) on the program as a game (Leach 2009 and O'Day 2016d), and "Vengeance on Varos" on the ideological nature of the program (O'Day 2016f). Other narratives reflect on their participation in different genres. Even the classical historical "Marco Polo" (1964), for instance, sees the Doctor in a historical travel log genre, through the presence of Polo as narrator over the shot of a parchment map, while "The Aztecs" (1964) deals with human sacrifice from a present perspective through the presence of the science fiction time travelers (O'Day 2016e), "The Deadly Assassin" (1976) reflects on its construction within the gothic genre through including a character named Chancellor Goth (Bernard Horsfall) (Barnes 1999, 12) and "Castrovalva" (1982) reflects upon the way it is composed of hard science behind a fairy tale façade through a tapestry, a symbol of textuality, existing in a fantasy locale yet being held up by mathematics (O'Day 2016b).

Role-play in "The Awakening" marks that story as commenting on the pseudo-historical. By contrast, the need for accurate role-play in "The Aztecs" highlights the fact that that story was a "classical historical." In "The Aztecs" Barbara (Jacqueline Hill) was taken for the High Priestess Yetexa, as she emerged from the Tomb of Yetexa wearing the goddess' ornaments, and, finding the Aztec practice of human sacrifice barbaric, she intended to eliminate it. This is what made Tlotoxl believe her to be a false goddess, a point which he is quite correct about. Barbara must learn to play the part of Yetexa properly and stick to recorded history. She cannot write her own script but is following one already written. Barbara is not playing herself but rather an established part. This makes "The Aztecs" metatextual. History is read from the present perspective of those arriving in the TARDIS and, although specific Aztec characters are fictional and did not really exist, the writer does not have the license to make everything up and cannot have the TARDIS crew change events.

Role-Play in "The Awakening" and Reflection on the Pseudo-Historical

Doctor Who is a drama series and its pseudo-historicals see aliens using the past for their sinister purposes. In "The Awakening," set in then-contemporary 1984, the theatrical Sir George Hutchinson re-enacts the English Civil War in the isolated village of Little Hodcombe (a dramatization of an historical event), to provide psychic energy for the alien Malus to reawaken (a science fiction element).

In the *Doctor Who* pseudo-historicals, real actors dress up in costume as characters in the narrative and there is attention to period setting. In "The Awakening," in the actual plot, characters from 1984 dress up as historical figures. For example, as noted in the DVD Production Notes, Sir George and Sergeant Willow (Jack Galloway) have red sashes on their costume and Colonel Wolsey (Glyn Houston) has an orange one, indicating which side they are fighting on in the English Civil War, Sir George and Willow being Royalists and Wolsey standing for Cromwell. Indeed, as Brown notes, anachronistic elements are set up from the opening scene (Brown 1997, 13). Horses pound along ridden by men in 17th-century clothing, while a woman (Jane Hampden [Polly James]) is clad in velvet trousers, a plush fabric for the 1980s (*ibid.*). Furthermore, as also mentioned in the DVD Production Notes, the parlor to Colonel Wolsey's house is in Stuart style, perfect in every detail. There is also a sense of historical accuracy where characters are not permitted to use modern-day technology like the telephone call-box, but must ride places to deliver messages to other characters.

In the case of the burning of the Queen of the May, which here unusually takes place at a battle fought in July, there is an attempt by Sir George to recreate the barbarism of the custom where "the toast of Little Hodcombe" would be "screaming" in order to provide psychic energy for the Malus' awakening. There is a difference between Sir George's recreation of history in a metadramatic way with the Doctor's and Colonel Wolsey's who replace Tegan as the intended May Queen with a straw dummy. Earlier, Jane Hampden has said that she knows what happens to a May Queen at the end of her reign and a distinction is drawn between Colonel Wolsey, who earnestly says he will not harm her, with Sir George. Colonel Wolsey indeed later remarks that the dummy is "not as attractive as Tegan" but that burning it is "more humane." The Doctor and Colonel Wolsey, unlike Sir George, recognize the playful nature to recreating history that occurs in many villages by replacing Tegan with a stand-in dummy that can easily be burnt but cannot be hurt, in contrast to aiding a science fiction monster. The straw dummy stands for the original Queen of the May but obviously is not the original Queen of the May, and its presence is therefore a way of recreating history but not in the sinister way of Sir George. The Doctor and Colonel Wolsey's offering of a dummy to be burnt reminds one of the most famous example of "burning the Guy" every November 5 in memory of the historical figure of Guy Fawkes and his plot to burn up the Houses of Parliament in the early 17th century (1605).

The burning of the May Queen is ceremonial. Not only is Tegan dressed up as the Queen of the May (something she is against) but also, as the cart driven by Colonel Wolsey makes its way through the village, people stand at the side of the road watching. This is spectacle and should be for the onlookers' enjoyment, showing how Sir George is perverting events. There is a somewhat ironic joyful incidental music track as the cart advances since this historical ceremony is not meant to be a mock-up of past events but is meant to be true-to-life with a real burning to assist the science fiction Malus. The joyful incidental music track is replaced by the ominous sound of drum beating at the place the burning is to take place. Again, indicating the perverting of a ceremony is Sergeant Willow's comment to the captured Doctor that he is just in time for the "show" and can have a "front seat." Willow has previously said that he is just obeying orders in getting Tegan to dress up to which Colonel Wolsey remarks "that's what they all say" highlighting the created drama.

Cross-cutting illustrates that Sir George is recreating the past in order to provide psychic energy for the Malus. Cross-cutting is a device which not only separates scenes but also connects them. There is a connection between the recreation of history and the Malus. For example, when Sir George's plan to burn the May Queen (in this case, Tegan) is thwarted, there is a shot of the Malus in distress in the church, bellowing smoke, and Sir George visibly disturbed on his horse, putting his hands to his head in agony. Sir George indeed states that he must get to the church, as he feels that the Malus needs him.

The point that past is being created in order to provide psychic energy is highlighted by the Doctor showing Will Chandler (Keith Jayne), who is actually from 1643, the tombstones in the church cemetery which indicate that the story is set in the then-present, 1984, far after Will's time. The Malus has remained in a type of tomb since 1643, however unlike those buried in the church cemetery is awakening in the 1984 present.

Furthermore, the point that the past is being recreated for a science fiction purpose is highlighted through reference to another historical event which followed the English Civil War by several centuries. As mentioned in the DVD Production Notes, this is World War II. Tegan says that it looks like a bomb fell on the church, to which Turlough replies that perhaps it did. This would not have been the case back in 1643 when Will Chandler originally witnessed the fighting between Cavaliers and Roundheads and the presence of the Malus in the church.

"The Awakening's historical content, then, is stage-managed by the villain Sir George in order to assist the Malus. Significantly, Sir George is the village magistrate and, while his role is traditionally to impose law and order, he creates an atmosphere of lawlessness, telling Jane Hampden that as the magistrate he will find himself innocent of any wrong-doing. Sir George surrounds himself by persons in military roles, Colonel Wolsey and Sergeant Willow, who help oversee the role playing of the war games. Sir George's typical role, then, is replaced by a different one in the role-playing drama.

"The Awakening" reflects specifically on a wide-range of *Doctor Who* pseudo-historical narratives which feature a futuristic villain or monster in a historical setting. This is the case as early as in "The Time Meddler" (1965) which saw the introduction of a member of the Doctor's own race, the Meddling Monk (Peter Butterworth), in "The Time Warrior" (1973–1974) where the alien Sontaran Linx (Kevin Lindsay) promises the medieval warrior, Irongron (David Daker), futuristic weapons to wage war on his enemies in return for a base from which to repair a spacecraft, in "The Masque of Mandragora" (1976) where alien energy possesses a Cult and aims to destroy the great thinkers of the Italian Renaissance and in "The King's Demons" (1983) where the Doctor's Time Lord nemesis, the Master (Anthony Ainley) schemes to prevent the signing of Magna Carta through the presence of an android impersonating King John (Gerald Flood). Even after "The Awakening," in "The Mark of the Rani" (1985), the actions of the Rani (Kate O'Mara), a Time Lady, threatens the Industrial Revolution since she extracts a fluid from worker's brains which make them aggressive and wish to attack those who stand for progress. In this way, the story is similar to "The Masque of Mandragora" since both concern a threat to man's move from the Dark Ages into scientific enlightenment. In "The Awakening" Sir George fits into the type of Irongron villain from "The Time Warrior" since both believe that they can control the monstrous, which is, in fact, using them.

Sir George is placed within a lineage of villains from history. Tegan is heard telling Sir George that history is filled with lunatics like him who fortunately end up locked away. These lunatics not only include real-life figures from history, which a character like Tegan would be familiar with from textbooks, but also *Doctor Who* villains who appear in the pseudo-historical narratives manipulating history. Sir George is just like these *Doctor Who* villains, here recreating history for devilish purposes.

At the end of "The Awakening" the villain Sir George gets his comeuppance and the monster is destroyed, as is typical of *Doctor Who* serials more generally. Peter Davison's Doctor sounds very Troughtonesque as he accuses Sir George of turning on his friend Colonel Wolsey and asks if Sir George had such feelings of hate before he activated the Malus. Additionally, although the Doctor and Sergeant Willow prevent Colonel Wolsey, knife in hand, of killing Sir George, Will Chandler pushes Sir George into the Malus saying, "It be better he be dead."

A comparison can also be drawn between different types of historian in the story: Jane Hampden is the village schoolteacher, much akin to Barbara Wright in early 1960s *Who*. Barbara Wright and Ian Chesterton (William Russell) were history and science teachers respectively at Coal Hill School and Barbara was an instructor of "purer history." Both Ian and Barbara stumbled aboard the TARDIS when following the Doctor's granddaughter Susan Foreman (Carole Ann Ford) who was a pupil at their school home. Barbara's role was to be able to explain things in history when the TARDIS materialized in past times such as in the period of "Marco Polo" and in the era of "The Aztecs." As noted earlier, history was also told from a present perspective and though Barbara found the Aztec practice of human sacrifice barbaric, the Doctor told her that she could "not rewrite history, not one line." Unlike the historian Andrew Verney (Frederick Hall) in "The Awakening" who (off-screen) has earlier told Sir George of the Malus' presence, Jane Hampden stands against the war games but for other reasons and needs her eyes opened to the science-fictional elements. Sir George tells Jane Hampden that as the village schoolteacher she should be more interested in their history and customs. In response, Jane Hampden remarks that it has all gone "beyond" a few high-spirited lads having fun and that someone will get hurt. But what Jane Hampden does not remotely suspect is that events are "beyond" the norm in that there is a science fiction element to the recreation of history. People will get hurt as a result of Sir George acting out the games for the Malus' presence.

"The Awakening" as Postmodern Pastiche

The *Doctor Who* classical historicals are historical fictions and employ features of adventure fiction. For example, "Marco Polo" includes a lengthy sword-fight. In "The Aztecs," Tlotoxl (John Ringham) is depicted as villainous, and speaks in an aside to the camera at the end of the first episode. Moreover, camera angles give the impression of Tlotoxl as villainous plotter where he is at the foreground and in the background of a shot at significant points, or where the camera lingers on him speaking after all other characters have left the scene. Also taken from Shakespeare's play *Hamlet* is the Doctor advising Itxa (Ian Cullen) that Ian Chesterton's strength can be drained in a fight through his wrist being scratched with a thorn. As there was a fight in "Marco Polo," there is a dramatic fight between the two with the episode ending being Tlotoxl calling for an overpowered Ian Chesterton to be killed. "The Aztecs" also sees Ian trapped in a tunnel which leads to the Tomb of Yetexa as it fills with water at the end of the third episode.

"The Awakening," meanwhile, is far from historically pure and uses conventions of fiction. While the story deals with the recreation of history, it also features generic elements of science fiction drama, and indeed of genres like the gothic, associated with *Doctor Who*, again showing how it is constructed. These include the underground secret passageway which leads from Colonel Wolsey's house to the decaying church, the Doctor silencing Jane Hampden and helping her evade Sir George and his pursuing men, the monster behind the crack in the wall in the church which awakens, and indeed leads to the *Doctor Who* episode ending with the Doctor engulfed in smoke and Jane Hampden screaming, the imprisonment of characters (Turlough and Andrew Verney) and the insane villain serving the monster.

It also recreates elements from earlier *Who* narratives in a type of postmodern pastiche. One such narrative is "The Daemons" (1971). As Brown notes, the isolation of the village, the awakening of an ancient alien presence and the disruption of a festival all echo this earlier narrative (Brown 1997, 72). Added to that is the destruction of the church by a monster at the climax. "The Awakening" also resembles "The Daemons" in that, as noted above, a science fiction premise is given to the Devil. Not only is there an image of the Malus on the stone in the church leading to the secret passageway but the Doctor also points Jane Hampden to a woodcarving of a man being chased by the Devil when she says that she has seen the Malus before. Similarly, in "The Daemons," it turns out that the Doctor is dealing with an alien race of Demons from the planet Demos. This race of horned beasts which includes Beelzebub, with horns being a symbol of power, has become engrained in Earth's religious culture. Furthermore, in "The Daemons" the Master (Roger Delgado) poses as the village vicar and, when he is not seen in his black vicar's outfit, is portrayed in a Satanic red cloak with a labyrinthine design, the maze having been a common Christian image for sinuousness and for not following a straight path to God. The pentangle is also a symbol of the Devil seen on the floor of the church and the church is guarded by a red-eyed gargoyle which moves with incredible speed.

"Pyramids of Mars" (1975) is also a narrative from the classic *Doctor Who* series where the Devil is given a science fiction rationale. Sutekh (Gabriel Woolf) comes from a race known as Osirans but with variations of his name being Set, Satan and Sadok, beings reviled on other worlds. Sutekh is imprisoned by his brother Horus in a pyramid and the story draws further on Egyptology with Sutekh's servants being robot Mummies and with a time tunnel existing in a sarcophagus. This story, furthermore, does not feature the locations of the village and of the Christian church.

The narratives of the early to mid–1980s produced by John Nathan-Turner and script edited by Eric Saward were notable for their post-modern pastiche. Not only is this the case with Cybermen and Dalek stories like "Earthshock" (1982), "Attack of the Cybermen" (1985) and "Resurrection of the Daleks" (1984) with scenes echoing earlier outings for these monsters, but also the pseudo-historical "The Visitation" (1982) with a spacecraft burning up and monsters crash-landing on 17th-century Earth in an escape-pod echoes "The Time Warrior" (1973–1974) and the Sontaran Linx's spacecraft crashing in medieval England. But such post-modern pastiche is especially key to a narrative which is about its construction as a narrative, with "The Awakening" echoing "The Daemons" and, to a lesser degree, "Pyramids of Mars." There is also an allusion to "The Visitation" and the Terileptils when the planet Raaga is mentioned.

As noted in the DVD Production Notes, the story is also indebted to the film *The Wicker Man* (1973). This was a British mystery-horror film and involved a police sergeant sent to a Scottish island village in search of a missing girl whom the townspeople say they have no knowledge about. There are strange rites that take place there, just as "The Awakening" is steeped in folklore. Furthermore, the psychic projection of the one-eyed man in "The Awakening" is indebted to the horror genre.

The alien Malus was supposedly also seen in the actual past by the figure of Will Chandler who, as noted above, crosses between two time zones from 1643 to 1984. Therefore, we see how not only in 1984 does Sir George Hutchinson mix history (recreating the English Civil War) and science fiction (this is done to enable the alien Malus to awaken from a dormant state) but, in terms of the plot, history and science fiction were mixed in 1643 when the real English Civil War gave the Malus energy. As Will Chandler says, the Malus made the fighting worse. Will Chandler's dress and speech are of a peasant from the earlier time-period. Therefore, the mixture of history and science fiction in 1643 is typical of the *Doctor Who* "pseudo-historical" while the 1984 recreation is a metafictional reflection on the "pseudo-historical." Will Chandler's presence in 1984 serves to verify the historical events that are being recreated like the burning of the Queen of the May and he is sided with the Doctor and not Sir George as he recognizes the evil nature of the Malus.

Conclusion

In conclusion, "The Awakening" is an unrepresentative *Doctor Who* story, neither a historical or a pseudo-historical but involving a stage-manager recreating the past in then-contemporary England (1984) in order to provide psychic energy for a science fiction monster. At the same time, by doing this, "The Awakening" reflects upon the pseudo-historical genre of many *Doctor Who* episodes where there is a mixture between history and science fiction. In some *Doctor Who* serials, the Doctor arrives in the past in his time and space machine, the TARDIS, where he finds science fiction mixed with history. It is hence an essential narrative, a vital part of the canon, for considering the use of history in "classic" *Doctor Who*. Finally, "The Awakening" is a postmodern pastiche and therefore is also situated in history and points to its fabrication in this way.

NOTES

1. I would like to thank Matthew Kilburn for inviting me to join the Oxford University *Doctor Who* Society where my interest in this narrative was awakened; Nicolas Pillai for providing vital archival material; and, as usual, Tim Harris for his support.

BIBLIOGRAPHY

Barnes, Alan. 1999. "Tales From the Crypt." *Doctor Who Magazine* 282: pp. 8–12.
Brown, Kate. 1997. "Recreations and Re-Enactments." In *In-Vision Doctor Who: The Awakening* 72. Edited by Anthony Brown. London: Jeremy Bentham. pp. 13–15.
Carr, E.H. 2001. *What Is History?* Basingstoke: Macmillan.
Currie, Mark, ed. 1995. *Metafiction*. London: Longman.
Leach, Jim. 2009. *Doctor Who*. Detroit: Wayne State University Press.
Lee, Patricia Ann. 1990. "Teaching Film and Television as Interpreters of History." In *Image*

as Artifact: The Historical Analysis of Film and Television. Edited by John E. O'Connor. Malabarg: Robert E. Krieger. pp. 96–107.

Marwick, Arthur. 1989. *The Nature of History.* Basingstoke: Macmillan.

O'Day, Andrew. 2016a. "*Doctor Who*: Peter Ling's "The Mind Robber—Absorbed in Fiction." https://www.academia.edu/524645/Doctor_Who_Peter_Lings_The_Mind_Robber_-_Absorbed_in_Fiction. Accessed 2 June 2016.

O'Day, Andrew. 2016b. "Difficult Television." https://www.academia.edu/524648/Difficult_Television_Part_I. Accessed 2 June 2016.

O'Day, Andrew. 2016c. "*Doctor Who's* 'Carnival of Monsters' and the Metafiction of Play." https://www.academia.edu/524643/Doctor_Whos_Carnival_of_Monsters_and_the_metafiction_of_play. Accessed 2 June 2016.

O'Day, Andrew. 2016d. "Dungeons and Doctors: 'The Five Doctors' and the Metafiction of the Game." https://www.academia.edu/524652/Terrance_Dicks_The_Five_Doctors_Doctor_Who. Accessed 2 June 2016.

O'Day, Andrew. 2016e. "History and Fiction in John Lucarotti's First Season *Doctor Who* Narratives." https://www.academia.edu/524641/History_and_Fiction_in_John_Lucarottis_Doctor_Who. Accessed 2 June 2016.

O'Day, Andrew. 2016f. "Whose Ideology? Media Manipulation in *Doctor Who's* 'Vengeance on Varos.'" https://www.academia.edu/524646/Doctor_Who_Philip_Martins_Vengeance_on_Varos_-_Whose_ideology. Accessed 2 June 2016.

O'Mahony, Daniel. 2007. "Now how is that wolf able to impersonate a grandmother?' History, Pseudo-History and Genre in *Doctor Who.*" In *Time and Relative Dissertations in Space: Critical Perspectives on Doctor Who.* Edited by David Butler. Manchester: Manchester University Press. pp. 56–67.

Sorlin, Pierre, 1990. "Historical Films as Tools for Historians." In *Image as Artifact: The Historical Analysis of Film and Television.* Edited by John E. O'Connor. Malabarg: Robert E. Krieger. pp. 31–38.

Tosh, John. 2002. *The Pursuit of History: Aims, Methods and New Directions in the Making History,* 3rd ed. London: Longman.

Waugh, Patricia. 1984. *Metafiction: The Theory and Practice of Self-Conscious Fiction.* London: Methuen.

Playing with History
Terrance Dicks, Fans and Season 6B

RHONDA KNIGHT

Terrance Dicks is one of the most frequent contributors to the *Doctor Who* franchise. He began working for *Doctor Who* as an assistant script editor in 1968. He became script editor later that year, serving in that role for five seasons. Afterward, Dicks wrote serials for his successors during Tom Baker's era. Outside of these direct contributions to the program, he helped build its fan base and franchise by writing the novelizations of over 60 televised serials and co-authoring the program's first "behind-the scenes" book, *The Making of Doctor Who* (1972) with Malcolm Hulke. After the program's cancellation in 1989, Dicks began composing original novels for the new tie-in markets and published 13 novels for ranges owned by Virgin Publishing and BBC Books. He is one of the few 1960s television writers who later wrote for all four ranges of tie-in novels. Through these various contributions to the *Doctor Who* franchise, Dicks offers a compelling case study in the evolution of *Doctor Who* fandom. Beginning with the ten-part serial "The War Games" (1968), which he co-wrote with Malcolm Hulke, Dicks has used reoccurring historical settings and characters to create a linked, adaptable multi-media narrative that first addressed *Doctor Who*'s emerging fandom and then engaged various types of *Who* fans when the fandom began to evolve.

A number of Dicks' works directly modify and develop the narrative that he and Hulke began in "The War Games." The aforementioned *The Making of Doctor Who* fills in gaps that the serial's ending creates. His tie-in novels *Timewyrm: Exodus* (1991), *The Eight Doctors* (1997), and the cross-range trilogy, *Players* (1999), *Endgame* (2000), and *World Game* (2005) showcase Dicks' strengths in researching and creating additional historical figures and scenes.[1] This body of work uses history to explore the questions that form the heart of *Doctor Who*: How can history be changed? What happens when history is changed through time travel? Who has the right to change history?

By addressing these questions that fascinate most *Doctor Who* fans, Dicks' publishing trajectory demonstrates a learning curve in which he discovers how to present original material to dedicated *Doctor Who* fans. His initial challenge was managing his penchant to insert formulaic continuity elements, such as references to previous texts (serials or novels), especially those of his own making. Dicks learned to address this distinct population of dedicated fans by incorporating their fan-generated contributions into the *Who* canon in his works. As a result, he has succeeded in creating a meganarrative that explores the nature of the unfettered power created by time travel focusing particularly on the ability to manipulate history.

Playing Games in "The War Games"

It is not hyperbole to say that "The War Games" was a watershed moment in *Doctor Who* history: the serial ends the Patrick Troughton era; it was the last serial broadcast in the 1960s; it was the last black and white *Doctor Who*; and it introduced the Time Lords. Yet, in spite of all of these important firsts and lasts, the merits of the serial itself should not be eclipsed by these landmark moments. Wood and Miles (2006, 270), for example, point out that serial's introduction of the Time Lords has overshadowed "the real point" of the serial, which is the war games that the enemies stage. Dicks (2009) explains the war games this way: "the basic concept is that these aliens kidnap people from different time zones, get the best fighters who survive and they're going to build them into an army to conquer the galaxy." The Earth time zones that the Second Doctor (Patrick Troughton) and his companions Jamie McCrimmon (Frazer Hines) and Zoe Heriot (Wendy Padbury) visit are World War I, the Roman Empire, and the American Civil War. Wood and Miles (2006, 283) argue that the idea of creating an army by kidnapping soldiers from different times is so quintessentially *Doctor Who* they are surprised that it did not appear earlier. Perhaps the Vietnam era was the appropriate time for Hulke and Dicks to introduce such a story. The serial's realistic images of violence juxtaposed with scenes of alien War Lords moving pieces on a table marked out like a game board certainly manifest the feelings many people in the 1960s had about the dehumanization of war.

Hulke and Dicks wrote "The War Games" to replace two serials that were abandoned; therefore, it is a very long serial (ten 25-minute episodes), which seems to be about different things in different moments. The kidnapping of Earth's soldiers by the alien War Lords dominates the first part of the serial, but when Hulke and Dicks decide to introduce the Doctor's own race, the serial, possibly inadvertently, becomes about the Time Lords. The writers introduce a Time Lord, called the War Chief (Edward Brayshaw), as a foil to the Doctor. In episode eight, the viewers learn that he is of the same race as the Doctor and is estranged from his people (just as the Doctor is). He uses his time-travel knowledge to build the machines the War Lords use to kidnap the soldiers. At the end of the serial, Hulke and Dicks leave the War Chief's fate unresolved. The viewers see a War Lord shoot the War Chief, and he seems to die. The program had already introduced the concept of regeneration in William Hartnell's last serial, "The Tenth Planet" (1966). So, even though "The War Games" does not suggest the War Chief's regeneration, fans might have wondered if he, like the First Doctor, survived and became someone else. Dicks will return to this point in later works.

The final two episodes of "The War Games" set up elements of Time Lord mythology that shape the future of the program and the *Doctor Who* universe. The Doctor explains to Jamie and Zoe that he must contact his people so that they can return the kidnapped soldiers to their appropriate Earth timelines, even though he knows that this contact places him in danger. Despite his attempts to escape, the Time Lords capture him and place him on trial. The viewers learn that the Doctor has broken the Time Lords' "most important law of non-interference in the affairs of other planets." However, the trial judges admit that the Doctor "has a part to play in the battle" against evil and sentence him to exile on Earth with a new appearance (episode ten). "The War Games" concludes with small images of the Second Doctor's face circling a larger version of the same image. The special effect recedes into the distance; thus the Doctor's regeneration is implied, which is the second unresolved issue Dicks will explore later in his career.

Specifically, production decisions and economic factors prevented the Second Doctor from having a regeneration scene like the one in "The Tenth Planet." During the sixth season of *Doctor Who*, the future of the program was under question. Many at the BBC believed that the show was "tired" and that it had reached the end of its natural life cycle ("War" 2009). The viewer numbers had been dwindling throughout the sixth season. Because of the program's uncertain future, producer Derrick Sherwin created an ending that could serve as the show's conclusion, if it did not return. In late March 1969, while "The War Games" was being filmed, Sherwin and Peter Bryant were searching for the next Doctor, in hopes the show would return (Howe, Walker, and Stammers 2005, 299–301, 323). The serial's tight schedule meant that the special effects of Second Doctor's regeneration scene had to be filmed at Ealing Television Film Studios on April 3 ("*Doctor*" 1995, 28). Jon Pertwee did not agree to play the Third Doctor until May 21, thus making the filming of a transformation scene impossible (Howe, Walker, and Stammers 2005, 324).

Playing with the Canon: Season 6B from Fanon to Canon

Because the conclusion of "The War Games" does not show the Second Doctor changing into the Third Doctor (Jon Pertwee), this scene has given fuel to a fanon, an extra-textual, therefore, non-canonical reading that is widely accepted by fans. Often, fans create these new "readings of characters or events," in service of "correcting perceived errors of continuity" (October n.d.). However, as Parrish (2007, 33) points out, fanons emerge only through the repetition of particular readings that creates a general acceptance among fans. These readings begin to seem like they are canonical and thus establish a fanon. One of *Doctor Who*'s most prevalent fanons is that of Season 6B. This fanon asserts that the Second Doctor's adventures do not end with "The War Games." Season 6B is an attempt at retroactive continuity, explaining the Second Doctor's later appearances in the program, namely "The Three Doctors" (1973), "The Five Doctors" (1983), and "The Two Doctors" (1985). As such, Season 6B creates an extra-canonical space in which stories may be told without altering the continuity of the Second Doctor's regeneration into the Third.

The continuity issues that make up Season 6B were first codified in *The Doctor Who Discontinuity Guide*, written by Paul Cornell, Martin Day, and Keith Topping. These authors are part of a second generation of script and novel writers who also grew up as fans of the program, and as such, they occupy a hybrid position as both *Doctor Who* authors and fans (Griffiths 1999, 49). In this dual position, Cornell, Day, and Topping (2013) explain that "we are here to celebrate the fan way of watching television," i.e., an acknowledgement of fans' attention to continuity. These authors resemble fans whom Henry Jenkins (2012) describes as textual poachers. He and John Tulloch (1995, 40) further explain the poacher paradigm: "[It is] fan activity reflect[ing] both a fascination with media content (which leads them to continue to work with and upon the original program material) and a frustration with the producer's inability to tell the kinds of stories they wish to see (which results in their progressive rewriting of the program ideology as the characters and situations become the basis for their own subcultural activity)." They further note the only power fans like these have "is *the power to gloss* and to write the aesthetic history of the show" (145), of which *The Discontinuity Guide* is an important example. In the case of Season 6B, close scrutiny of various *Doctor Who* serials by textual poachers provides them with clues they can weave into a narrative that explains why the Second Doctor can appear alongside his former and future incarnations in three separate serials. Dicks subsequently embraced the narrative space of Season 6B as a way to revisit the characters and situations of "The War Games" and by populating it with new enemies known as the Players, who appear in a trilogy of novels. Like the War Lords, the Players see humans as game pieces they can manipulate for their own purposes.

Because of the complexities of Season 6B, only the three points pertinent to Dicks' use of it are discussed here.[2] First, proponents of Season 6B argue that the scene of the Second Doctor's spinning images in "The War Games" does not depict his regeneration but the effects of a transmat upon the Doctor, sending him to Gallifrey (Morley 2014). Dicks embraces this alternate fan interpretation and uses it as a plot point in *Players* and *World Game*, two subsequent *Doctor Who* novels. Second, supporters of Season 6B believe that the Second Doctor begins *working for* the Time Lords after he is taken to Gallifrey by the transmat. The Second Doctor's appearance in Robert Holmes' "The Two Doctors" indicates that he is clearly now the Time Lords' agent. Dastari (Laurence Payne), the head of the space station, inquires if the Second Doctor "act[s] on their instructions," to which the Doctor replies: "It's the price that I pay for my freedom" (episode one). Third, fans note that in "The Two Doctors," the Second Doctor possesses state-of-the-art gadgets and demonstrates better control of the TARDIS than previously. In episode one, Jamie notices a new control on the console, which the Doctor identifies as "the Time Lords' dual control," which contains a remote device that allows him to summon the TARDIS to his location. When the Sixth Doctor (Colin Baker) sees this remote device later in "The Two Doctors," he exclaims that he's always wanted one of those. The Second Doctor replies: "Some of us have earned these little privileges" (episode three). Adherents of Season 6B see this exchange as evidence that the Time Lords manipulate the Second Doctor's memory after he stops working for them. Otherwise, wouldn't the Sixth Doctor remember having had this remote in his past? Also, another new gadget, a TARDIS-homing watch, appears in the Third Doctor's first serial, "Spearhead from Space" (1970), which also causes fans to believe that the Doctor—before he finally regenerated—obtained more gadgets while working for the Time Lords.

At one level this fanon signals fan desires to make decades of *Doctor Who* programs a cohesive, comprehensive text rather than a progression of televised ephemera, created for the moment with little regard to what came before or what might come after. In the Forward to *The Discontinuity Guide,* Dicks (2013) says when he was script editor, the program did not have "a 'Bible,' a book of rules and facts in which continuity was set in stone." Elsewhere, Dicks (2010, 8) observes that in the pressure-packed atmosphere of making *Doctor Who* the creators were not thinking about "shows that were over and done with" but working to finish new episodes, noting that re-watching an old serial required "a private viewing" from the BBC tape, if it had not been erased. Therefore, fans today have a luxury *Doctor Who*'s creators did not. They may watch serials with little or no gaps between them with a remote in their hands to check continuity. As such, the vicissitudes of television production create the continuity gaps observant fans can write their own stories into.

Playing to the Fans: The Making of Doctor Who *and* Timewyrm: Exodus

Yet, before fan publications like *The Discontinuity Guide*, Hulke and Dicks wrote *The Making of Doctor Who*, the first non-fiction book about the program, and Dicks began publishing in BBC's new novel range. Hulke and Dicks were among the first to recognize that there was a fandom who wanted to not only peek behind the scenes of the program but to also relive the important plot points of the almost decade-long story. Mat Coward (2015, 74) calls it a "revolutionary book that first transformed passive viewers into active fans, able to watch our favourite programme from backstage, as it were, as well as on the screen." Tulloch and Jenkins (1995, 4) explain that a fandom is initially defined by the desire to connect to the program through "relations of consumption and spectatorship." *The Making of Doctor Who*'s blurb demonstrates the multiple kinds of spectatorship it offers, beginning with the plot-based question "What happened when Doctor Who was put on trial by the Time Lords?" and continuing with the promise of insider knowledge, "learn how the Cybermen and the Daleks came into being and how the special effects work" (Hulke and Dicks 1972). It is no coincidence that the first line of the blurb mentioned above refers to "The War Games." The section of the book that recounts the Doctor's many adventures uses the Second Doctor's trial as an organizing conceit and offers a series of memoranda, purportedly from "the secret files of the Time Lords," as a frame narrative to summarize the on-screen adventures of the first two Doctors (39). Submitted by his Time Lord defense counselor, accounts of each serial through "The War Games" serve as the Second Doctor's evidence. Although the Time Lords admit that "he had always tried to do good and to fight evil," he is sentenced—just as in "The War Games"—to exile on Earth with a new appearance (55). Even though the book's outcome of the trial is the same as the serial's, Hulke and Dicks claim to present a different, more authentic version of the trial for the fans who purchase the book.

Dicks' next continuation of "The War Games" is *Timewyrm: Exodus* which functions as both a sequel to the televised "The War Games" and to John Peel's novel, *Timewyrm: Genesys*, which precedes it in the Virgin New Adventures range, featuring the Seventh Doctor (Sylvester McCoy). *Exodus* cultivates its audience by providing internal references to the *Who* canon and external references to historical events. Ora McWilliams and Joshua Richardson (2011) distinguish the importance of both types of references. They explain that "the purpose of the internal reference is to create a privileged, referential universe for its most dedicated fans. Such a system of connection encourages fandom by giving a form of insider knowledge that lionizes fan devotion and text consumption" (114). On the other hand, external references "situate the program in the center of a web of texts" (114), which fans find empowering because they frequently discuss texts by referencing other texts. *Exodus*'s internal references tie it to "The War Games" and *Genesys* by using enemies established in both. The Timewyrm, a parasitic, transcendental entity, occupies and manipulates significant figures in Earth's history; in Peel's novel she embodies the Akkadian goddess Ishtar, and in Dicks' novel she invades the mind of Adolf Hitler. Dicks incorporates the renegade Time Lord from "The War Games" as Hitler's advisor Doctor Kriegslieter (German for "war chief"). Kriegslieter is an ugly, deformed figure in the novel. His deformity, Dicks explains, comes from his incomplete regeneration, caused by his wounding during "The War Games." Kriegslieter explains that he barely survived and stayed "on the War Lord planet as a medical curiosity," plotting revenge for the Doctor (1991, 187). Kriegslieter, still aligned with the War Lords, realizes that the best way to find the Doctor is to interfere with Earth's history. Dicks deploys this unresolved detail from "The War Games" as a way to add depth to his book's villain while also providing a continuity element for the fans.

Exodus develops "layered plot strands," providing readers with twists on events they already know (Russell 1991, 39). The Seventh Doctor and Ace (Sophie Aldred) arrive in London during the 1951 Festival of Britain and find a Britain that has surrendered to the Nazis. The Doctor must turn to a record of the past, albeit the false one, to determine where history has gone awry; he must use his knowledge of Earth's history to defeat those who are trying to change it. In the alternate 1951, he searches the archives for the moment the current timeline diverged from the expected one; here he learns that Dunkirk is the key moment of change (Dicks 1991, 62). Aided by civilians, the British Army had not escaped; instead, the German army forced its surrender (61). Alternate history plots enable Dicks to focus on "fine points where history was in the balance," and this World War II plot is significant to Dicks "because [the British] might so narrowly have lost" (Russell 1991, 39). Therefore, *Exodus* places the Doctor in important moments in Hitler's life, such as the Beer Hall Putsch, so that he can manipulate history. The Doctor explains to Ace that their actions should be minimal: "Changing history is a delicate operation—like brain surgery. You don't start by sawing the patient's head off" (107). The Seventh Doctor shows a reluctance to "muck about" with history, even when he knows that he must correct the damage done by the Timewyrm and Kriegslieter. In ensuring that "one of the most terrible wars in human history ... happened on schedule," the Doctor saves "true history" (228, 135). *Exodus* sets up a paradoxical pattern that will occur in Dicks' subsequent novels: the Doctor must protect history from being toyed with by outsiders; however, in fulfilling this role he must actively interfere with history, which he believes should be avoided.

Playing Too Much: Alienating Fans with The Eight Doctors

What is especially important in Dicks' adoption of Season 6B is that he— as a representative of *Doctor Who* creators in Jenkins' poacher paradigm— actually acknowledges and supports the fan-writers who gloss and produce new texts and situations. By doing so, Dicks canonizes their work. This marks an important level of cooperation between fans and creators that is often absent within a fandom. Dicks embraces this narrative space as a place to develop the themes and characters from his original serial; Dicks, however, is not immediately sure how to explore this space. His first publication after the *Discontinuity Guide*'s articulation of Season 6B, *The Eight Doctors*, does little to explore Season 6B's possibilities because this book had more immediate marketing goals. The novel was the first in BBC's new range of books featuring the Eighth Doctor (Paul McGann). In 1997, after the broadcast of the Fox TV-movie *Doctor Who* (1996) that introduced the Eighth Doctor, the BBC did not renew Virgin Publishing's license to produce new *Doctor Who* books. From 1991, Virgin had overseen the New Adventures range, featuring the Seventh Doctor, and in 1994 had added the Missing Adventures range, featuring stories with earlier incarnations. The market for these Virgin books was "adult science fiction" readers; therefore, these books contained adult situations, such as sex and drug use (Russell 1990, 50). When the BBC decided to promote its new Eighth Doctor through a new book range, Terrance Dicks was the obvious choice to inaugurate it because of his long association with the program and established publishing history for *Doctor Who* tie-in books. The BBC also started the Past Doctors Adventure range that mirrored Virgin's Missing Adventures.[3] However, the first editor of the BBC books was Nuala Buffini, an executive who was not a fan of the program and whose only creative charge was to commission books that were less controversial than the Virgin ranges. Buffini, therefore, did not have the knowledge to realize that Dicks' inaugural novel, which many could see as an homage to the program, could also be perceived by the fans as an insult (Sandifer 2012; Sullivan 1997).

The Eight Doctors' premise is that the Eighth Doctor, in the events immediately following the movie, suffers amnesia, caused by a device the Master places in the TARDIS. To restore his memory, the TARDIS takes him back to a pivotal moment in each of his former lives, where he interacts with his earlier selves and regains each incarnation's memories. The premise seems like perfect marketing, introducing new fans to the various Doctors and providing established fans a nostalgic journey. Yet, many fan reviews note that the book is poorly-plotted and dominated by failed continuity fixes, obscure internal references, and self-plagiarism. *Doctor Who* novelist and reviewer Craig Hinton claims to have coined the term *fanwank* to describe this type of writing.[4] In his memorial blog post for Hinton, Topping (2006) defines fanwank: "a continuity reference thrown into a story and having little relevance to the plot, but there purely as a device to please fans." Matt Hills (2010, Ch. 2) shows that fanwank is a designation often wielded by dedicated fans, which demonstrates their anxiety over "negative fan stereotypes," such as infantilism and insularity. The anxiety emerges when dedicated fans look at works created specifically for them and think about how the casual fan might view these works as strange or trivial. The designation fanwank is then both an expression of fan anxiety and a reaction against poorly-conceived works that try to pander to dedicated fans. *The Eight Doctors* constructs a particular view that *Doctor Who* fans are satisfied by mere gestures towards the program's long history without the author providing narrative substance in those references.[5]

The Eight Doctors' two chapters that revisit "The War Games" illustrate the ways Dicks' attempts to write a referential, fan-pleasing text miss the mark. Landing at almost the same time and location as the Second Doctor, the Eighth Doctor learns about the war games and follows parts of his predecessor's path (through some broadly-drawn rehashing of the series' dialogue) to the War Lord headquarters, where he meets his Second incarnation. For this book, Dicks creates a time-travel convention that makes time stop when the two versions of the Doctor meet, so that the memory transfer can take place. During this out-of-time moment, the Eighth Doctor advises his previous self to ask the Time Lords for help in sending the soldiers back to their respective timelines. He uses his own existence as evidence that the Second Doctor's punishment is not "temporal dissolution" (Ch. 5). With his newly-restored memories of his first and second incarnations as reference material, the Eighth Doctor coaches the Second Doctor in how to convince the Time Lords that he should be allowed to continue fighting evil in the universe (Ch. 5). Dicks' revision of this scene weakens the original serial, as the Second Doctor's sacrifice, shown through his resolve to do right, and his purposeful rhetoric, only emerge through the Eighth Doctor's influence. This book stands in stark contrast to *Exodus*, which skillfully builds upon "The War Games." Instead, it demonstrates that Dicks has not yet learned how to address dedicated fans who want to exercise their insider knowledge but not be pandered to by revisions of existing serials. The next time he returns to "The War Games" plot, he introduces his new enemy, the omnipotent Players, in a novel of the same name. This novel demonstrates that Dicks has learned more about fan audiences and their desires.

Playing with History: The World as Game Board

In the Players trilogy, Dicks addresses different fan constituencies by combining historical settings and characters with internal references to *Who* and its history. In their study of *Doctor Who* audiences, Jenkins and Tulloch (1995, 90) define several types of fans through ethnographic interview techniques. One group, Australian high school boys, explained that they especially liked episodes that provided "'twists' to historical events" because these episodes were grounded in prior, accepted knowledge. Obviously, this pleasurable aspect of some *Doctor Who* serials appeals to a much wider viewership. The Players trilogy addresses this specific type of fan as well as other dedicated fans by creating villains who are specifically interested in changing Earth's history; Dicks accomplishes this by moving between numerous historical figures and time periods, by providing substantive internal references to the *Doctor Who* canon, and, finally, by using Season 6B as a frequent setting.

Dicks (1999, 33) revises many aspects of the War Lords in his creation of the Players, "mysterious transcendental beings who [treat] human history as a giant chess game," especially in their desire to objectify humans (vi–vii). They live by the credo: "Winning is everything—and nothing / Losing is nothing—and everything / All that matters is the Game." Throughout the trilogy, historical figures, such as Winston Churchill, Napoleon Bonaparte, the Duke of Wellington, Harry S. Truman, and Josef Stalin, become pieces in the Players' games. Individual Players travel to historical moments masquerading as humans so that they can manipulate human history. The Players "may work together or alone, co-operate or compete. But [they] always work through others." One of the rules of the Game is "the hand of the Player must never be seen" (2000, 1). A female Player explains their motives: "'All the wealth, all the pleasures of this world are within our grasp' ... 'We are rich, we do not age—and we are bored, Doctor, so bored'" (1999, 297). The Players' omnipotence and multi-dimensionality means that the Doctor can encounter them in multiple times and multiple places, which allows Dicks to explore specific historical moments.

The first and third books of the trilogy, *Players* and *World Game*, specifically revisit scenes and characters from "The War Games." Dicks composed the middle book, *Endgame*, for the Eighth Doctor Adventures range; as such, it is situated in a story arc that places the Doctor on Earth with amnesia, where the Eighth Doctor has no knowledge of his previous encounters with the Players. Because Dicks had to include the Doctor's amnesia into *Endgame*, he was able to introduce new readers to this enemy as the Doctor learns about them (again). Yet, because of this publishing constraint, the third novel *World Game* is finally able to develop the Players' roles as enemies to mankind. While each of these three novels have specific goals, each continues the central theme of "The War Games": the manipulation of Earth's history by a powerful enemy.

In *Players,* a Sixth Doctor novel, Dicks creates a scenario so that he can feature the Second Doctor and revisit the setting of "The War Games." Both Doctors interact with the Players as these enemies attempt to alter the events of World War II by assassinating Winston Churchill before he becomes Prime Minister and by preventing pro-Nazi King Edward VIII's abdication. The Doctor meets Churchill on three separate occasions: as the Sixth Doctor, during the Boer War and during the abdication crisis, and in his second incarnation, during World War I, just after the events of "The War Games." This plot device gives Dicks the opportunity to revisit "The War Games" and continue its story. Dicks handles this insertion as a flashback the Sixth Doctor shows Peri Brown (Nicola Bryant) on a thought scanner. The Sixth Doctor tells Peri before he was sentenced to regeneration and exile, he did "odd jobs" for the Time Lords, a direct reference to Season 6B (1999, 77). Peri sees the Second Doctor returning to World War I to check on the Time Lords' restoration of the timeline. The Second Doctor encounters Lady Jennifer Buckingham (Jane Sherwin) and Lieutenant Jeremy Carstairs (David Savile) as they appeared in "The War Games." The three of them save Churchill from an assassination attempt and are subsequently imprisoned by (and escape from) the Players who are impersonating European nobility. The remainder of the novel follows the Sixth Doctor and Peri as they interact with Churchill during the abdication crisis and try to preserve Earth's history. The Sixth Doctor approaches this responsibility gleefully: "if you interfere with interference, is it still interfering? You might say they cancel each other out. In a way, interfering with interference is a form of non-interference in itself!" (1999, 131). He and Peri arrive in 1936, early in Edward VIII's reign, where they work to establish themselves as upper-class foreigners, so that they can "sit back and let" British society come to them (149).

By allowing the Doctor to settle down in a specific point in time, a luxury in which the television program can rarely indulge, Dicks details historical context concerning Edward VIII's problematic accession and Churchill's withdrawal from politics, and his subsequent return. Dicks' alternate history develops the long-standing rumor that Wallis Simpson was romantically involved with the German ambassador to Britain, Joachim von Ribbentrop. Dicks transforms Edward VIII's famous radio broadcast that announced his abdication into an attempt to dissolve the government and create a police state, controlled by Sir Oswald Mosley and his Blackshirt troops. The historical plausibility of *Players* is an aspect certain fans of the program could appreciate, especially those mentioned above who like stories with historical "twists."

Endgame was written as the fourth book in the Eighth Doctor Adventures' Earthbound arc, in which the amnesiac Doctor is stranded in England from 1890 to 2001. The six books in the series follow the Doctor chronologically. *Endgame,* set in 1951, explores the Cambridge Five spy ring during the

Cold War. The Eighth Doctor is recruited by Kim Philby, one of the Cambridge Five: "You appear from nowhere, and disappear just as suddenly. You have no real friends, no family, no official existence. You have outstanding combat skills, and a knowledge of codes, disguise, escape and evasion. If you are not a spy, Doctor, who are you?" (2000, 87). Philby wants the Doctor to participate in Tightrope, an alliance of double agents working to prevent war: "The aim is to hold the stalemate in place, redress the balance when it tips too far, keep the political and military idiots under control" (2000, 81). The Doctor thinks he is "finished with being involved" (2000, 45), but when the Doctor sees that Earth's history is again being tampered with he realizes he must act.

Situating this novel in the middle of a purposeful arc aids Dicks' second use of the Players as enemies. The fact that books two and three in the arc[6] already treat the time periods of the World Wars forces Dicks to move away from these settings he uses so frequently. Furthermore, the Eighth Doctor's memory loss means that he does not remember his previous encounters with the Players, which allows him to react, once again, with horror to their actions. Vanessa Bishop's review (2000, 44) asserts that the Doctor must relearn right and wrong and "for once" he is not defined by aliens. Yet, because he is earth-bound and has been living as a human for more than 60 years, his reaction to the Players' actions carries not only horror but also an understanding of humanity. He asks the Players: "Can't you imagine the joy of holding a new-born child? The shock of a cold shower? The wonder of a rainstorm on a sunny day? … the loss of a lover's departure? The fading memory of a stolen kiss?" (2000, 218). This sympathetic speech redeems this novel's uncaring, depressed Doctor, whose amnesia has left him without identity or purpose. Dicks gives the fans a nice glance at a "human" Doctor without moving towards fannish wish-fulfillment narratives that erase all his distance and alienness.

The Doctor's amnesia also limits Dicks' "usual excesses of continuity" (Smith n.d.). His big gesture to continuity appears in the book's second prologue, which returns to the conclusion of *Exodus* and provides a chance encounter between the Seventh and the Eighth Doctors. At the end of *Exodus*, the Doctor and Ace return to the Festival of Britain to make sure that the timeline has been corrected. Dicks picks up this scene in *Endgame*. The Seventh Doctor sees a "good looking" man with "unfashionably long" hair emerge from the Dome of Discovery and registers "a flicker of recognition" but loses it (1999, 4). The amnesiac Eighth Doctor does not recognize his former self or Ace and envies the happiness he sees in them. This opening is the type of internal reference all *Who* fans could appreciate because it can work on several levels. Casual fans will appreciate the use of the Seventh Doctor and Ace and do not need to know that this is a reference to *Exodus* for it to work. Dedicated fans who have read *Exodus* will grasp the link between the two books and will note that the Seventh Doctor's earlier pessimism is abating as he and Ace set out to a funfair. This scene demonstrates that Dicks has learned how to reference his own works, but in a way fans can comprehend, according to their own level of *Doctor Who* knowledge.

The last book in the trilogy, *World Game*, returns to Season 6B as a setting and further illustrates Dicks' progress in creating purposeful continuity elements through internal and historical references. He fully embraces the possibilities of Season 6B and offers correctives to his earlier, more tentative, explorations. Dicks introduces another version that "corrects" the Second Doctor's trial, which he has already shown in three different ways in "The War Games," *The Making of Doctor Who*, and *Players*. The novel opens by stating that the following is a "genuine and original" relation of the trial, recently "released under the provisions of the Gallifreyan Freedom of Information Act." Dicks then revisits the two most meaningful elements of the Second Doctor's trial: he offers the Doctor's truncated speech about being proud of his actions, and the Time Lords concede that he has "a part to play in the struggle" against evil. Yet, in this new record, the Doctor is sentenced to death rather than exile to Earth (2005, 3–4). Dicks immediately countermands this purported authentic death sentence by creating a situation in which the Second Doctor is needed. *World Game* outlines this situation and creates the Second Doctor as "an agent [the Time Lords] can control, and if necessary, disown," which, of course, is the founding tenet of Season 6B (2005, 8). The novel briefly summarizes the Second Doctor's return to 1915 France and his adventures there with Churchill that happened in *Players*. He then travels to the eighteenth century, where he interacts with Napoleon, the Duke of Wellington, Robert Fulton, and other human game pieces that the Players are manipulating. As this lists shows, Dicks incorporates plenty of fan-pleasing interactions with historical characters as the Doctor once again saves the world.

The internal references *World Game* offers provide a closure of Season 6B for the fans. Dicks sutures the conclusion of the novel to the troublesome opening of "The Two Doctors," which shows the Second Doctor and Jamie arriving at Space Station Camera without a female companion.[7] Jamie worries that the Doctor will not be able to pilot the TARDIS accurately to retrieve Victoria (Deborah Watling) from her graphology lesson. Fans have always seen this exchange in "The Two Doctors" as a sloppy gesture to continuity by scriptwriter Robert Holmes. Dicks incorporates this into the fabric of the Second Doctor's time while working for the Time Lords. After the Doctor completes the *World Game* assignment, he asks for his own TARDIS back and Jamie as his choice of companion. The Time Lords agree, saying they will have to "adjust [Jamie's] memory" (2005, 280). The Doctor adds "and account for whoever he thinks is missing. Let him believe we've dropped off Victoria somewhere for some reason… Graphology! That sounds like Victoria" (2005, 280). With these words, Dicks completes his contribution to

Season 6B, connecting the ending of "The War Games" to the beginning of "The Two Doctors." The fans now have reasonable answers to the discrepancies and continuity errors "The Two Doctors" caused.

Conclusion

Dicks' achievement as a writer for dedicated fans manifests in the way he learned to manage his trademark references from his numerous contributions to *Doctor Who*. All of his books that reference "The War Games" focus on the same warnings about power, corruption and violence. He encapsulates this message in *World Game*, when the Second Doctor faces two seemingly arbitrary adversaries that the Players pit against him. The first is a vampire, which is a reference to Dicks' serial "State of Decay" (1980) and his subsequent novel *Blood Harvest* (1994); the second is a Raston Warrior Robot, which he created for the serial "The Five Doctors." At first these seem to be Dicks' gratuitous self-references akin to those that appeared in *The Eight Doctors*, yet Dicks—in a way that he had not previously—demonstrates his message through his continuity elements. The Second Doctor realizes that these adversaries come from the Death Zone on Gallifrey. Dedicated fans will know that this is a reference to the time when the Time Lords abused their power, and Dicks has the Doctor explain that once the Time Lords "kidnap[ped] ferocious alien life forms and set them to fight each other" for their entertainment (2005, 171). Through this explanation, the Doctor shows that the Time Lords were once no different than the War Lords or the Players, and Dicks shows how power is a corrupting force. The Time Lords, who espouse non-interference as the basis of their society and chastise the Doctor for trying to help civilizations, once used their great power to dehumanize and objectify weaker life forms—a theme whose message is as important today as it was when "The War Games" first aired during the Vietnam Era.

The trajectory of Dicks' historical texts illustrates a significant case study, showing how a *Who* insider—familiar with creating televised ephemera and novelizations—learned to create original-content novels for dedicated fans. He recognized the potential of "The War Games" for continued narratives— in both its theme and as a cultural touchstone in the program's history. Through his many works, Dicks emphasizes his strength in historical content and learns to manage his weakness in adding excessive continuity elements. His foray into original content demonstrates the difficulties of writing for dedicated fans, a group who, at best, communicates mixed expectations to content producers. By adopting and endorsing the fanon of Season 6B, Dicks shows an important willingness to listen to fans at a time in *Who* fandom when fans were the most powerless. As Dicks says: "Fans are a small but important subgroup when there's a show, but when there's no show, in a sense the fans are all there is" (Griffiths 1999, 48–49).

NOTES

1. The books' positions in their respective ranges are as follows: *Timewyrm: Exodus* (Virgin New Adventures #2), *The Eight Doctors* (Eighth Doctor Adventures #1), *Players* (Past Doctor Adventures #21), *Endgame* (Eighth Doctor Adventures #40), and *World Game* (Past Doctor Adventures #74).

2. Besides *The Discontinuity Guide*, full discussions and examinations of Season 6B can also be found in the following: Kistler 2013, "Sidebar: Season 6B"; Wood 2007, 57–63; Parkin and Pearson 2012, 718–19.

3. For more on the novel ranges, see Kistler 2013, "Chapter 18" and Howe, Walker, and Stammers 2005, 782–87.

4. In an interview for Doctor Who Online, Hinton says that he used the term in a review for Jim Mortimore's *Blood Heat* in *Doctor Who Magazine* #205 (Hinton 2003). I have read the review, and the word is not there (Hinton 1993).

5. Although it was critically unsuccessful, *The Eight Doctors* was named by a 1999 study as the bestselling original *Doctor Who* novel in any range (Griffiths 1999, 50).

6. Steve Emmerson's *Casualties of War* (2000) set in 1918, and Paul Leonard's *The Turing Test* (2000), set in 1945.

7. The Second Doctor traveling without any female companion only happens in the extra-narrative space between "The Faceless Ones" and "The Evil of the Daleks" in season four (1967). This is another piece of evidence that "The Two Doctors" occurs after "The War Games."

BIBLIOGRAPHY

Bishop, Vanessa. 2000. "Shelf Life." *Doctor Who Magazine*. December 2000. pp. 41–44.
Cornell, Paul, Martin Day, and Keith Topping. 2013. *The "Doctor Who" Discontinuity Guide*. 1995. Reprint, London: Gateway. Kindle edition.
Coward, Mat. 2015. "*Doctor Who* and the Communist." *Doctor Who Magazine*, May 2015. p. 74.
Dicks, Terrance. 1991. *Timewyrm: Exodus*. London: Virgin.
Dicks, Terrance. 1994. *Blood Harvest*. London: Virgin.
Dicks, Terrance. 1997. *The Eight Doctors*. London: BBC Books. PDF edition.
Dicks, Terrance. 1999. *Players: Fiftieth Anniversary Edition*. Reprint, London: BBC Books, 2013.
Dicks, Terrance. 2000. *Endgame*. London: BBC Books.
Dicks, Terrance. 2005. *World Game*. London: BBC Books.
Dicks, Terrance. 2009. "Audio Commentary for 'The War Games.'" *The War Games*. London: BBC Video. DVD.
Dicks, Terrance. 2010. Introduction to *Wiped! "Doctor Who's" Missing Episodes*, by Richard Molesworth. 2010. Revised, Prestatyn, Denbighshire: Telos, 2013.
Dicks, Terrance. 2013. Foreword to *The "Doctor Who" Discontinuity Guide*, by Paul Cornell, Martin Day, and Keith Topping. 1995. Reprint, London: Gateway. Kindle edition.
"*Doctor Who* Archive: 'The War Games.'" 1995. *Doctor Who Magazine*, November. pp. 20–32.
Emmerson, Steve. 2000. *Casualties of War*. London: BBC Books.
Griffiths, Peter. 1999. "And Now for Something Completely Different." *Doctor Who Magazine*, March 1999. pp. 47–50.
Hills, Matt. 2010. "'The *Doctor Who* Mafia': Fans as Textual Poachers Turned Gamekeepers." In *Triumph of a Time Lord: Regenerating "Doctor Who" in the Twenty-First Century*, Matt Hills. London: I. B. Tauris. Kindle edition.
Hinton, Craig. 1993. "Shelf Life." *Doctor Who Magazine*. October 1993. pp. 48–49.
Hinton, Craig. 2003. "Live Chat with Craig Hinton, *Doctor Who Online*. www.drwho-online. co.uk/chat-craighinton.doc. (Accessed January 7, 2015).

Howe, David J., Stephen James Walker, and Mark Stammers. 2005. *The Handbook: The Unofficial and Unauthorised Guide to the Production of "Doctor Who."* Tolworth: Telos.

Hulke, Malcolm, and Terrance Dicks. 1972. *The Making of "Doctor Who."* London: Target.

Jenkins, Henry. 2012. *Textual Poachers: Television Fans and Participatory Culture.* 2d edition. London: Routledge.

Kistler, Alan. 2013. *"Doctor Who": A History.* Guildford: Lyons. Kindle edition.

Leonard, Paul. 2000. *The Turing Test.* London: BBC Books.

McWilliams, Ora, and Joshua Richardson. 2011. "Double Poaching and the Subversive Operations of Riffing: 'You kids with your hula hoops and your Rosenbergs and your Communist agendas.'" In *In the Peanut Gallery with Mystery Science Theatre 3000: Essays on Film, Fandom and the Culture of Riffing*, ed. Robert G. Weiner and Shelley E. Barba. Jefferson: McFarland. pp. 110–120.

Morley, Christopher. 2014. *"Doctor Who*—Season 6B and the Celestial Intervention Agency." *Warped Factor.* Available at http://www.warpedfactor.com/2014/08/doctor-who-season-6b-and-celestial.html. (Accessed January 7, 2015).

Mortimore, Jim. 1993. *Blood Heat.* London: Virgin.

October, Dene. n. d. "Fan Cultures." https://fanculturesblog.wordpress.com/4–2/. (Accessed December 17, 2016).

Parkin, Lance, and Lars Pearson. 2012. *Ahistory: An Unauthorised History of the "Doctor Who" Universe.* 3d Edition. Des Moines: Mad Norwegian.

Parrish, Juli J. 2007. *Inventing a Universe: Reading and Writing Internet Fan Fiction* (Unpublished doctoral dissertation). University of Pittsburgh, Pittsburgh. http://d-scholarship.pitt.edu/8963/1/Parrish2007.pdf. (Accessed December 17, 2016).

Peel, John. 1991. *Timewyrm: Genesys.* London, Virgin.

Russell, Gary. 1990. "An Open Book." *Doctor Who Magazine*, November 1990. pp. 48–50.

Russell, Gary. 1991. "Off the Shelf." *Doctor Who Magazine*, October 1991. pp. 39–42.

Sandifer, Philip. 2012. "My Dear Doctor, You Must Die." *Eruditorum Press.* http://www.eruditorumpress.com/blog/my-dear-doctor-you-must-die-the-eight-doctors/. (Accessed January 7, 2015).

Smith, Robert. n. d. "Endgame." *The Cloister Library.* http://mysite.science.uottawa.ca/rsmith43/cloister/endg.htm. (Accessed 7 January 2015).

Sullivan, Shannon Patrick. 1997. "*Doctor Who* in Books." *Doctor Who News.* http://www.doctorwhonews.net/1997/06/doctor-who-in-books.html. (Accessed January 7, 2015).

Topping, Keith. 2006. "Craig Hinton." *From the North …* http://keithtopping.blogspot.com/2006/12/craig-hinton.html. (Accessed January 7, 2015).

Tulloch, John, and Henry Jenkins. 1995. *Science Fiction Audiences: Watching "Doctor Who" and "Star Trek."* London: Routledge.

"War Zone: The End of an Era." 2009. Produced by Steve Broster. *The War Games.* London: BBC Video, 2009. DVD.

Wood, Tat. 2007. *About Time 6: The Unauthorized Guide to "Doctor Who."* Des   Moines: Mad Norwegian.

Wood, Tat, and Lawrence Miles. 2006. *About Time 2: The Unauthorized Guide to "Doctor Who."* Des Moines: Mad Norwegian.

Doctor Who Unbound
and Alternate History

KAREN HELLEKSON

Introduction

The literary genre of the alternate history posits "what if" scenarios related to the outcomes of historical events: what if America had never had a revolution and was still a colony of Great Britain in the 1960s? What if Hitler had prevailed during World War II? Known in the field of history as counterfactuals, alternate histories link cause and effect. By changing a major or minor event, a completely different outcome may ensue. As a genre, the alternate history "explore[s] the consequences of an imagined divergence from specific historical events" (Alkon 1994, 68). Both historians and fiction writers have exploited the genre to explore the nature of causality, to critique the Great Man theory of history, to valorize individual agency—and much more. My own work has focused on the alternate history as a mode of fictive exploration of agency and alterity (that is, otherness), with the alternate history making the world appear other in order to make a point about the agent himself or about the larger forces of history. Most alternate histories treat history as ultimately genetic (concerned with origins, or with cause and effect) (Hellekson 2001).

The alternate history, however, is not limited to real-world historical events; it can also include fictional ones. The *Doctor Who* universe is no exception: it has its own series of alternate histories, including *Doctor Who Unbound*, a range of six full-cast, stand-alone audio dramas. These "what ifs" include: what if the Sixth Doctor (Colin Baker) had lost his trial? What if the First Doctor (William Hartnell) and Susan (Carole Ann Ford) had never left Gallifrey? What if the Third Doctor (Jon Pertwee) had not advised UNIT, instead ending up in a different time period after his forced regeneration?

Only one release, the fifth, "Deadline" (2003), is not directly set within the *Doctor Who* milieu. Instead, it is a metatext about the very existence of *Doctor Who* as a TV program. The *Unbound* series is thus highly mediated: it addresses agency by altering the Doctor, thus permitting us to hold the one against the other and judge. Instead of making a larger point about the purpose of history, it addresses concerns of agency—of one person's ability to act and change the world around him. The Doctor is the pivot around which all revolves.

In this regard, the *Unbound* audio series addresses the Great Man theory of history, famously addressed by Thomas Carlyle (1840), who noted, "They were the leaders of men, these great ones; the modellers, patterns, and in a wide sense creators, of whatsoever the general mass of men contrived to do or to attain; all things that we see standing accomplished in the world are properly the outer material result, the practical realization and embodiment, of Thoughts that dwelt in the Great Men sent into the world." The Doctor, the embodiment of a Great Man, is able to affect outcomes; he acts as a cause that brings about an effect. The *Unbound* audios address history in a larger sense via theme and via changes within the franchise's built world, but the focus is not on the ultimate goals of history but on a Great Man who has the power to both affect and effect history.

These "what ifs" require a departure from canon—that is, the authoritative, official texts that aired. *Doctor Who Unbound* can be divided into three groupings according to theme, which revolve around the Doctor's inherent nature: helpful and good in a tight spot, the same as that seen in canon; a passive, rather than active, genius; and actually evil. These groupings provide a useful structure for making essential some of the concerns inherent in the texts: readings of the character of the Doctor and metacommentary on the notion of creative imagination—the ontological underpinning of the entire *Doctor Who* TV program in all its iterations, and an expression of the Great Man theory by providing agency to individuals, who have the power to alter events and thus bring about what we might call history. As Gavriel Rosenfeld notes, "The presentist character of alternate histories allows them to shed light upon the evolving place of various historical events in the collective memory of a given society" (2002, 90). In the *Unbound* audios, that collective memory is that of the *Doctor Who* story world as presented in canon, but the point still holds: the audios shed light on the canonical character of the Doctor and the canonical events he brings about.

These three character-themed groupings permit us to draw conclusions about the nature of (a)historical discourse in the *Doctor Who* universe. In "Sympathy for the Devil" (2003) and its sequel, "Masters of War" (2008), as well as in "Exile" (2003), the alternate Third Doctor's (David Warner and Arabella Weir, respectively) fundamental nature as someone who helps others and attempts to solve problems remains. In contrast are the audios that present the Doctor as not active—that is, as passive. In "Auld Mortality" (2003), the alternate First Doctor (Geoffrey Bayldon) never left Gallifrey; he is now an eccentric old novelist. In its sequel, "A Storm of Angels" (2005), the Doctor is not a doer but a dreamer. These audio dramas are explications of the creative process and act as metatexts for the impulse to create *Doctor Who*. Next, "Deadline," in which a former TV writer, the stand-in for the Doctor (Derek Jacobi; the text does not intend any specific Doctor), wonders what his life would have been like if that TV show he'd been working on, *Doctor Who*, had ever made it into production, is about a passive, failed creative genius. The audio drama becomes a densely allusive metatext. Finally, "Full Fathom Five" (2003) and "He Jests at Scars" (2003) provide alternate evil Doctors; the former posits a Doctor (David Collings)—it's never stated which one—who believes that the ends justify the means, and the latter posits a Doctor-Valeyard (Michael Jayston) who glories in destruction as he continually alters the time line.

By linking the character of the Doctor with the alternate history, *Unbound* explores the value and meaning of the primary *Doctor Who* text by considering what-if scenarios. The audios also link to the larger genre of the alternate history by addressing concerns of agency that link to the genetic theory of history: people act, and as a consequence, events happen, bringing about an effect. Cause and effect thus intertwine, the retrospective analysis of which we call history. The character of the Doctor is uniquely positioned to address historical concerns of cause, effect, and agency.

Big Finish and Doctor Who *Audios*

Big Finish,[1] a company founded in 1999, creates full-cast audio dramas, complete with music and sound effects, for a number of franchise properties. The company began with books and audios featuring a solo Bernice Summerfield (Lisa Bowerman), originally a Seventh Doctor (Sylvester McCoy) companion created for the Virgin New Adventures line of books launched after *Doctor Who* went off the air. Their main *Doctor Who* range features cast members from the original run of *Doctor Who* (1963–1989), plus the 1996 Paul McGann film, and includes all the still-living actors who originally played the Doctor before the program's reboot in 2005.[2] The *Doctor Who Unbound* series is among the Big Finish spin-off properties, although in these audios, the Doctor has of course been recast. Several other characters, voiced by the original actors, recur in their canonical roles: Nicholas Courtney as Brigadier Alistair Lethbridge-Stewart, Carole Ann Ford as Susan, Michael Jayston as the Valeyard, and Bonnie Langford as Melanie Bush. These familiar voices and the voice talents of the alternate Doctors (including such luminaries as Geoffrey Bayldon, Derek Jacobi, and David Warner), along with sound effects and incidental music, help create an immersive experience.[3] The texts reward close knowledge of not only the original *Doctor Who* but also some of the other spin-offs, including the novels. One fan has cataloged many of these allusions online—certainly more than I noticed myself (Bates 2016). Indeed, as I have noted elsewhere, the alternate history as a genre rewards specialist knowledge: when inside the story world, it is wonderful to find a point of discontinuity, either of a character or an historical event, which then reorients the reader or listener vis-à-vis the story (Hellekson 2001; 2013). Certainly this is the case for *Doctor Who Unbound* in terms of the *Doctor Who* universe's own history.

The audios in the *Unbound* series, which run about an hour each for the ones released in 2003, and which run about two hours for the two sequels, need not be listened to in any particular order. The last two, which were released several years after the original six-episode 2003 run, although sequels, stand alone as enjoyable stories. Good fan-created synopses of the audios are available online ("Doctor Who Reference Guide").

The Doctor as Active Helper

"Sympathy for the Devil" and its sequel, "Masters of War," bring an alternate Third Doctor together with classic *Doctor Who* companion Brigadier Alistair Lethbridge-Stewart. In "Sympathy for the Devil," the point of divergence is quickly identified: the Third Doctor, after being forced to regenerate by the Time Lords and then sent into exile on Earth with an inhibitor on his TARDIS so he can't travel properly, never becomes UNIT's scientific advisor. In fact, the Doctor, to his dismay, misses the 1970s altogether. Instead, he runs into a retired and embittered Brigadier, owner of a British-style pub, in Hong Kong the day before the United Kingdom hands Hong Kong over to China in 1997. The crash of an invisible plane leads China and the United Kingdom to attempt to be first on the scene to examine the technology and question any survivors. The Doctor and the Brigadier band together to find out what is going on and discover the Master (Mark Gatiss) at work.

Alone in the Brigadier's closed pub, an alternate Lethbridge-Stewart fills the Doctor in on what happened after the Doctor left: "I was a career embarrassment. Passed over. Laughed at. Things like that start to build up on one's record…. Things were bad back in the '80s, Doctor." Listeners are left to infer what things were like in the *Doctor Who* story world without the Doctor and his expert help and guidance. We are also left to wonder how the Brig has changed, thanks to the historical differences that resulted from the Doctor's absence, some of the details of which the Brig delineates. How much of the

Brigadier's career success relied on the Doctor on the scene to increase UNIT's success rate and bolster its prestige? Quite a bit, apparently.

In a Buddhist temple near the crash site, the Doctor talks with the Abbot (Trevor Littledale), to whom he identifies himself with Chinese wordplay, each version of *hu* pronounced slightly differently, in a telling scene that explores the Doctor's identity:

ABBOT: And your name?
DOCTOR: Sometimes they call me *hu*.
ABBOT: The tiger?
DOCTOR: For my courage, supposedly. Sometimes *hu*.
ABBOT: The fox.
DOCTOR: For my cunning, they say. But I personally prefer *hu*.
ABBOT: Ah. He who tends to the sick.
DOCTOR: Outside China, people normally just say "The Doctor."

This scene emphasizes the nature of the Doctor: he represents all these things, in the canonical *Doctor Who* world and, we hope, in this alternate reality. This alternate Doctor is in essence a different pronunciation of *who*, the Doctor.

Its sequel, "Masters of War," is likewise a straight-up adventure that teams Warner's Doctor with the Brig as they work together to defeat a canonical adversary. Unlike "Sympathy for the Devil," it is not set at a specific historical moment; instead, it takes place on Skaro, home of the Daleks, where our two protagonists help some Thal resistance fighters. The bad guy is Davros (Terry Molloy), who first appeared in *Doctor Who* in 1975 in "Genesis of the Daleks," a Fourth Doctor (Tom Baker) story. Thus the alternate Third Doctor would never have encountered Davros before; they have no history together. Indeed, the alternate Doctor tells Davros, "I've never heard [the Daleks] mention you," to which Davros responds, in a line clearly designed to create retroactive continuity, "So you've met the renegades. I sometimes wonder how they're faring." The twist in the story is that the Daleks are actually attempting to protect the Thals against a common enemy, the Quatch.

The world created in "Masters of War" is free of the Fourth Doctor's involvement in "Genesis of the Daleks," but this is a minor part of the story, which focuses first on the Thal's struggles and then on the Dalek–Thal attempt to repel the Quatch. According to the Tardis Data Core wiki, which lists the time line differences, "The Daleks seen in the story were created by Davros to have a degree of compassion so they would not turn on him. This led to them developing the idea that because Daleks were superior to all other life, they had a duty to protect that life" ("Masters of War Audio Story)" n.d.). The surprise of the alternate here is the surprise of the Daleks' behaving so unlike their murderous TV counterparts, as introduced in 1963–1964 in "The Daleks." It is also interesting to hear the Doctor and Davros meet for the first time. Of these two related audios, "Sympathy for the Devil" better explores the notion of the alternate because of its focus on the Doctor's and Brigadier's relationship, which in "Sympathy for the Devil" has already been established, so the latter's story's interest lies more in its plot and in the interest of seeing the Doctor and Davros meet for the first time. These audios are fun stories that fit nicely within the canonically established world: the Doctor may be different, and the Brig may seem greatly changed to us by the Doctor's absence, but we recognize both these old soldiers.

Like "Sympathy for the Devil" and "Masters of War," "Exile" also features an alternate Third Doctor, here played by a woman, Arabella Weir. In this silly episode, which features lots of drinking, burping, and vomiting, the Doctor works in a Sainsbury's grocery store, hiding from the Time Lords and hanging out with coworkers in pubs. This Doctor committed suicide to force a regeneration—which, it turns out (at least in this version of the *Doctor Who* universe), causes Time Lords to change sex. By doing so, the Doctor has escaped the Time Lord's justice, but at the cost of having stay in hiding. (Indeed, two Time Lords are hilariously undercover, searching for the Doctor.) The Doctor must ignore strange events and weird happenings, even if the Master may be lurking somewhere—but of course, the Doctor can't not get involved.

The Doctor, through a convoluted sequence of events, becomes convinced that Princess Anne is going to be blown up via a buildup of toxic gas while she is presiding over an official opening of a Sainsbury's parking lot—the plot of a malign alien influence, likely the Quarks. However, the Doctor is wrong, and after accosting Princess Anne in a misguided attempt to save her, the Doctor is summarily fired. The Doctor, contemplating a bottle of poor-quality vodka, ruminates on the situation: "That's why I'm on this planet, that's why I'm hiding, because the Time Lords are looking for me. They want to punish me for being *me*. So if I *do* do anything that's too *me*, they'll find me. If I let people know who I really am, if I did everything I can really do … then that would be the end of *me*." The alternate Third Doctor realizes that it's no good staying alive and undercover: "that would be the end of *me*." The attempt to save a not-in-danger Princess Anne was the result of a good impulse based on a misinterpretation of existing intel (and likely also vodka), but its significance is greater than the resulting farce: the Doctor must once again get involved, even if it means capture by the Time Lords— as indeed, alas, happens. The two Time Lords sentence the Doctor to death rather than exile. But the Doctor has done the right thing. The moral of the story is what is moral about the Doctor: he acts to help people because he wishes to make things better, and as a Great Man, he has the ability to bring about events. One must be true to oneself, regardless of the consequences— in this case, continuing to get involved, rather than sitting on the sidelines, as the Time Lords would prefer.

"Sympathy for the Devil," "Masters of War," and "Exile" all have rip-roaring plots, full of adventure. Although it's fun to trace the *Doctor Who* universe's differences without Pertwee's canonical Third Doctor, the three are linked by the Doctor's alterity. We assess the differences on the basis of character rather than plot. We know what the Third Doctor is supposed to be like, and we read the alternate Doctors against that standard. Listeners use knowledge of the Doctor as presented in canon as a frame to judge these alternative Doctors. These audios present the Doctor as an active agent despite the Doctor's alternate otherness. He is someone true to his name: a healer, someone who fixes things. The Doctor remains an active agent; his presence, or absence, alters events and people around him—the point of canonical *Doctor Who*, where the Doctor and his bag of tricks always save the day. These audios reward knowledge of classic *Doctor Who* episodes, thus focusing on the fictive history presented by the series by laying another fictive history against it; but they also reaffirm the Doctor as an active agent with a moral compass—a Great Man.

The Doctor as Passive Genius

"Auld Mortality" and its sequel, "A Storm of Angels," posit a world in which the First Doctor never left Gallifrey with his granddaughter, Susan. It is unclear whether this clearly elderly Doctor, voiced by Geoffrey Bayldon (who declined the role of the Doctor twice, as the First and Second Doctors), is the same as the one originally created by William Hartnell or a regeneration (Wolverson 2010), although Bayldon includes some of Harnell's distinctive First Doctor vocal tics. In this alternate world, the Doctor is a celebrated author. His sojourns in time and space are flights of fancy, not literal. In "Auld Mortality," a grown-up Susan seeks out the Doctor on the eve of her ascension to the presidency; he is unable to meet with her because he is inside his illegal possibility generator, a device that lets him run various scenarios—in this case, traveling with Hannibal and his talking elephant over the Alps.

When the Doctor and Susan finally meet, he tells her, "From every moment, there are infinite possibilities. They branch out, treelike, in every direction, over and over, tangling through each other.... It draws you in— the possibilities blind you with diversity. Far safer to stay at home." He now ruefully remembers the day he considered taking a TARDIS and going into exile—for us, the reality of what happened: "Once, like a mirror, I thought I saw myself, spiraling between worlds in an old TARDIS, just as I planned to do so long ago! Imagine that! But I can't, can I?" He prefers the safety of his imagination. This alternate Doctor did the safe thing—the right thing. But perhaps it is not too late: he proposes to Susan that they take his TARDIS (they find the console buried under papers on his desk) and do now what they failed to do years ago. At the end of the audio drama, playing out the notion of simultaneous choice, their voices overlap as he suggests they go and stay, and she responds both yes and no, her voice heavy with resignation at her duty or full of delight at the reprieve from an unwanted task. We don't know how it ends, but that is the point: they both go and stay, each possibility equally true. As the Doctor puts it, "Who needs a TARDIS?" We only need our imaginations—the true possibility generator.

In the sequel, "A Storm of Angels," we think that the question has been answered: Susan said yes, and she and the Doctor have been traveling for a while in the TARDIS. This time, their ship, disguised as a barrel, takes the Doctor and Susan to a 16th-century ship in space captained by Francis Drake, with Gloriana (1533–1603) ruling the world. Could this accelerated, space-faring culture have occurred as a result of the Doctor's contact with Leonardo da Vinci? Did the Doctor's meddling so greatly alter history? But when another Susan appears, scolding the Doctor for messing with the time line and ready to march him back home, it becomes clear that Susan actually said no; she "became ceremonially archived" on Gallifrey, as the Doctor puts it, and ascended to the presidency. "Why did you stay behind, hm?" he asks her. "You have such dreams! Was it family, or duty?" The Susan traveling with the Doctor is a creation of the possibility generator, now nearly out of power and failing, which manifests as Susan's being ill. However, the episode ends on a ray of hope, as the Susans, without telling the Doctor (but of course he knows), switch places. The Gallifreyan president stays with her grandfather and the adventuring, false Susan takes her place on Gallifrey. The structure of the plot continues the theme of the possibility of imagination: it is both true and not true that Susan came with the Doctor. The endings of both audios emphasize the simultaneous and doubled nature of possibility, which ties back into the nature of time itself: it is not necessarily linear but can loop and change. The Doctor is a Great Man only in made-up scenarios; yet his exploits in the possibility generator show an adventuring spirit and a desire to help, with the Doctor's moral compass firmly pointing north.

"Deadline" is the only audio drama in the *Unbound* series that steps outside the *Doctor Who* universe. Derek Jacobi's Martin Bannister, the Doctor character, is a retired writer who lives in an old-age home, where he is hectored by the voices of characters in a TV show he worked on that never got off the ground: *Doctor Who*. Instead, fans prefer to focus on his work on TV cop show *Juliet Bravo* (and a real TV program that aired 1980–1985). When his estranged son comes to visit, announcing the existence of a previously unknown grandson, he feels like he can perhaps redeem his wrecked life. But his wardrobe may be a TARDIS, and Susan (Genevieve Swallow) is calling to him.

The episode ends when Martin locks himself inside his wardrobe as his son and caretaker pound on its door. The pounding and calling fade into the quiet hum of the interior of the TARDIS, and Susan appears. He says to her, "But you are dead. Are you sure you're not dead?" Her response: "That's up to you." She then tells him he has "a final decision" to make: "This TARDIS of ours is an erratic old thing. We never know where it will take us next. Once we leave, I doubt we'll be able to return.... And I suspect that if you step outside now, we'll never find the TARDIS again. It will just be a wardrobe full of suits you'll never have a reason to wear.... I'll look after you. Are you ready?" A frightened Martin, wavering voice now firming, answers in the tone of a hero, "Yes. Let's find new worlds to explore!"

In "Auld Mortality" and "A Storm of Angels," we wanted the alternate Doctor to follow his dream: to move from writer of adventures to doer of adventures, to move from passive to active—to do as we think he was meant to do: take his TARDIS and Susan, and leave Gallifrey for endless adventures in time and space, where he can, as a Great Man, effect change and save people. Yet the Doctor does not do this. He stays in the possibility generator. We must be satisfied with the idea that all possibilities are simultaneously true. We worry that, bound to a single space and time, he is in what Baydon's Doctor in "A Storm of Angels" calls a "terrible, stifling trap." In "Deadline," Martin's decision to stay with Susan means he has left reality behind, with the stifling trap that of the figurative TARDIS and literal wardrobe, into which he shuts himself. The world of that unmade television program, *Doctor Who*, that he enters may be the dementia of an unlikeable old man who destroyed his own life. Like Baydon's Doctor, Jacobi's Doctor leaves reality behind and chooses his imagination, and we know he won't be able to go back. Yet in this case, it is tragic, not noble—imagination twisted and made bad.

The alternate history genre here provides the listener with a mode of reading the text: we hold these passive, imagining Doctors against our ideal of the canonical Doctor, active and keen to fight injustice. The commonality with canon, the character quirk that aligns with our understanding of the Doctor, is the alternate Doctors' imaginations. It is no surprise that these two alternate Doctors are writers—those who dream and spin out words but do not act. Part of Martin's annoyance with fans' remembering his work on *Juliet Bravo* (Martin's scene with a fan writer is a great counterpoint to real-life fan obsession with *Doctor Who*) is that he thinks that the show was terrible; the work he really wanted to—the imaginative, quirky job, *Doctor Who*—never got made. These Doctors' other worlds and places are not literal but rather created, one in the possibility generator and the other in dementia.

By addressing themes of otherness and creativity, the audio dramas become metatexts that comment on the nature of *Doctor Who* itself as a show that provides a springboard for endless adventures. These audios also thematically address alternate historical concerns: personal history as fraught and tinged with dementia, coloring agency by calling into question the actor's competence to accurately view the world (as indeed the alternate history fails to do—the very point is that it is not accurate), or the actor's ability to view the world at all, as the probability generator overrides the world by subsuming those inside it, treating agency as a spectacle or game. Imagination without action is laid against views of history as generative, with change brought about by agents like the Great Man, which is the mode of history that *Doctor Who* as a franchise normally exploits. These audios focus on that disconnect.

The Doctor as Evil

Two audios posit the Doctor as, if not evil, then willing to go places that the canonical Doctor will not go. (This is also the mode of the Doctor in Big Finish's War Doctor audios featuring John Hurt, the first series of which was released in December 2015.) In "Full Fathom Five," the Doctor revisits the site of a years-old failed biological experiment deep underwater. He hires a submarine pilot to take him down but then has to confront not only the results of the experiment but also the angry daughter, Ruth Mills (Siri O'Neal), of a man who died 27 years ago in the radioactive fallout of the station's destruction. Mills confronts the Doctor, demanding an explanation, and he tells her everything that happened all those years ago—including his shooting a scientist who was conducting illicit and dangerous human experiments in an attempt to create a supersoldier. Mills is understandably shocked, as the kindly man who cared for her during her traumatic childhood has been revealed as a cold-blooded killer. He tells her, "There are far greater things to consider than whether one person lives or dies. There could be no witnesses to these experiments. He had to die…. This is not about right and wrong. This is about doing what is best." As this remark illustrates, the point of difference for "Full Fathom Five" is, "What if the Doctor believed the ends justified the means?" ("Full Fathom Five (Audio Story)" n.d.). The alternate Doctor's explanation reveals him to be a different man than the canonical Doctor.

When Mills discovers that the Doctor has not only lied to her for all these years about her father's death—he knew the whole time what had happened—but also that he contrived the entire escapade to ensure the complete destruction of the research and to get his TARDIS back, she stands over him with a gun and shoots him, regeneration after regeneration, in what stands as the most chilling scene in the *Doctor Who* franchise. "One down," she says after she shoots the product of the first regeneration. "I wonder how many more lives this bastard has left."

Similarly, in "He Jests at Scars," which I have discussed elsewhere

(Hellekson 2013), the Doctor's character is fundamentally different, but in this audio drama, the Doctor is not strictly the Doctor but rather a Sixth Doctor–Valeyard hybrid, thus amplifying the character difference that plays out in canon, when we are actually shocked that the Valeyard is an iteration of the Doctor, as his behavior is so against the Doctor's. In this story, an embittered Melanie Bush (Bonnie Langford) has been sent by the Time Lords to stop the Doctor after the Matrix shows them their future destruction. The Doctor-Valeyard seized control of the Matrix after the Valeyard, whom we discover in the canonical *Doctor Who* was a future version of the Doctor, won the Trial of a Time Lord (season 23, 1986). The Doctor-Valeyard has been repeatedly altering the time line, creating paradoxes and then attempting to undo them, which only muddles things further. As the Doctor-Valeyard tells Mel, "I disturbed time. Then I disturbed another bit, to put right the first. Then I changed things. I changed this part of the Third Doctor's life, that bit of the Eighth. I moved the First Doctor's compass. I stole the Seventh Doctor's hat. All tiny things, all of which changed their lives, the lives of his companions, his friends, his enemies, the planets, the stars, the galaxies! … Dominoes. Like dominoes, one time line falls, the others come cascading down." This insight is in line with genetic alternate history protocols: a cause–effect chain of events occurs, "a temporal spread between causes and, at least, their remote effects" (Simpson 1995, 53). Something small snowballs into something big, and change occurs. In "He Jests at Scars," the Doctor-Valeyard's endless tinkering with time has resulted in changes so profound that they threaten to wipe out the Doctor-Valeyard's very existence.

Further, the Doctor-Valeyard proves himself to not be the helpful Doctor of canon; he kills callously, sometimes to make a point, sometimes just because he can. This Doctor is not our Doctor. As in "Auld Mortality" and "A Storm of Angels," a kind of possibility generator has been put to use. The TARDIS has been running possibilities to save the Valeyard from himself, and Mel discovers that she has been inside a sort of possibility generator rather than questing through the real universe in search of the Doctor-Valeyard. What is real and what is not? Does it matter? The result is the same: people react to a situation, then change. When Mel set out on her quest to find the Doctor, she hoped to touch that part of the Doctor-Valeyard that was still the Doctor. She does not succeed. Further, during her long quest, she too has been altered for the worse.

When Mel confronts the Doctor-Valeyard, he tells Mel that as a result of his meddling, as well as the endless cascade of difference that results from action, he is literally afraid to move: "And I realized that I had to stop, to stay still, because if I moved as much as a millimeter, I might change my own destiny, kill an earlier body too soon, and I'd vanish, cease to exist." The dominoes work not only on the level of big action—stealing the Seventh Doctor's hat, which results in a galaxy-level change—but on the level of tiny movements. Every move, every gesture, becomes fraught with uncontrollable results. In the audio's bleak ending, Mel and the Doctor-Valeyard exist in the TARDIS together, unable to move until the end of time. This stasis reflects the enormity and the delicacy of history: every move has consequences, and every agent has immense power. To avoid catastrophic consequences, one must not move.

This complex, troubling story deals with the alternate on several levels. We have a different Mel and a different Doctor—a Doctor-Valeyard. He tells Mel, quoting the Shakespeare play the title is drawn from, *Romeo and Juliet:* "I so wanted the Doctor's lives, so wanted to live, to be real.... I couldn't become the Doctor, not the true Doctor. I hadn't got his courage, his wisdom or experience. He jests at scars that never felt a wound. All I had was inexperience. I believed I could be him, but couldn't." This summarizes the entire audio drama: we do not recognize the Doctor here. Unlike the other audios in the *Unbound* series, the Doctor character is not presented as any sort of dreamer; nor is he someone who attempts to solve problems. Instead, the Doctor-Valeyard glories in chaos, only to reject it; he seeks a new existence, only to regret it; he seeks to change, which ends in his inability to move because of the domino-like cascading of cause and effect.

These audios posit a Doctor so different that we do not recognize him; we cannot approve of his actions. These alternate histories' focus on character and agency highlight their intertwining: the one affects the other, coloring actions with ethical meaning. They highlight how much we rely on the Doctor's intentions when he acts. We long for a Great Man, who can alter history as a "natural luminary shining by the gift of Heaven" (Carlyle 1840), but here we have only a Man, someone whose agency can affect the universe but who is not worthy of that power.

Conclusion

As a series, *Doctor Who Unbound* presents us with two intertwined points of difference: the character and agency of the Doctor, and the nature of the *Doctor Who* world. It shows how the one affects the other, compounding the effects of both. The genre of the alternate history displaces reality in order to comment on it; Paul Alkon (1994, 83) notes that the genre "may serve to provide enhanced awareness of what the past was like and of our relationships to it as well as to our present historical moment." The alternate scenarios cause us to question notions of contingency and cause and effect. The *Unbound* stories provide metacommentary, both directly and obliquely, on the very point of *Doctor Who* as a text: creative imagination. Indeed,

"What if?" is the primary question behind the canonical *Doctor Who*. *Unbound* pushes it further, thus pushing the overarching theme of *Doctor Who* into relief. As I've noted elsewhere, "the goal of the alternate history is to bring to the fore historical and temporal concerns" (Hellekson 2001, 22). The *Unbound* series does so within the context of the *Doctor Who* universe.

History depends on a similar understanding of cause and effect. Canonical *Doctor Who* would have us believe that a single extraordinary person—a Doctor, a Great Man—can greatly affect the outcome of events. The program demonstrates that a single person has agency and can bring about change. It follows, then, that we are thus not passive in the face of events. We can bring them about, and doing so has real stakes and real meaning. *Unbound* examines these stakes, asking us, as listeners, to consider scenarios generated by creative imagination. The audios become a possibility generator. We lay our understanding of what is against what might be as these alternate scenarios are run. The Doctor as an active doer, as a passive watcher, and as a malevolent entity are all held against the Doctor of canon, who is a moral Great Man. The texts comprising *Doctor Who Unbound* ask us to consider and judge the Doctor and events, with alterity wedging open the imagination.

NOTES

1. https://www.bigfinish.com/.
2. Big Finish obtained licenses for post-reboot Doctors and in 2016 released some Tenth Doctor audios featuring Big Finish stalwart voice actor David Tennant.
3. August 2016 saw the release of a new sequence of Bernice Summerfield audios featuring Summerfield with Warner's *Unbound* alternate Third Doctor.

BIBLIOGRAPHY

Alkon, Paul. 1994. "Alternate History and Postmodern Temporality." In *Time, Literature and the Arts: Essays in Honor of Samuel L. MacEy*. Edited by Thomas R. Cleary. Victoria: University of Victoria Department of English. pp. 65–85.
Bates, Alden. n.d. "The DiscContinuity Guide: Doctor Who Unbound." *Tetrapyriarbus*. http://www.tetrap.com/drwho/disccon/unbound/. Accessed June 13, 2017.
Carlyle, Thomas. 1840. *On Heroes, Hero-Worship, and the Heroic in History*. http://www.gutenberg.org/cache/epub/1091/pg1091.txt. Accessed June 13, 2017.
"Doctor Who Reference Guide." n.d. *Doctor Who Reference Guide*. http://www.drwhoguide.com/who.htm. Accessed June 13, 2017.
"Full Fathom Five (Audio Story)." n.d. Wiki. *Tardis Data Core*. http://tardis.wikia.com/wiki/Full_Fathom_Five_(audio_story). Accessed June 13, 2017.
Hellekson, Karen. 2001. *The Alternate History: Refiguring Historical Time*. Kent: Kent State University Press.
Hellekson, Karen. 2013. "Doctor Who Unbound, the Alternate History, and the Fannish Text." In *Fan Phenomena: Doctor Who*. Edited by Paul Booth. Bristol: Intellect Books. pp. 128–135.
"Masters of War (Audio Story)." n.d. Wiki. *Tardis Data Core*. http://tardis.wikia.com/wiki/Masters_of_War_(audio_story). Accessed June 13, 2017.
Rosenfeld, Gavriel. 2002. "Why Do We Ask 'What If?' Reflections on the Function of Alternate History." *History and Theory* 41: 90–103.
Simpson, Lorenzo C. 1995. *Technology, Time, and the Conversations of Modernity*. New York: Routledge.

Wolverson, E. G. 2010. "Doctor Who Unbound—Auld Mortality." *Doctor Who Reviews*. http://www.doctorwhoreviews.altervista.org/UN01.htm. Accessed June 13, 2017.

List of Audios

"Auld Mortality." 2003. Director: John Ainsworth. Writer: Eddie Robson. *Doctor Who Unbound*. Big Finish.

"Deadline." 2003. Director: Nicholas Briggs. Writer: Robert Shearman. *Doctor Who Unbound*. Big Finish.

"Exile." 2003. Director and writer: Nicholas Briggs. *Doctor Who Unbound*. Big Finish.

"Full Fathom Five." 2003. Director: Jason Haigh-Ellery. Writer: David Bishop. *Doctor Who Unbound*. Big Finish.

"He Jests at Scars." 2003. Director and writer: Gary Russell. *Doctor Who Unbound*. Big Finish.

"Masters of War." 2008. Director: Jason Haigh-Ellery. Writer: Eddie Robson. *Doctor Who Unbound*. Big Finish.

"A Storm of Angels." 2005. Director: John Ainsworth. Writer: Eddie Robson. *Doctor Who Unbound*. Big Finish.

"Sympathy for the Devil." 2003. Director: Gary Russell. Writer: Jonathan Clements. *Doctor Who Unbound*. Big Finish.

The Vikings
at the End of the Universe
Doctor Who, *Norsemen*
and the End of History

MARCUS K. HARMES

The Vikings were seafaring people from a variety of Scandinavian kingdoms, active in the eighth to 11th centuries as raiders, colonizers and traders
in the Irish Sea, Normandy, Frisia and further to Constantinople. The name
Norse is not exclusively interchangeable with Viking, although Norsemen
were Vikings. The Norsemen in particular moved west to raid and settle in
the north of England as well as in Ireland and Scotland (McEvedy 1961, 50).

Their dramatic and often violent history is adapted into drama, narrative, and design in *Doctor Who*. This essay examines the adaptation of Viking
history in *Doctor Who*, although the combination of Vikings and *Doctor Who*
may not be immediately obvious. Vikings have only been portrayed directly
in the series twice; one of those was long ago in 1965's *The Time Meddler* and
the other in 2015's *The Girl Who Died*. However, the adaptation of the historical record of Vikings can be oblique and indirect, and images and allusions
that are recognizably Norse have appeared in stories from 1965 into the
revived series. The program constantly borrows from texts and genres of all
types (Marlow 2009; Harmes 2014) but there is a constellation of *Doctor Who*
serials where Norse references appear. These range from *The War Machines*
in 1966 in which a mad computer is called WOTAN, to 1983's *Terminus* whose
protagonists are named from Norse myth, to the Gods of Ragnarok in *The
Greatest Show in the Galaxy*, and to the very Viking-like character Gantok in
The Wedding of River Song. A number of the Doctor's companions—Rose
Tyler, Martha Jones, Donna Noble and River Song—have characteristics of
the Valkyries (Larsen 2010, 120–139; Burke 2010, 140–183). These stories, char-

acters, and their sources testify to a broader set of questions concerning the meaning that can be extracted from history for popular cultural outputs.

One particular story from 1963 to 1989 *Doctor Who* is my focus: *The Curse of Fenric* (1989).[1] In studying that story, one issue is of capital importance: no actual living Vikings appear in *Fenric*. Its historical setting is the 1940s not the early Middle Ages. *Fenric*'s Vikings are allusive, suggestive presences, participating in the narrative and the texture of the story by loose adaptation of their history in the north of England. By adapting allusively from the history of the Vikings, the creative team responsible for *Fenric* adopted a mode of storytelling where the Vikings opened spaces for other textual traditions, including antiquarian ghost stories, 1980s horror cinema and the history of the Second World War. These could be brought into dialogue with Viking history and mythology as eerie historical resonances bubble up from the past to threaten the future.

Because it adapts from Viking mythology, *Fenric* is concerned with not only the past but also the fulfillment of history. Two points about the Vikings and the adaptation of their history in *Fenric* will shape the discussion of this essay in particular. One is that the story positions history and historical records as ominous; the other is that the future is threatening. The story draws upon the eschatological threads of Viking mythology and is preoccupied with the end of the world and the end of time. Characters in *Fenric* speak of a future where the earth is dying. Full destruction in the story is averted because the Doctor saves the day, of course, whereas the historical fulfillment of Norse myth would have lay in the destruction of the world. In this way, the major creative impulse of the historical source, which is the expectation of the ending of things, comes into collision with the narrative necessity for the Doctor to avert catastrophe. Adaptations of history and historical narratives do transgress or deviate from original sources. When the history of the Vikings meets *Doctor Who* the adaptation of history is truncated. There may be Vikings in *Doctor Who*, but their world cannot end.

A Space Helmet for a Cow: Vikings in Doctor Who

The first appearance of the Vikings in on-screen *Doctor Who* was 1965's *The Time Meddler*. This serial was a timely historical adventure in that it was set shortly before the Norman Conquest of 1066 and was broadcast when Britain was gearing up for large-scale 900th anniversary celebrations of the Conquest in 1966. It was timely but also to an extent timeless as well, as the general history of 1066 was still taught in the British history curriculum, as well as being known in popular culture through W.C. Sellar's and R.J. Yeatman's enduringly popular spoof history text *1066 and All That* published in 1930 but still in print in the 1960s.

In *The Time Meddler*, the First Doctor's (William Hartnell) TARDIS brings him and his companions to the Northumbrian coast shortly before the Conquest, where they become embroiled in an adventure involving an alien time traveler, Anglo-Saxons, and Vikings. The Doctor finds a helmet on the beach; it has two horns poking out of it. Whereas the Doctor's companion Steven (Peter Purves) expresses disbelief that they really have landed in 1066 and that the helmet is real, the Doctor has no such doubts. "What do you think it is, a space helmet for a cow?" he asks irritably as well as rhetorically. That settles it, then: they're holding a real Viking helmet in the real 1066. Except, as has been pointed out endlessly by historically conscious fans, Vikings did not really have horned helmets; in fact, the Celts did (Chadwick 1970, 48). The intention of the Doctor's line was serious, and the serial's writer Dennis Spooner was saying that the helmet was authentic. Since 1965, however, the interpretation of this scene has undergone strange metamorphosis. In 1965 *Doctor Who* was still at times clinging to the idea it was educational, and the story set in 1066 was also meant in part to be a history lesson; landing in 1066 was one of many historical experiences for the First Doctor (Cull 2001, 101–102). In 1965 the Doctor was being serious in chiding his companion for his ignorance and informing the watching school children about what 11th-century Vikings wore. Since 1965 the scene has taken on a raucously extra-diegetic meaning, with the Doctor's authoritative claims to be holding a real Viking helmet subverted by our knowledge that the helmet is inaccurate. The fact that *The Time Meddler* is actually about an alien time traveler leaving anachronisms in 11th-century England (a wrist watch, an electric lamp, a gramophone), and the meddler was played by comedy star Peter Butterworth (McKee 2007, 242), only adds to the fun that what was meant to be serious and authentic is now challengingly fake, even if the mixture also confused contemporary viewers (O'Mahony 2007, 59).

Themes and creative impulses from Viking culture and history were out of sight in 1970s *Doctor Who* but then re-appeared throughout the 1980s, which was the final decade of the program's 1963–1989 production. The adaptation of the Vikings in this decade is less direct and more allusive than their straightforward portrayal in *The Time Meddler*. But there is a significant irony that the adaptations, while transgressive and indirect, are more serious than the purported history lesson delivered in 1965.

All 1980s *Doctor Who* serials were overseen by John Nathan-Turner, producer from 1980 to 1989, who oversaw stories which imaginatively reconfigured Vikings (Rafer 2007, 128). *Terminus* from 1983 was set in outer space but its thematic and visual cues were Viking. Like *Fenric*, the story's structure and focus adapted from mythologies preoccupied with the end of time as the

Fifth Doctor (Peter Davison) manages to avert the destruction of the universe. The script and the design intersect with Viking theme and nomenclature as the "Vanir," a type of guardian at a space hospital in the future, take their name and the appearance of their armor from Viking sources. Their giant dog, the Garm, is a further adaptation from Viking mythologies.

In 1988's *The Greatest Show in the Galaxy*, the Seventh Doctor (Sylvester McCoy) and his companion Ace (Sophie Aldred) visit the "Psychic Circus." There they are menaced by robot clowns, a werewolf, the conniving and murderous circus staff, the walking dead, and finally the Gods of Ragnarok. The story's director (Alan Wareing) uses strong visual styling to emphasize the horror behind the circus. White-faced clowns drive around in a hearse, a dusty workshop is full of robots which activate and attack, and the big top is a slaughterhouse where the performers die in gruesome ways while watched by a suspiciously small and quiet audience of a father, mother and their little girl. These three are actually the "Gods of Ragnarok," demanding sacrifices and overseeing the slaughter of the innocent.

Galaxy adapts from more than the Vikings. The trope of the sinister circus has been a mainstay of horror films since at least the 1930s, when Tod Browning's *Freaks* fused the fairground with the grotesque, although even earlier the expressionistic horror *Das Cabinet des Dr. Caligari* (1919) was set in a fairground. Circuses have returned periodically in horror cinema, including as the setting of the climax of *Horrors of the Black Museum* (1959), as the framing device for a portmanteau horror in *Torture Garden* (1967) and as principal settings in *Circus of Horrors* (1960), *The Evil of Frankenstein* (1964), *Circus of Fear* (1966), *Vampire Circus* (1971), *The Mutations* (1974) and *The Funhouse* (1981) (Newman 1996, 68–69). The circus clowns are an uncanny presence and their capacity to frighten is reinforced by real-life notoriety such as the clown killer John Wayne Gacy. The fictional variations on Gacy such as Stephen King's *It* (1990), *American Horror Story: Freak Show*'s Twisty the Clown (2014), Papa Lazarou in *The League of Gentlemen* (1999) or even Krusty the Clown (from *The Simpsons* 1989–present) at his most grotesque, continue to register in popular culture.

The clowns and the gods in *Galaxy* are a fusion of two cultural resources: horror cinema with Vikings. The combination is shown on screen by the juxtaposition of the bright billowing circus tent with ancient stones that mark the entry to the Gods of Ragnarok's domain. The deities presiding over this mayhem are inflected after Viking themes, as the name Ragnarok indicates. Ragnarok is eschatological: the death of the gods and the passing of the world (Sørensen 1997, 206; Steinsland 2013, 149). As with most *Doctor Who* stories, *Galaxy* ends with the defeat of preternatural evil by the Doctor. In this specific instance, it is through the fulfillment of Ragnarok itself, the moment in Norse myth when the gods are destroyed (Ellis 1964, 37). He brings order to a chaotic situation, a point of dramatic urgency indicated in *Galaxy* by the Doctor's comment: "Things are getting out of control quicker than I expected." Forced to perform before the Gods of Ragnarok, the Doctor in fact turns the tables, taunting and teasing the gods with a range of tricks and eventually tricking them into causing their own destruction. In this respect, the Doctor takes on characteristics of another Norse mythological figure, Loki the trickster god and maker of mischief (Fraser 1981, 244). The Doctor's magic tricks briefly entertain the deities, but in time he turns the tricks against them, using a mirrored amulet to reflect the gods' own destructive rays and bring down their entire domain.

The Curse of Fenric from 1989 contains the most direct representations of Vikings since 1965. No Vikings appear but their language, their longboats and their history all impact on the narrative. In this serial, the Doctor is visiting a military base in Northumbria during World War II. The base houses a gigantic cipher-cracking computer, the Ultima Machine, operated by Dr. Judson (Dinsdale Landen). The base's commandant, Commander Millington (Alfred Lynch), is obsessed with Vikings, and most particularly with the eschatological myths concerning the Great Ash, that is, the final battle between the Gods, and the end of the world. More ominously still, runic writing starts to burn itself onto a wall in a nearby church crypt and vampiric creatures emerge from the graveyard and from the sunken wreck of a Viking longboat off the coast.

These 1980s stories are not set in the medieval period, yet as the plot summaries above show, the serials are steeped in Norse history and mythology, and the dynamics of the plot are driven by the Doctor's need to avert an apparently inexorable destruction (or else bring about the twilight of the Gods of Ragnarok). Sometimes the influences appear as part of the *mise en scène*. For example, actual runic writing, the script of the Vikings, appears on screen in *Fenric* as do the remains of a dragon-headed longboat. In other instances, the Viking influence is in nomenclature (Ragnarok, the Garm, whereas Fenric is a slight variation on Fenrir, another Viking name). More deeply still, the Viking influences penetrate the means of telling stories and the narrative preoccupations of each with eschatology and the end of history.

These stories are not distinctive in being *Doctor Who* stories that are adaptations of historical legend or folklore. But if we say that the writers of these *Doctor Who* stories were "adapting" Vikings, a shift in both terminology and methodology is necessary. There is no single point of origin; for example, the novel *Great Expectations* can be adapted into a film *Great Expectations* and have largely the same plot and characters, but with Vikings there is no such singular point of origin. There are the Prose Edda by Snorri Snurluson and the Eddic poems, a collection of poetry in Old Norse, which provided evocative and atmospheric descriptions of the end of time used in *Fenric*. There are historical records such as the *Anglo-Saxon Chronicle* and the *Historia de Sancto Cuthberto* with references to the Northumbrian King Raegnald (Campbell 1942, 86). There are also archaeological remains showing what the Vikings and their longboats looked like. There is, however, no one coherent source. That point is significant. *Fenric*, like many other *Doctor Who* stories, evokes sinister settings, generates fear and promotes a disturbing and uncanny gothic atmosphere. To consider for a moment Helen Wheatley's assessment of what she terms "gothic television," there is her emphasis on dread, terror, the uncanny and the supernatural. More important, Wheatley points out that there is not a single coherent or definitive meaning of this type of genre-based television, when ideas and scripts are an assembly of many different text types and elements (Wheatley 2006, 3). The horror trappings of these *Doctor Who* stories interact with Norse history which is an aggregation of texts and traditions.

Adapting Norsemen

These Viking texts and traditions are subject to constant adaptation, and the *Doctor Who* stories are in a trajectory of adaptations that have been taking place since the medieval period. Oral legends and stories have been adapted to written works (Sigurdsson 1988, 245). Works expressing a pagan cosmogony and cosmology (or understandings of the beginnings and the operation of the cosmos) were in time adapted to a Christian emphasis following the conversion of the Scandinavians and Icelanders to Christianity. These adaptations have taken centuries and the majority of them are recent to the past two centuries. Indeed, for many centuries after the eleventh little was known or remembered of Vikings. Their now widely recognized longboats were lost to history until archaeological discoveries of the late 19th and early 20th centuries (Meier 2006, 25). Since the late 19th century, Vikings have become a familiar and fruitful source of adaptation in popular culture, including in the gothic mayhem of these *Doctor Who* stories. For example, texts and legends have been adapted to music, and the most malicious adaptation was the appropriation by fascist ideologues in Germany and Norway of Viking heritage, an association used as the inspiration for the Norsefire fascist Chancellor Susan in *V for Vendetta* (Žižek 2009, 47).

Original documentary records of the Vikings situate them among supernatural portents and sinister events, including the storms, winds and signs in the sky that presaged their raid on the abbey at Lindisfarne in AD 793 according to the *Anglo Saxon Chronicle* (Hodgkin 1952, 473) to the walking dead in medieval romances (Simpson 2003, 390), a point used in *Galaxy* when the Gods of Ragnarok reanimate the dead (Palsson and Edwards 1985, 58). Vikings had their own eschatological myths but were also incorporated into religious teachings about the end of the world by those they attacked. Churchmen saw in their ferocious attackers clear signs of judgment and doomsday (Palmer 2014, 209). These characteristics readily translate into the horror-inflected serials in *Doctor Who*. With these thoughts in mind, it is now time to consider specifically *Fenric* and its Viking adaptations.

Ghost in the Machine: Vikings, Computers and World War II

Fenric was one of the last stories made in the original 26-year run of *Doctor Who*. I have argued elsewhere the stories of the 1989 season are distinguished by their depth and the maturity of their themes, in ways indicative of their place in the later history of the program (Harmes 2013, 206). *Fenric* is representative of the other stories from 1989 in terms of the wide but tightly controlled range of sources that inform plotting, characters and themes. Vikings do not "appear" as such, although a sunken longboat with its dragon-headed prow is glimpsed under the water. Both their history and their mythology are however a constant presence in the story. "Why is everyone round here so interested in Vikings?" Ace asks at one point, after hearing about Viking curses, seeing Viking inscriptions and handling chess pieces. Historically, it is valid to posit, as the story does, that there would be a Viking wreck off the Northumbrian coast and that there would be runic carvings scratched into walls (Keynes 2007, 157; McLeod 2015, 9; Meier 2006, 97; Thompson 2002, 126). Chess men are a prominent motif in a story which ultimately centers on a battle of wits between the Doctor and his antagonist Fenric, fought out via a chess game which is a strong visual association with the Viking-era Lewis chessmen (Robinson, 2004). Further resonances include the sunken longboat under water which various characters warn is beset by dangerous currents, a point that parallels the historical circumstances of the loss of longboats in coastal currents (Meier, p.31). There are sinister implications in local place names. The adversary, Fenric, is released from a flask that had been brought on a longboat from Constantinople. A spirit trapped in a flask is a mainstay of ghost stories (Simpson 1997, 13) but the flask coming from the east is an historical allusion to the trading routes that Viking ships reached along and the presence of Vikings in Byzantium and the wide distribution of artifacts, including vessels of the type Fenric is trapped in (Mikkelsen 1996; Meier, 6). Its supernatural guardian in *Fenric*, the Ancient One, recalls the watchmen of medieval Icelandic literature (Jakobsson 2011, 289).

Most penetrating is the intersection between the standard *Doctor Who* narrative of an evil force threatening the world and its confrontation and containment by the Doctor, as the point of intersection is the Viking mythology pertaining to twilight, to destruction, and the end of the old order in the world. Viking eschatological myth is intrinsic to *Fenric's* plot dynamics. As typical with a *Doctor Who* story, the Doctor confronts and defeats a menace. The story emulates the Norse myth of Fenrir, a wolf and an enemy of the gods, whom the gods chained but who is one of the "agents of destruction" of Ragnarok (Samplonius 2013, 114; Burstrom 2015, 260). These notions drive the plotting of Ian Briggs' script, over the course of which the audience learns that much earlier the Doctor fought and defeated Fenric in a game of chess, confining him in a flask. Exerting preternatural influence of those he calls his "wolves," or the descendants of Vikings who had obtained the flask, Fenric has manipulated history to create a convergence of circumstances that will lead to his release in Northumbria in 1943. Meanwhile the base's commander believes "The Viking legends will come true. The treasure will be brought to us, and with it all the dark powers of Fenric shall be ours." As an antagonist his motivation derives from belief in Viking curses.

Part of this narrative concerns the Doctor's arrival at the military base in Northumbria in 1943. Dr. Judson is a fictional analogue to Alan Turing (Orthia 2010, 121), suggested by the discussion between Judson and the Doctor of the Prisoner's Dilemma. Judson is using "Ultima" to crack U-Boat ciphers. But the complex narrative also includes the Doctor's meeting with the Reverend Mr. Wainwright (Nicholas Parsons), vicar of the nearby St Jude's Church, where the churchyard is full of the descendants of Norse settlers in the region and the church crypt contains spooky runic inscriptions. The plot threads of the computer at the military base and the runes in the church crypt coalesce because Dr. Judson has been testing the code breaking capacity of his computer by translating the runes. There is a further link: St Jude's contains a dreadful evil: a strange poisonous substance is leeching through crypt walls and the poison will be used to create chemical bombs at the military base. The massive "Ultima" machine we see operated by Dr. Judson is a composite of the Colossi, a set of electronic digital computers, and Alan Turing's electromechanical Bombe. Both were intrinsic to breaking the encrypted messages of the German High Command. One of the operators of an actual Colossus at Bletchley Park during the Second World War has left on record this evocative description of a Colossus: "its sheer bulk and apparent complexity; the fantastic speed of thin paper tape round the glittering pulleys…; the uncanny action of the typewriter in printing the correct scores without and beyond human aid; the stepping of the display; … and the strange rhythms characterizing every type of run" (Good, Michie and Timms 1945). Turing himself wrote of superstitions about electronic computers that people held into the 1950s (Turing 1950, 439), and this atmospheric account of the Colossus brings to mind the impressive prop seen on screen in *Fenric*, a massive black machine with analogue dials, filling a room and spitting out computations on paper. Yet there is something that is more sinister than impressive and more supernatural than electronic about the Ultima, and the uncanniness mentioned in relation to the Colossus applies here. Deep in Ultima's electronic structure is a vessel of green poisonous liquid from the church crypt. Realizing that a group of Russian soldiers have infiltrated the base to steal Ultima, and predicting that following the war Russia and Britain would no longer be allies, the camp's insane commander intends to let the Russians steal the computer. It is pre-programmed to explode and release the poison in Moscow (Orthia 2010, 121). The machine takes on a yet more sinister aspect when Ace realizes that in shape and design the ancient runes are akin to a computer program language. Judson runs this program and the computer tape began to print out of control, as if the machine was possessed. "Let the chains of Fenric shatter" reads Dr. Judson in puzzlement as the computer's rotor mechanism whirls madly and ticker tape spurts out the names of the Vikings who were lost at sea when the longboat sank: Estrid, Sigvald, Hakon, Fridrek, Wulfstan, Ingiga. The language of the computer echoes the Eddic poetry's descriptions of Ragnarok and which proclaims "the wolf will break its bonds" (Crawford 2015, p.11).

Thus *Fenric* showed something much older than the (for 1943) state of the art Ultima Machine. The story mobilizes the history of the church building and of Northumbria as ominous and dangerous intrusions into the narrative. The story's monsters are the "Haemovores," or blood eaters; in other words, vampires. It is not surprising that a character mentions that the action is taking place near to Whitby, which is where Dracula came ashore in Bram Stoker's novel. The Haemovores are awakened to go on a killing rampage by the reading aloud of ancient runic writing. This notion—that language, especially an ancient and esoteric one, has the power to summon supernatural forces—brings to mind a number of texts, but none as immediately pertinent as the *Ghost Stories of an Antiquary* (1904) by M.R. James (d. 1936). This writer of ghost stories was himself a philologist and bibliographer and his actual scholarship with manuscripts and ancient languages suffuses his writings, including non-fiction writing on medieval ghost stories (James 1922). In "Casting the Runes," a message on a piece of paper written in Viking script is an agent of terrifying danger: anyone holding the paper dies. In "Oh, Whistle and I'll come to you, my lad," a Latin inscription *"quis est iste qui venit"* on a whistle summons a preternatural menace. The same impression of the lively but dangerous potency of ancient writing runs through both literary theory and popular culture, from renaissance theories on the determinative functions of language (Wilkins 2012, 16) to manifestations in popular culture such as the Substitutiary Locomotion spell that animates empty suits of armor in Disney's *Bedknobs and Broomsticks* (1971). The same sense that words are lively informs *Fenric*'s narrative. Dr. Judson reads a runic inscription that says, "I've heard the magic words that will release great powers." The local vicar's grandfather had translated the runes, but the Reverend Mr. Wainwright realizes their affective danger. Reading out loud the runes, speaking the names of the descendants of Norse settlers and running the computer program unleash an ancient evil and raise the grotesque Haemovores from the sunken longboat. The Doctor reads in translation the sinister inscription: "We hope to return to the North Way, carrying home the oriental treasures from the Silk Lands in the east, but the dark curse follows our dragon ship." As he speaks, the dead awaken as both the runes and the computer program are motivating forces that reanimate the malevolent dead; in that regard they follow a characteristic of James's ghost stories (Moshenska 2012, 1195).

The adaptations of Viking folklore in *Fenric* are therefore densely layered. The Viking mythology that is the basis of the plot dynamics participates in an adaptive process with other sources. Because the story is so preoccupied with Vikings, their ancient writings and the impact of history on the present, the story has a strongly antiquarian flavor, a point of entry for the historical and antiquarian gothic, supernatural themes reminiscent of James' ghost stories. *Fenric* is an adaption of his work, where antiquarian research unearths sinister discoveries and is a way for history to be brought onto the screen. Early in the story the Doctor is told the church is built on old Viking graves, and the Vicar repeats a Northumbrian superstition: "They say evil was once buried here" and there is an "old Viking curse" around the area. As if realizing that he is appearing in a story adapting from the ghost stories of M.R. James, the Doctor acts as an antiquarian and goes to the church to consult the parish registers. Registers are large volumes in which a vicar records the names of the buried, the married, and the baptized in the parish. The Doctor finds a vital clue to unraveling the horror unfolding by looking in the registers at St. Jude's. The idea that churches could be sinister locations is long-established in English writing, with accounts of ghostly church bells and other sinister occurrences dating from the medieval and early modern periods (Mandeville Caciola 2014, 318; Mackinnon 2007, 255–267), and transmitting as a type of "ecclesiastical gothic" through literary episodes such as the late night visit to the crypt of Cloisterham Cathedral in *The Mystery of Edwin Drood* and the killer church bells in Dorothy L. Sayers' *The Nine Tailors* (Conrad-O'Briain 2011) and the many details of church furnishings in James' stories (Conrad-O'Briain 2010). This potential is exploited in *Fenric* when the registers make clear to the Doctor that the graves around the church contain the bodies of the descendants of Vikings, bodies that are now rising from the dead as the computer prints their names. There is also a degree of antiquarian speculation about the architecture of St Jude's, which the Doctor's companion thinks looks less like a church and instead looks like it has been fortified (Harmes 2014).[2] M.R. James' ghost stories also show antiquarian research, or what Helen Conrad-O'Briain refers to as the "practical scholarship," as intrinsic to the investigation of an mystery, including research in the British Library in "Casting the Runes," in a museum in "The Stalls of Barchester Cathedral," into a Latin cryptogram in stained glass in "The Treasure of Abbot Thomas," strange rubrics in prayer books in "The Uncommon Prayer Book," or around the archaeological remains of a Templar church in "Oh, Whistle and I'll come to you, my lad." The Doctor's research into the parish registers is pure antiquarianism, akin to the searching in old manuscript folios in "Canon Alberic's Scrapbook," but like James' stories it contains sinister implications as the names in the records are of the dead descendants of Vikings, and reading their names causes their corpses to rise from the sea and graveyard.

While plot mechanics in the serial derive from James' Edwardian ghost stories, major aspects of style and focus in *Fenric* derive from far more current horror tropes. These testify to a particular type of genre television identified by Wheatley, noted above, where stories do not have a clear or easily identifiable nature but draw together different elements. Ian Briggs' script suggests a prior relationship with John Carpenter's 1980 horror film *The Fog* and the same director's 1987 film *Prince of Darkness*. The parallels are close and obvious. In *The Fog* a seaside community is attacked by monstrous figures that rise from the sea and go to the church, as do the Haemovores. In both an ancient flask containing pent-up evil falls out of a crack in the wall of the church and the local priest's grandfather has left behind writings which have ominous warnings about a local curse. In both the community's priest is killed by the creatures. In *Prince of Darkness* green liquid under an old church is a dangerous and sinister source of power, ancient writings contain alarming warnings and a church is attacked by a horde of the possessed. However, it may be more accurate to say that Briggs, like Carpenter, was an adapter of Nigel Kneale's science fiction.[3] Kneale's 1958/1959 science fiction serial *Quatermass and the Pit* showed that an ancient menace had left historical clues in the archive of Westminster Abbey and the name of a street, Hob Lane. Kneale, Carpenter, and then Briggs convey an impression of the lively but disquieting history, where historical records can alarm and where menace comes back to the surface (Covell 2013).

The mayhem unleashed in *Fenric* unites the history of computing, 1980s horror, and James' antiquarianism, but underpinning the mayhem are the eschatological portents of Norse myth, which bring together the sinister resonances from Northumbrian history with the threats from the future. The myths are sinister, an aspect clearly exploited in *Fenric*'s uncanny computer prophecies, the sunken vessel, dangerous currents, and the walking dead.

The twilight of the gods would, according to mythological sources, see monsters walk, creatures emerge from the sea, a vessel of the dead sail, all leading to a final battle (Ellis, 38). The insane Commander Millington provides commentary on the events unfolding around him, perceiving in the preternatural events the signs of the end of the world. "The dead man's ship has slipped its mooring," he declares, echoing the account of Ragnorok in the prose Edda (Sturluson 2005, 72); he also believes in the Great Ash of Viking mythology and accepts the Doctor likening the poison to "the Well of Hvergelmir, deep beneath the ground where broods of serpents spew their venom over the roots of the Great Ash Tree" (Tonnelat 1968, 250). Reading the translation of the runes in the church, he finds they say: "I warn of the day when the earth shall fall asunder, and all of heaven too. The Wolves of Fenric shall return for their treasure, and then shall the dark evil rule eternally"; he adds his own meaning to the words: "This is it. The final battle."

Yet the point of departure, or where the adaptation takes from a source but recreates it, is in denying the fulfillment of Ragnarok. Across its history, *Doctor Who*'s narratives only ever showed the end of the world in other contexts besides the current world related to the viewing audience. Parallel worlds could be destroyed (as they were in *Turn Left*) but not the world as we the viewers know it, including historical settings such as the World War II time period in *Fenric*. In his most recent adventure with Vikings, 2015's *The Girl Who Died*, the Twelfth Doctor (Peter Capaldi) made clear that the stakes were very small: "The earth is safe, humanity is not in danger. It's just one village." Indeed, *The Girl Who Died* showcased a very different type of Vikings to the portentous and sinister aspects stressed in *Fenric*. In 2015 the emphasis was on Viking daily life: the village, its blacksmith and crafts and its children, rather like a television version of the Yorvik Viking Centre. The small scale of the drama is very different to *Fenric*, where the end of the world itself is threatened. The crisis and the danger derive from Viking mythology, which spoke of the complete destruction of an old order and the creation of a new (Jones 1984, 319). Coterminous with the destruction of the world was the end of the gods themselves (Tonnelat, 250).

However inspiring the Viking sources may be, they have undergone dramatic revision in order to intersect with the cosmology promoted within *Doctor Who*, where the world cannot end. In this regard, the Viking narratives are almost stunted but have to be so the adaptation will creatively merge with the pre-existing diegesis where each week the Doctor saves the world. The Doctor has averted not just a short-term threat but the future destruction of the entire world. Although *Fenric* borrows trappings (the church, the creatures, the coastal community) from *The Fog*, it does not borrow what is at stake. The deadly fog is only a local curse, whereas *Fenric* speaks to a final ending which the Doctor averts. The story moves beyond the history of computing, beyond the Jamesean antiquarianism to speak to environmental concerns about the end of the world and potential disaster which the Doctor averts. Millington, the insane commander, had anticipated that the release of Fenric would be the end of world via an environmental disaster: "And the Great Serpent shall rise from the sea and spew venom over all the Earth." The serpent is represented on screen by an ancient, grotesque Haemavore which has the task of releasing poison (Rafer 2007, 133–134). Fenric itself says of the chemical bombs: "There's enough poison in here to contaminate the world forever" and orders his minions to release the poison into the ocean and irreversibly pollute the earth's oceans. Modern biological warfare is the conduit for the myth. Being *Doctor Who*, the possibility of alternative futures arises and the Doctor can foresee what will happen if the poison is released: "Thousands of years in the future, the Earth lies dying, the surface just a chemical slime." Also because it is *Doctor Who* the Doctor prevails in the end: the poison is not released, Fenric is destroyed, and the world does not end.

Conclusion

Vikings, their history, and their mythology received sustained but complex treatment in the final years of *Doctor Who*'s original production run. The complexity is that the Vikings appear allusively among other adaptive sources. A strong central concept defines both stories. In *Galaxy* it is the horrors of the circus, a series of tropes, settings and events that came from the cinema of the decade. Similarly the binding agent in *Fenric* is the adaptation from *Fog* which provides the setting (the church and the seaside), the plot dynamics (an ancient curse and the killing of the priest) and the appearance of the monsters rising from the sea. The horror cinema pervades both *Doctor Who* stories but so does the Viking eschatology. The future of the world itself is at stake and the history comes dangerously to life.

NOTES

1. *The Curse of Fenric* now exists in three versions: the original 1989 broadcast; a slightly expanded VHS release; and the DVD release which included the original and a "movie length" version. The VHS release is the version used for this paper.

2. Appropriately, the medieval church used as the location was St Laurence in Hawkhurst, Kent, described in the Pevsner architectural guide as "bold and battlemented" (Newman 2012, 284).

3. Carpenter credited the screenplay for *Prince of Darkness* to "Martin Quatermass."

BIBLIOGRAPHY

The Anglo-Saxon Chronicles. 1995. Translated by Anne Savage. Twickenham: Tiger Books.
Anon. 1985. *Two Viking Romances*. Translated by Hermann Palsson and Paul Edwards. Harmondsworth: Penguin.

Anon. 2015. *The Poetic Edda: Stories of the Norse Gods and Heroes.* Translated by Jackson Crawford. Indianapolis: Hackett.

Burke, Jessica. 2010. "Doctor Who and the Valkyrie Tradition, Part 2: Goddesses, Battle Demons, Wives and Daughters" in *The Mythological Dimensions of Doctor Who,* edited by Anthony Burdge, Jessica Burke and Kristine Larsen. Crawfordville, FL: Kitsune Books. pp. 140–183.

Burstrom, Nanouschka Myrberg. 2015. "Things of Quality: Possessions and Animated Objects in the Scandinavian Viking Age" in *Own and Be Owned: Archaeological Approaches to the Concept of Possession,* edited by Alison Klevnas and Charlotte Hedenstierna-nson. Stockholm: Department of Archaeology and Classical Studies, University of Stockholm. 23–48.

Campbell, A. 1942. "Two Notes on the Norse Kingdoms in Northumbria." *The English Historical Review* 57, no. 225: 85–97.

Chadwick, Nora. 1970. *The Celts.* Harmondsworth: Pelican Books.

Conrad-O'Briain, Helen. 2010. "'The Gates of Hell Shall Not Prevail Against It': Laudian Ecclesia and Victorian Culture Wars in the Ghost Stories of M.R .James" in *The Ghost Story from the Middle Ages to the Twentieth Century: A Ghostly Genre,* edited by Helen Conrad-O'Briain and Julie Anne Stevens. Dublin: Four Courts Press. pp. 47–60.

Conrad-O'Briain, Helen. 2011. "Providence and Intertextuality: LeFanu, M.R. James, and Dorothy Sayers' *The Nine Tailors.*" *The Irish Journal of Gothic and Horror Studies* 9. http://irishgothichorrorjournal.homestead.com/HConrad-OBriain.html. Accessed March 18, 2016.

Covell, Adam. 2013. "An Ancient Evil: M.R. Hames and Nigel Kneale." *The Celluloid WickerMan.* http://celluloidwickerman.com/2013/12/23/an-ancient-evil-m-r-james-and-nigel-kneale/. Accessed December 23 2013.

Cull, Nicholas. 2001. "'Bigger on the Inside…': Doctor Who as British Cultural History" in *The Historian, Television and Television History,* edited by Graham Roberts and Philip M. Taylor. Luton: University of Luton Press. pp. 95–11.

Davidson, H.R. Ellis. 1964. *Gods and Myths of Northern Europe.* Harmondsworth: Penguin.

Frazer, James. 1981. *The Golden Bough: The Roots of Religion and Folklore.* New York: Avenel Books.

Good, Jack, Donald Michie, and Geoffrey Timms. 1945. *General Report on Tunny: With Emphasis on Statistical Methods.* http://www.alanturing.net/turing_archive/archive/index/tunnyreportindex.html. Accessed March 18, 2016.

Harmes, Marcus. 2013. "Religion, Racism and the Church of England in *Doctor Who*" in Doctor Who *and Race,* edited by Lindy Orthia. Bristol: Intellect. pp. 199–212.

Harmes, Marcus. 2014. *Doctor Who and the Art of Adaptation.* Lanham, MD: Rowman & Littlefield.

Harmes, Marcus. 2014. "Why does your church look like a fortress? God and the Gothic in *Doctor Who* and Hammer." *Science Fiction Film and Television* 7, no. 1: 99–116.

Hodgkin, R.H. 1952. *A History of the Anglo-Saxons,* 2 vols. Oxford: Oxford University Press.

Jakobsson, Armann. 2011. "Vampires and Watchmen: Categorizing the Mediaeval Icelandic Undead." *Journal of English and Germanic Philology*: 281–300.

James, M.R. 1922. "Twelve Medieval Ghost-Stories." *The English Historical Review* 37, no. 147: 413–422.

James, M.R. 2011. *Collected Ghost Stories,* edited by Darryl Jones. Oxford: Oxford University Press.

Jones, Gwym. 1984. *A History of the Vikings,* 2d ed. Oxford: Oxford University Press.

Keynes, Simon. 2007. "An Abbot, an Archbishop, and the Viking Raids of 1006–7 and 1009–2." *Anglo-Saxon England* 36: 151–220.

Larsen, Kristine. 2010. "Doctor Who and the Valkyrie Tradition, Part 1: The Valiant Child and theBad Wolf" in *The Mythological Dimensions of Doctor Who,* edited by Anthony Burdge, Jessica Burke and Kristine Larsen. Crawfordville, FL: Kitsune Books. pp. 120–139.

Mackinnon, Dolly. 2007. "Hearing the Reformation: Earls Colne, Essex" in *Hearing Places:*

Sound, Place, Time and Culture, edited by Ros Band, Michelle Duffy and Dolly Mackinnon. Newcastle upon Tyne: Cambridge Scholars. pp. 255–267

Mandeville Caciola, Nancy. 2014. "Revenants, Resurrection, and Burnt Sacrifice" *Preternature* 3, no. 2: 311–338.

Marlow, Christopher. 2009. "The Folding Text: *Doctor Who*, Adaptation and Fan Fiction" in *Adaptation in Contemporary Culture: Textual Infidelities*, edited by Rachel Carroll. pp. 46–60. London: Continuum.

McEvedy, Colin. 1961. *The Penguin Atlas of Medieval History*. Harmondsworth: Penguin.

McKee, Alan. 2007. "Why is 'City of Death' the Best *Doctor Who* Story?" in *Time and Relative Dissertations in Space: Critical Perspectives on* Doctor Who, edited by David Butler. Manchester: Manchester University Press. pp. 233–245.

McLeod, Shane. 2015. "The *Dubh Gall* in Southern Scotland: The Politics of Northumbria, Dublin, and the Community of St Cuthbert in the Viking Age, c.870–950CE." *Limina: A Journal of Historical and Cultural Studies* 20, no. 3: 1–21.

Meier, Dirk. 2006. *Seafarers, Merchants and Pirates in the Middle Ages*. Translated by Angus McGeoch. Woodbridge: Boydell Press.

Mikkelsen, Egil. 1998. "Islam and Scandinavia during the Viking Age" in *Byzantium and Islam in Scandinavia: Acts of a Symposium at Uppsala University, June 15–16, 1996/Studies in Mediterranean Archaeology*, edited by Elisabeth Piltz, vol. CXXV: 39–51.

Moshenska, Gabriel. 2012. "M.R. James and the Archaeological Uncanny." *Antiquity* 86: 1192–1201.

Newman, John. 2012. *The Buildings of England: Kent: West and the Weald*. New Haven: Yale University Press.

Newman, Kim, ed. 1996. *The BFI Companion to Horror*. London: Cassell.

O'Mahony, Daniel. 2007. "'Now how is that wolf able to impersonate a grandmother?' History, Pseudo-History and Genre in *Doctor Who*" in *Time and Relative Dissertations in Space: Critical Perspectives on Doctor Who*, edited by David Butler. Manchester: Manchester University Press. pp. 56–67.

Orthia, Lindy. 2010. "'Enlightenment was the Choice': *Doctor Who* and the Democratisation of Science." Australian National University PhD.

Palmer, James T. 2014. *The Apocalypse in the Early Middle Ages*. Cambridge: Cambridge University Press.

Rafer, David. 2007. "Mythic Identity in *Doctor Who*" in *Time and Relative Dissertations in Space: Critical Perspectives on* Doctor Who, edited by David Butler. Manchester: Manchester University Press. pp. 123–137.

Robinson, James. 2004. *The Lewis Chessmen*. London: British Museum Press.

Samplonius, Kees. 2013. "The Background and Scope of Vǫluspá" in *The Nordic Apocalypse: Approaches to* Vǫluspá *and the Nordic Days of Judgement*, edited by Terry Gunnell and Annette Lassen. Turnhout: Brepols. pp. 113–146.

Sigurdsson, Gisli. 1988. "On the Identification of Eddic Heroic Poetry in the View of Oral Theory" in *Poetry in the Scandinavian Middle Ages*. The Seventh International Saga Conference. pp. 245–255.

Simpson, Jacqueline. 1997. "'The Rules of Folklore' in the Ghost Stories of M.R. James." *Folklore* 108: 9–18.

Simpson, Jacqueline. 2003. "Repentant Soul or Walking Corpse? Debatable Apparitions in Medieval England." *Folklore* 114, no. 3: 389–402.

Sørensen, Preben Meilengracht. 1997. "Religions Old and New" in *The Oxford Illustrated History of the Vikings*, edited by Peter Sawyer. Oxford: Oxford University Press. pp. 202–224.

Steinsland, Gr. 2013. "*Vǫluspá* and the Sibylline Oracles with a Focus on the 'Myth of the Future'" in *The Nordic Apocalypse: Approaches to* Vǫluspá *and the Nordic Days of Judgement*, edited by Terry Gunnell and Annette Lassen. Turnhout: Brepols. pp. 147–160.

Sturluson, Snorri. 2005. *The Prose Edda*. Translated by Jesse Byock. London: Penguin Books.

Tonnelat, E. 1968. "Teutonic Mythology" in *New Larousse Encyclopaedia of Mythology*. Translated by Richard Aldington and Delano Ames. London: Paul Hamlyn. pp. 245–280.

Thompson, Victoria. 2002. *Dying and Death in Later Anglo-Saxon England*, Woodbridge: Boydell and Brewer.

Turing, Alan. 1950. "Computing Machinery and Intelligence." *Mind* 59, no. 236: 433–460.

Wheatley, Helen. 2006. *Gothic Television*. Manchester: Manchester University Press.

Wilkins, Kim. 2012. "'Words of Art': Magic and Language in Early Modern England" in *The British World: Religion, Memory, Society and Culture: Refereed Proceedings of the Conference Hosted by the University of Southern Queensland, July 2nd–July 5th 2012*, edited by Marcus Harmes, Lindsay Henderson, Barbara Harmes and Amy Antonio. Toowoomba. pp. 15–26.

Žižek, Slavoj, 2009, "From Job to Christ: A Paulinian Reading of Chesterton" in *St. Paul Among the Philosophers*, edited by John M C Aputo and Linda Martin Alcoff. Bloomington: Indiana University Press, 2009. pp. 39–60.

Ape-Man or Regular Guy?
Depictions of Neanderthals and Neanderthal Culture in Doctor Who

KRISTINE LARSEN

*I must stop thinking of myself as different—*Das, *Only Human*
(Roberts 2005, 235)

Introduction

Anne Hamilton argues that fiction featuring Neanderthals[1] focuses on the interactions between them and anatomically modern humans[2] because "we are only interested in defining ourselves through comparison with Neanderthals, not viewing their behavior" (2005, 89). While such juxtaposition can encourage a critical examination of prehistoric (and modern) human history and culture, Neanderthal behavior itself is a topic of general interest that we find reflected within popular culture. This fascination with Neanderthals is due, in part, to the fact that there remain several fundamental questions concerning our relationship to them. These include their precise placement in the human family tree as well as the issue of Neanderthal extinction, and the possible role that anatomically modern humans may have played in their disappearance. Was this the first genocide perpetrated by humans, or did they simply *become* us, through interbreeding? Either way, a careful reconstruction of Neanderthal genetics and culture is vital in understanding human prehistory.

Four Doctors[3] have had significant interactions with Neanderthals: the Second (Patrick Troughton) in the rejected episode storyline "The Return of the Neanderthal" (1967), the Fifth (Peter Davison) in the short story "Observation" (Farrington 2004), the Seventh (Sylvester McCoy) in the serial "Ghost Light" (1989) and its expanded novelization (Platt 1990) as well as the novel

Timewyrm: Genesys (Peel 1991), and the Ninth (Christopher Eccleston) in the novel *Only Human* (Roberts 2005). Due to its emphasis on travel throughout history without restrictions as well as the titular character's habit (whether intentional or accidental) of removing people from their native time, *Doctor Who* provides a unique lens through which to view any extinct population. Not only can they be observed in situ (thus opening up a doorway into a long dead way of life), but also in anachronistic situations that not only produce ample opportunities for both humor and tension, but in the process provide the viewer/reader with a fresh lens through which to view our modern society. In particular, the integration of Neanderthals into the mythos of *Doctor Who* provides three distinct intersections with history. Firstly, works such as *Only Human* and "Observation" that view Neanderthals in their original time provide an opportunity for reflection on Neanderthals as an integral (albeit not completely understood) part of the biological history of humanity. Secondly, works such as *Timewyrm: Genesys*, "Ghostlight," and *Only Human* that take Neanderthals out of their natural time period and insert them into other eras of human history (ancient Mesopotamia, Victorian rural England, and modern London, respectively) focus attention on the similarities between Neanderthals and anatomically modern humans, as they try and pass for "human." Lastly, all of these works provide a mirror that reflects our changing viewpoint of the Neanderthal as depicted through the history of popular culture.

Taken as a whole, these works invite us to meditate upon the not insignificant question: what does it really mean to be "human"? Such discussion also provides a valuable lens through which to examine a charge that has been levied against *Doctor Who*, namely that it perpetrates blatant stagism—the belief that "primitive" people are caught in an earlier stage of development than sophisticated Europeans and with effort can be elevated to the "more advanced" European stage of development (Orthia 2013, 272). In her critique of the series, Lindy Orthia gives myriad examples of stagist language and presumptions, from history teacher Barbara Wright's (Jacqueline Hill) belief that the Aztecs should be saved from the European genocide because they are on the verge of "civilization" (*ibid.*, 277) to repeated references to Leela (Louise Jameson) as "primitive" and "semi-intelligent" (*ibid.*, 281–282).

This essay begins by surveying our changing knowledge of, and stereotypes concerning, Neanderthals, then explores how this evolving viewpoint has been reflected in other works of popular culture (specifically H.G. Wells's short story "The Grisly Folk" [1921], William Golding's novel *The Inheritors* [1955], Isaac Asimov's short story "The Ugly Little Boy" [1957], and Jean Auel's best-selling novel *The Clan of the Cave Bear* [1980]), before considering what lessons we can glean from the myriad historical interactions between the Doctor and Neanderthals.

Who Was the Neanderthal?

The term Neanderthal refers to a close human relative, who entered the fossil record about 300,000 years ago and became extinct around 30,000 years ago. Their biological designation is *Homo neanderthalensis*, signifying them as a distinct species from anatomically modern humans. Some scientists argue that Neanderthals were actually a variant of our own species, and prefer the designation *Homo sapiens neanderthalensis* (similar to our *Homo sapiens sapiens*). They are named for the first identified fossils, collected in 1856 from the Neander Valley (Neander Tal) in Germany (Drell 2000, 1). Two earlier sets of fossils had been collected from Belgium and Gibraltar in 1830 and 1848, respectively, but not identified as humanoid remains until later (*ibid.*).

The anatomical differences between Neanderthals and ourselves include a slightly shorter height yet stockier build, curved femurs and lower arms, shorter arms and legs, and a distinctive shape to the ribcage (narrow at the top and wide at the bottom). The most obvious differences involve the skull (appearing flatter and more elongated in side profile with an obvious occipital bun at the back) and the facial features (large brow ridge, receding lower jaw with the corresponding lack of a modern chin, jutting midface, full cheeks, and large nasal opening) (Harvati 2010, 2–3). Indeed, the anatomical differences of the face and skull are in particular utilized to identify the Neanderthal characters of *Timewyrm: Genesis* and *Only Human* as such. Neanderthals are often illustrated as being inordinately hairy (another trait frequently utilized in *Doctor Who* to distinguish Neanderthal characters), despite the fact that there is no direct evidence to support this. Indeed, the opposite was more probable, given that the Neanderthals existed during both glacial and interglacial periods in which average temperatures were comparable to the present day and having copious amounts of body hair would have been unnecessary (Drell 2000, 7). Berman (1999, 291) explains that the "association of wild hair, a hairy body, and a "natural" state frequently occurs cross-culturally and diachronically. The wild aspect of naturalness carries with it connotations of primitivism, of animal-like behavior, of standing outside of civilization, of power, of lawlessness, of amorality, of sexual abandon, of perversion, of madness." Therefore the widespread stereotype of Neanderthal as hirsute is a natural outgrowth of other stereotypes of these humanoids as brutish and less highly evolved than modern humans.

The enduring public stereotype of the Neanderthal as an apish, stooped brute (a caricature mocked, for example, in the infamous GEICO caveman ad campaign, featuring the tagline "So easy a caveman can do it"[4]) owes its genesis to the work of French paleontologist Marcellin Boule, who described a skeleton found at Le Chapelle-aux-Saints, France, in 1908. In his reconstruction of the skeleton, Boule accentuated what he saw as the apish characteristics, giving the spine an abnormally large curve that resulted in a "stooping posture and slouching gait. The head was thrust forward—emphasizing the elongated shape, protruding face, and large brow-ridges—the knees bent, and the toes diverging" (Drell 2000, 6). Boule argued that "it is probable, therefore, that Neanderthal Man must have possessed only a rudimentary psychic nature, superior certainly to that of anthropoid apes, but markedly inferior to that of any modern race whatever. He had doubtless only the most rudimentary language" (Trinkaus and Shipman 1993, 302). In this view, Neanderthal was inferior to ourselves, an evolutionary dead end.

The pendulum swung in the other direction in the 1930s–1950s, when discoveries of purported burials sites cast Neanderthals in a decidedly human (and humane) light, along with the discovery that Boule had (apparently) intentionally misinterpreted the Neanderthal stance based on an obviously arthritic individual (Trinkaus and Shipman 1993, 302–303) to suit his own anti-evolutionary prejudices. During these decades the Neanderthal was seen as a possible direct ancestor of present-day humans.[5]

Our view of the intelligence of Neanderthals has also evolved over time. While the brain size of the Neanderthal is comparable to our own (relative to body size), brain size alone is not a definitive indicator of intelligence. The relative sizes and complexities of brain structures and neural connections between these structures are also important. Since quantifying these parameters is difficult at best when relying on fossil evidence, archaeological evidence serves as an admittedly equivocal proxy. Mellars (1996, 368) cites several areas of debate during the late 1980s and early 1990s concerning Neanderthal cognitive abilities, including evidence for "symbolic expression or behavior" and language. The first category includes the use of pigments, decorative and symbolic objects, burial practices and other rituals (including religion). While the archaeological record initially suggested limited Neanderthal engagement in these practices, more recent discoveries support the view that Neanderthals were, indeed, engaging in symbolic representations in artwork and ornamentation as well as creating sophisticated tools even before their encounters with our direct ancestors (Wong 2015, 40). In addition, as Mellars (1996, 366) argues, a simplistic lifestyle is not compelling evidence that Neanderthals were cognitively simplistic. A progressive interpretation of Neanderthal artistic culture is clearly seen in the novelization of *Ghost Light*, where Nimrod covers the walls of a tunnel beneath the mansion in a detailed mural "reminiscent of prehistoric cave paintings" (Platt 1990, 74).

In terms of Neanderthal burial sites, one of the most famous examples is the so-called "Flower Burial" in Shanidar Cave in Iraq. In 1968 pollen expert Arlette Leroi-Gourhan found a suspicious excess of fossil flower pollen at that site. Archaeologist Ralph Solecki interpreted this as evidence that the

Neanderthal buried their dead with flowers (including some with potentially medicinal purposes), the source for the title of his popular level book, *Shanidar: The First Flower People* (Trinkaus and Shipman 1993, 339–341). Solecki bolstered his argument that the Neanderthals had compassion with details about another skeleton found in Shanidar (*ibid.*, 340). This approximately 40-year-old man had died after having lived many years with a number of what should have been fatal injuries, apparently only surviving because he had been well-tended to by his family and perhaps others. The religious practices of Neanderthals have also been long debated. Amateur archaeologist Dr. Emil Bächler located Neanderthal tools in a cave in Switzerland circa 1920, and interpreted the finding of cave bear fossils in the same location—especially a skull with a "femur thrust through its cheekbone"—as evidence of a ritual involving these large predators. His reports led to other purported examples of bear cults, however, upon closer inspection the evidence does not support the claim (Tattersall 1995, 96–97). In the mythos of *Doctor Who*, the religious beliefs of Neanderthal characters is most clearly explored in "Ghost Light" (especially its novelization), as this essay will demonstrate in a later section.

Perhaps the greatest debate concerning Neanderthal behavior surrounds their ability to use spoken language. In 1971 speech analyst Phillip Lieberman and anatomy professor Edmund Crelin argued from skull reconstructions that the Neanderthal larynx was positioned in such a way that Neanderthals would have had difficulty pronouncing some vowels. Although their work was largely refuted, it focused attention on the problem of defining what constitutes human language (Trinkaus and Shipman 1993, 353–355). Interestingly, as James Shreeve argues, different aspects of language could have evolved over time (related to the sophistication of the overall intelligence), for example the concept of past, present, and future tense (1995, 308). While the debate continues, in 2007 it was announced that the FOXP2 gene sequence associated with language in modern humans had been located in the Neanderthal genome, in a form that was more representative of that in modern humans than in chimpanzees (Smith 2007). Of necessity, with the exception of the short story "Observation," all Neanderthals in the universe of *Doctor Who* have the ability to speak, either in a native tongue that is easily translated by the TARDIS, or in the vernacular of that historical time and place (e.g., ancient Mesopotamia or Victorian England).

Since Neanderthals and Cro-Magnons co-inhabited Europe for several millennia, the question of interbreeding has long been considered. James Shreeve explains the possibility of co-habiting without interbreeding through the concept of "mate-recognition" (1995, 203). He considers that the facial features of the two types of humans were sufficiently different such that they would not recognize members of the other group as potential mates. More simply put, each group thought the other too alien—too ugly—to be attracted to them. However, as Tattersall (1995, 202) argues, rape perpetrated by Cro-Magnons would not have been out of the realm of possibility. In his words, "it's highly improbable that viable offspring could have been produced by the resulting unions" (*ibid.*).

Despite these predictions, in 1999 the skeleton of a young child was unearthed in a 24,500 year old burial site in Abrigo do Lagar Velho, Portugal that was purported to have a mixture of anatomical traits suggesting that it was a Neanderthal-modern human hybrid (Duarte et al. 1999, 7604). The discovery was sufficiently revolutionary to have been reported on the front page of *The New York Times*, where it was clarified that, as Neanderthals had become extinct several thousand years previously, the child was not the direct result of interbreeding, but rather was expressing traits from an earlier Neanderthal ancestor (Wilford 1999, 1). This discovery was questioned when a 2004 analysis of Neanderthal mitochondrial DNA (passed through matrilineal lines) demonstrated no evidence of interbreeding and suggested that there was "an almost complete sterility between Neanderthal females and modern human males" (Currat and Excoffier 2004, e421). These scientific doubts were clearly ignored by Gareth Roberts in the writing of *Only Human*, as potential interbreeding between Neanderthals and 20th-century humans is strongly suggested.

While White (2015, n.p.) notes that as late as 2009 "incontrovertible evidence for or against Neanderthal and modern human admixture has yet to be identified," the following year, a draft sequence of the entire Neanderthal genome was published, revealing that between "1–4% of the genome of present-day Non-Africans" derives from the Neanderthal genome (Green et al. 2010, 471). The relatively low percentage of Neanderthal DNA extant in present-day humans has been explained as a byproduct of the interbreeding process, for example that the presence of Neanderthal alleles decreased male fertility in hybrids (Sankararaman et al. 2014, 354). As Ann Gibbons muses, "Neanderthals and modern humans made imperfect mates" (2014, 471).

However rare these incidences of interbreeding of Neanderthals and Cro-Magnons may have been, their inconvertible existence is an important point to consider when discussing the extinction of the former. A number of scenarios have been suggested for their extinction, including an inability to adapt to changing climates (surprising given their success during the previous 250,000 years of climate fluctuations), competition with modern humans for limited resources, low birthrate and high mortality, or even genocide by more aggressive *Homo sapiens* (Harvati 2010, 7). But evidence of shared tool technology between the two groups suggests that the Neanderthals' demise was more quiet than dramatic. As James Shreeve notes, in terms of evolution "you do not have to fail to go extinct. You have only to succeed a little less often than someone else" (1995, 337). In this viewpoint of Neanderthal extinction, there was no violent genocide propagated by our Cro-Magnon ancestors; rather, we merely out bred the Neanderthals. The role of Cro-Magnons in the downfall of Neanderthals (including the potential roles of both genocide and outbreeding) has been explored in both the *Doctor Who* short story "Observation" and the novel *Only Human*. There is therefore much food for thought in contemplating Neanderthal/Cro-Magnon interactions, which has resulted in a rich variety of Neanderthal-based fiction over the 20th century and into the 21st, including the mythos of *Doctor Who*.

Neanderthals in Popular Culture

One of the first classic tales of Neanderthal interactions with modern humans, H.G. Wells's 1921 short story "The Grisly Folk" paints a less than flattering picture of a brutish Neanderthal straight out of Boule—an "ugly, strong, ungainly, manlike animal" (Wells 2008, 4)—who, Wells reasons, "must have fought and met" with the "true men" (*ibid.*). Wells' tale in fact pictures "the beginning of an incessant war that could end only in extermination" (*ibid.*, 17), including the kidnapping of a human child by Neanderthals. In contrast we have William Golding's 1955 novel *The Inheritors*, which casts Neanderthals as the gentle, simple-minded victims of aggressive modern humans. Alterman describes Golding's Neanderthals as specifically lacking "abstract reasoning power" (1978, 5), playing into debates of Neanderthal intelligence. They are telepathic but possess a limited spoken language, and practice a matrilineal religion. They are, as Alterman stresses, decidedly alien. In this tale the Neanderthals are killed off one by one by our ancestors, until the last Neanderthal child is adopted (albeit not without prejudice) by a group of modern humans.

The trope of a Neanderthal child adopted by present-day humans is central to Isaac Asimov's 1957 short story "The Ugly Little Boy." The titular character, named Timmie by his nursemaid, the symbolically named Edith Fellowes, is kidnapped from the past through time travel technology owned by the research corporation, Stasis Inc. While she comes to love Timmie as her own child, Edith is originally repulsed by the appearance of the Neanderthal, "horribly ugly from misshapen head to bandy legs" (Asimov 1959, 191). She is equally surprised by the fact that he initially laps milk from a saucer like a kitten and the fact that he has a native tongue "made up of gutturals and elaborate tongue-clickings" (*ibid.*, 193). The author—a trained biochemist—lends his opinion on Neanderthal's taxonomical positioning through the words of a Stasis Inc. employee: "*Homo neanderthalis* is not a truly separate species, but rather a subspecies of *Homo sapiens*. Why shouldn't he talk?" (*ibid.*). The child's humanity becomes obvious to Edith when he is out of her sight and she hears his cries of loneliness and fear: "it was a child; what did the shape of its head matter? It was a child that had been orphaned as no child had ever been orphaned before. Not only its mother and father were gone, but all its species" (*ibid.*, 196). She teaches Timmie to speak English as well as read (in line with Asimov's opinion regarding Neanderthal's place in human evolution), and comes to see Timmie as a normal human child, in contrast describing "an ordinary boy on the street" as ugly, finding "something bulgy and unattractive in his high domed forehead and jutting chin" (*ibid.*, 201–202). On the other hand, in the eyes of Stasis Inc. Timmie is a simply commodity, an experiment, and when the experiment is slated to be terminated (with the boy to be returned to his own time, despite the fact that it would be akin to releasing an animal raised in a zoo or a household pet back into the wild) Edith first tries to smuggle the child out of the lab, and when that fails, sends the two of them back into the past together.

A similarly sympathetic view of Neanderthals is found in Jean Auel's 1980 bestselling novel *The Clan of the Cave Bear*. An orphaned modern human girl, Ayla, is adopted by a clan of Neanderthals, despite the fact that they view her as one of the hideously ugly Others. As noted by Trinkaus and Shipman (1993, 341), Auel utilizes Solecki's interpretation of the Shanidar burials in the creation of the character Creb, a severely physically challenged shaman well-versed in herbal magic and hallucinogenics. Auel's story also incorporates other (sometimes dubious) scientific research on Neanderthals of her time, including the Leiberman-Crelin hypothesis of limited vowel usage, as well as suggestions that Neanderthals utilized sign language in addition to spoken language (DePaolo 2000, 433).

As the title of the novel suggests, Auel also borrows the unsubstantiated claims by Bächler for a cult surrounding the worship of cave bears. In the novel, the Cro-Magnon Ayla has a much more fluent command of language—even as a young child—than the Neanderthal adults, whose reliance on hand gestures is heavy and use of symbolic and abstract language is severely limited. A prime example is the difficulty Auel's Neanderthals have in conceptualizing numbers and generalizations (e.g., trees as opposed to specific types of trees) (2011, 126).

In addition to scientific hypotheses and evidence, Auel also incorporates pseudoscience, in having the Neanderthals being telepathic (as in the case of Golding's story) and born with a racial memory related to a person's profession (for example, identifications and uses of medicinal herbs in the case of wise women), which left their brains with insufficient room for innovation and learning. The relatively simplistic brains of Auel's Neanderthals also apparently have great difficulty with deception, with Neanderthals said to lack the concept of lying (Auel 2011, 65), despite the fact that deceptive behavior is common among apes (Angier 2008, n.p.). Interestingly, a similar difficulty in grasping the subtleties of fiction is a characteristic of the Neanderthal Das in *Only Human* (as I will explore in a later section).

The Neanderthals' view of Ayla as ugly leads to a concern that she will never find a mate, in keeping with the previously mentioned concept of mate-recognition. Despite this, there are two Neanderthal-modern human hybrids in the novel, both the product of rape. Ayla gives birth to a "deformed" child after being raped by the son of the Neanderthal leader of the clan, while the Neanderthal girl Oda gives birth to another hybrid following a similar encounter with a band of Cro-Magnon males.

The trope of telepathic Neanderthals utilized by Golding and Auel was almost adopted in *Doctor Who*, in the rejected 1967 storyline entitled "The Return of the Neanderthal," penned by Roger Dixon. In the proposed story, the Doctor and Jamie (Frazier Hines) travel to Terunda, where a band of telepathic Neanderthals has been fostered. The Doctor grants them their request to return to Earth, where they reveal their plans to dominate modern humans. Fortunately for the 20th century, the Neanderthals have been altered by the Terundans—conditioned like lab rats to modify their behavior in order to avoid pain—and die en masse once one of them commits an act of violence (Sullivan n.d.). The stagist message of this storyline is clear: Neanderthals are depicted as inherently violent savages who must be treated like wild animals and domesticated in order to be allowed to co-exist with the civilized and advanced Terundans. While this serial was never realized, there have been a number of interactions in both televised episodes and published stories between the Doctor and Neanderthals, two circa 1990 and two in the early 21st century. These depictions are now explored in detail, situating them against both the historical evolution of our scientific understanding of Neanderthals and the works of speculative fiction discussed above.

Butlers and Sidekicks: Neanderthals in Doctor Who *Circa 1990*

The Doctor and Ace (Sophie Aldred) become embroiled in a complex Victorian mystery in the serial "Ghost Light" and its novelization (Platt 1990).[6] The evolution subplot of "Ghost Light" aligns well with the Social Darwinism/Eugenics plotlines central to many of the Dalek stories of the McCoy era and the series as a whole (Larsen 2013b). Also central to this serial is the "renegotiation" of English identity during the Victorian Era, especially "through the impact of multiculturalism" (Harmes 2013, 200). The pro- and anti-evolutionary sides of 1883 England are represented by the scientist Josiah Samuel Smith (Ian Hogg), the current lord of the mansion Gabriel Chase, and the Reverend Ernest Matthews (John Nettleton), respectively. But not all in Gabriel Chase is as it superficially appears. The Seventh Doctor and Ace materialize in a child's playroom turned laboratory in the mansion, where the inappropriately dressed (for 1883) Ace is considered barbaric and uncivilized, in stark contrast with Nimrod (Carl Forgione), the well-mannered butler, who is, surprisingly, a Neanderthal. As described in the novelization, "His shoulders were hunched and his long arms dangled at his sides. A course mass of brown hair surrounded his monkeyish face with its flattened nose and protruding jaw. The bright, brown eyes were set beneath a broad bony ridge across the forehead" (Platt 1990, 40). Note the use of the hirsute Neanderthal trope and the incorrect depiction of the Neanderthal as having a jutting chin. The television version of Nimrod is fitted with the proper prosthetics and makeup to appear as a Neanderthal from the neck up, as well as fitted with thick hair on the backs of his hands. Walking with visibly stooped shoulders in a slightly shuffling gait, Nimrod appears very much the stereotype of the Boule era Neanderthal. However, his heavy mutton chops are an exact fit with the fashion of the day, ironically mirroring those of the evolution-denying reverend.

In addition, Nimrod's manners and ability to use language are identical to the modern humans around him. Ironically, Nimrod terms the prisoner in Josiah's basement a "poor silent brute" (Platt 1990, 62), however over the course of the episode the female character Control (Sharon Duce)–representing the constant, unchanging part of an experiment—evolves into a fine Victorian lady. It is revealed that Josiah is the other piece of that experiment, and has evolved at a dramatically accelerated rate from lower forms of life into a Victorian gentleman. Once "Light" (John Hallam), the angelic appearing alien whose spacecraft sits beneath the mansion and in whose grand experiment Josiah and Control are merely parameters, is released from his stasis, the nature of the grand experiment is explained. Light's mission is to survey and catalogue life on various planets, but he finds Earth to be a particular challenge due to the propensity of life here to evolve and change. Nimrod is revealed to be the "last specimen of the extinct Neanderthal race," collected by Light as part of his survey. He is particularly appreciated by Light, because his species "knew when to stop evolving" (*ibid.*, 137). However, in Darwinian terms, to stop evolving is to risk becoming extinct. It also highlights the prejudice found in this story; whereas Control and Josiah can rise to the Victorian aristocracy, Nimrod is forever relegated to the role of brutish butler despite his refined manners and wardrobe.

Fortunately, Nimrod is treated with the respect by the Doctor and Ace (despite the fact that she gives him the affectionate yet stereotypical nickname Tarzan), who both understand that while Nimrod is a Neanderthal, he is also a human being. In contrast, he is treated as merely a servant (or worse) by the other characters, relegating him to a subhuman class not for his species, but rather his perceived socio-economic/racial position. For example, Inspector Mackenzie (Frank Windsor) describes Nimrod as a "nasty looking customer. Must be a foreigner," which the Doctor calmly corrects, "Neanderthal." Displaying his own lack of intelligence by misunderstanding the reference, Mackenzie adds, "Ah, gypsy blood. I can see it in him. Lazy workers…. No self-control, these Mediterraneans. Too excitable. Nasty tempers, too" ("Ghost Light," episode two).

The novelization explores Nimrod's internal thought process on several occasions, in ways the broadcast episodes cannot, the most interesting centering on his views of both the Victorian Era and his positioning in time: "Nimrod had learned the lore of language and etiquette and subservience … [b]ut there were older memories that he could not forget, lore that few people of this age remembered. No one here listened to the wilderness of the words and the waters. Their thoughts were turned in on themselves…. In this place, time flowed faster than in the old wild world, even though the sun still travelled the same course…. Nimrod would be the stationary point which events moved around. He would watch as he always had watched and listened, because he would then have new tales to tell" (Platt 1990, 47–48). Nimrod therefore situates himself as similar to a fixed point in time (to use the vernacular of *Doctor Who*), who believes he does not evolve in any meaningful way despite the trappings of modern culture that have been thrust upon him. However, Ace understand that he has, indeed, evolved in some respects. For example, she marvels at Nimrod's use of modern oil paints to construct Paleolithic paintings that are "more refined" in technique than the original (*ibid.*, 74).

Nimrod's internal thoughts in the novelization also focus on his religious beliefs. He believes Light to be the manifestation of his tribe's deity, a fire god named the Burning One. While Nimrod appears to blindly follow Light in the televised serial until near the end, in the novelization it is clear that Nimrod is engaging in higher order thought throughout the adventure, as he weighs the wisdom of following the tradition of his tribe and obeying Light versus evolving (in the stagist sense of moving beyond what are viewed as the superstitions of his previous life) and placing his trust in the Doctor (Platt 1990, 47–48). The Doctor gains this trust through his knowledge of and sensitivity to Neanderthal customs. First, he gives Nimrod a cave bear tooth, which Nimrod accepts with reverence and awe, explaining in the televised version "The fang of a cave bear! A totem of great power" ("Ghost Light," episode one); in the novelization it is termed "a totem of great power bestowed only by the greatest elders of my tribe," which Josiah derides as "Primitive fiddle-faddle" (Platt 1990, 46). The supposed cave bear cult of Neanderthals previously described is clearly referenced here as a second example of Neanderthal religious belief. In the novelization it is also revealed that Nimrod had been his people's storyteller, keeper of the memories of his tribe. His internal thoughts reveal that he is able to deal with the abstraction of memories and the concept of keeping someone alive through them: "His family, his people and his world were long dead. They lived only in his thoughts now. If he lost their memory, they were gone for ever" (*ibid.*, 108). Another instance of cultural sensitivity is shown by the Doctor when Nimrod gives his word to the Time Lord that the insane explorer Redvers Fenn-Cooper (Michael Cochrane) is being properly cared for. The Doctor gives the culturally appropriate response, "Only the madmen may see the path clearly through the tangled forest" ("Ghost Light," episode one).

In addition, the euphemistic use of the term "going to Java" within the serial to denote a person being drugged and becoming part of the mansion's exotic zoo (or worse) is more than just a nod to a distant, exotic travel destination in the Victorian Era. In 1891 another important human fossil, the so-called "Java Man," *Pithecanthropus erectus* (later *Homo erectus*), was discovered in Java by Eugène Dubois. This discovery played a pivotal role in the reconstruction of human evolution, as it was quickly ascertained that this fossil represented an earlier (and clearly more primitive) human form than the Neanderthal. The scientific debate over the correct Linnaean classification for Neanderthals is also played with in the story, as Josiah ridicules the Doctor and Matthews in the novelization as "sub-species in the genus *Homo Victorianus*" (Platt 1990, 49). More specifically, when Josiah "devolves" Matthews into an apelike creature and puts him into stasis (essentially turning him into a diorama in a natural history museum) the caption *Homo Victorianus Ineptus* is appended to his exhibit (*ibid.*, 116).

In the 1991 novel *Timewyrm: Genesys*, author John Peel interweaves mythology and history as the Doctor and Ace travel to ancient Mesopotamia not long after the events of "Ghost Light" and meet another Neanderthal out of his native time–Enkidu, the legendary companion of the equally legendary King Gilgamesh. While the tale itself is interesting in its interweaving of Mesopotamian politics and religion with alien aggression (for example, the alien masquerades as the goddess Ishtar), only the Neanderthal subplot will be discussed here.

Enkidu's identity as a Neanderthal is established early in the novel: "Enkidu took a little getting used to.... He was tall, brooding and muscular, but hardly from the same stock as Gilgamesh and his men. Instead of the long, oiled beards of the men of Uruk, Enkidu had long, dark hair all over the exposed portions of his body. The bony ridges above his eyes projected forwards, his chin jutted out equally savagely ... a prime specimen of a Neanderthal Man, supposedly long-dead by this point in history" (Peel 1991, 43). In keeping with the characterization of Nimrod, Peel also incorrectly includes

a jutting chin and utilizes the hairy stereotype, but in this case, with mythological precedent, as the literary version's "whole body was covered thickly
with hair" (Gardner and Maier 1985, 68). Enkidu, the Wild Man of Mesopotamian legend, also has to be taught how to eat and drink like a civilized
man. Indeed, other individuals besides Peel have pondered the possibility
that the mythological character could represent someone of Neanderthal
ancestry (e.g., Sanderson 1967).

Throughout the story, Enkidu's otherness is highlighted by the author
through the use of designators such as "the Neanderthal" (Peel 1991, 187),
"the Neanderthal soldier" (*ibid.*, 183), and "the ape-man" (*ibid.*, 182). En-Gula,
the acolyte to Ishtar, muses to herself that Enkidu and the Doctor are "a hairy
half-human creature and a strange madman" (*ibid.*, 163). Agga, the king of
Kish, derides Enkidu as "the ape-man that moves at Gilgamesh's behest" (*ibid.*,
158), while one of the king's soldiers refers to Enkidu as "the ape" (*ibid.*, 48).
Similarly, when Enkidu's cloak falls aside in a drinking establishment, one of
the patrons exclaims "Look at that fur! … Only one person looks like that—
the monkey-man that Gilgamesh of Uruk keeps as his pet!" (*ibid.*, 96). Gilgamesh affectionately refers to his friend as "you hairy monster" (*ibid.*, 136),
but it is not established whether or not Enkidu finds this as humorous as his
king.

As in the case of Nimrod, Enkidu is clearly intelligent and capable of
symbolic and abstract thought. He is wary of strangers and rash actions, and
waxes philosophical when discussing their imprisonment with the Doctor,
warning, "Do as I shall: get rest while you can. Who knows when we shall
need our strength" (Peel 1991, 163). Peel explains to the reader, "For all of his
apparent similarity to an ape, Enkidu had a keen brain," and the Doctor com-
pliments Enkidu by exclaiming, "I've always been impressed by the reasoning
powers of the Neanderthaler. Met one of your relatives a few thousand years
from now who was pretty bright, too," a reference to Nimrod (*ibid.*, 145).
Enkidu is comforted to learn of Nimrod's existence, lamenting (as Nimrod
does), "After me, my race is gone forever from the Earth…. My people will
never be remembered" (*ibid.*, 164). In the end, it is made quite clear that
Enkidu is far more thoughtful and wise than the "lout" Gilgamesh (*ibid.*,
218). Enkidu explains to Ace that his "ideas are strange, I warn you. I think
that Uruk and Kish would get along better if they were allies, rather than
enemies. When I was a child, my mother told me that the reason my people
died out is that we could not co-operate; these hairless humans took advantage of that folly, and managed to destroy my race. I've always been afraid
that the same thing might happen to all humans one day" (*ibid.*, 71). Note
that Enkidu considers himself to *be* "human." It is interesting to consider
how Enkidu's family survived to present day, despite the fact that they deemed
their kind to be "extinct." Where, then, did his parents meet? Is there merely

a tiny breeding population existing within the larger human world? Was there dramatic inbreeding among the surviving population? This is never explained within the story.

There is also a reference to the potential of interbreeding between Neanderthals and Cro-Magnons. Enkidu apologizes to Ace for his appearance, but she assures him that she was merely musing how he resembles an "old mate" of hers. Enkidu misunderstands, and assumes that she had taken "one of my kind as a lover once in the past," to which she explains that she is merely referring to a friend (Peel 1991, 58). Enkidu is relieved that Ace does not find him "repulsive"; on the contrary, Ace explains, "Compared to some people I've met, you're positively gorgeous." She muses to herself that Enkidu is a "regular guy," in contrast with Gilgamesh, "a right royal pain in the arse" (*ibid.*). Therefore, both of the Seventh Doctor's adventures with Neanderthals consistently paint them as intelligent and decidedly human, a refreshing exception from the program's usual stagist perspective.

Neanderthal Evolution and Extinction in 21st-Century Doctor Who

The unanswered question of Neanderthal extinction plays a pivotal role in the 2004 Fifth Doctor short story "Observation." Penned by Ian Farrington for the 2004 anthology *Short Trips: Life Science,* the story is told through the eyes of the companion Turlough (Mark Strickson). The Doctor decides to spend six months camped out on 40,000 BC Earth monitoring the very first interaction between Neanderthals and modern humans, in order to discover what really happened: "Did they fight? Mate? Co-inhabit? Develop tools? Were the Neanderthals instrumental in the development of Humanity? Or were they, as some have argued, more of an evolutionary cul-de-sac—wiped out by the Cro-Magnons, or by something else?" (Farrington 2004, 62). The impatient redhead takes the TARDIS six months into the future, returning to find a disturbed Time Lord and a dead Neanderthal.

Upon reading the Doctor's journal entry, Turlough discovers that, although the two human subspecies passed a short geographical distance from each other, they had not seen each other during his six-month absence. Despite his efforts to remain hidden from both groups, the Doctor had been spotted by a Neanderthal approaching from the opposite direction, who had subsequently fallen to his death. Turlough notes another Neanderthal first spying on him and the corpse from a higher elevation, then running away, leading the companion to hypothesize that the Neanderthals may consider the Doctor—and hence modern humanoids—to be a threat. With the Cro-Magnons and Neanderthals now approaching from different directions,

Turlough realizes that the Doctor's presence in that space-time coordinate has possibly caused the very event that he hopes to observe. If that is the case, is the Doctor then responsible for a prehistoric genocide? There are two particular points of interest to note in this tale. The first is that the physicality of the two groups of humans is never described. The Cro-Magnons are merely called "humanoids" and Turlough identifies them as "human" when viewing them through binoculars (Farrington 2004, 61). The second is that while the Doctor refers to both groups as "proto-human species" (Farrington 2004, 62)—thus placing them on equal footing—Turlough clearly distinguishes between them, describing the Neanderthals as "creatures" (*ibid.*, 66).

A converse point of view is espoused by Rose Tyler (Billie Piper) in the Ninth Doctor novel *Only Human*, a work that examines human evolution through the lens of the extraterrestrial Doctor, as well as reflects the heavy emphasis placed on mortality in the Eccleston and Tennant years (Larsen 2013a). Due to the decidedly unethical experiments of a time traveling mad scientist, Chantal Osterberg, a member of the genetically perfected human species born some 400,000 years in the future, the Neanderthal Das is sent back to present-day England. He is described as "short" with heavy features, including "an enormous nose, seemingly flattened out at the edges, a huge lumpy brow and thick bushy eyebrows" (Roberts 2005, 34). In addition, Das's body is "covered in coarse, thick hair" (again, the hirsute stereotype) and "his body went straight from stomach to groin," a nod to the different chest shape of the Neanderthal (*ibid.*, 27). When Rose tentatively dubs him "Not a human," the Doctor counters "Depends on your definition" (*ibid.*, 34). Das is brought to the TARDIS, where he is able to communicate in English thanks to the Universal Translator. Rose is surprised when Das reasons that he is now in the future, "A time to come," with the Neanderthal retorting "You think I'm stupid…. Your lot always think we're stupid" (*ibid.*, 42). The storyline bifurcates at this point, with the Doctor and Rose Tyler taking the TARDIS back to the England of 26,185 BC to investigate how Das came to be transported to the 21st century, while Captain Jack Harkness (John Barrowman) is tasked with acclimating Das to his new environment, as the Neanderthal cannot be sent back into the past without killing him during the dematerialization process.

In the prehistoric storyline, the Neanderthals are depicted as possessing a well-defined culture and spoken language and are far more humane than either the genetically engineered humans of the Osterberg Corporation (who claim to have travelled back into the past in order to learn how the Neanderthals became extinct) or the Cro-Magnon tribe known as the "Family" with whom the Neanderthals are in direct competition. While both the Neanderthals and Cro-Magnons refer to each other as "Them," only the Cro-Magnons are warlike. They justify their aggression by describing the Neanderthals as "not normal," uncomfortably reminding Rose of the "casual racism of some of her own grandmother's friends back home" (Roberts 2005, 150–151). Rose is also distressed to learn from the Doctor that the peaceful Neanderthals—people who are "just like us"—are doomed to soon die out at the hands of the Cro-Magnons (*ibid.*, 45). Not only do the Doctor and Rose save both humanoid groups from the machinations of Osterberg and her genetically engineered "superhuman" predators, the Hy-Bractors—what Osterberg calls an "upgrade of the human race" (*ibid.*, 214)—but a truce is brokered between the local groups of humanoids, through the marriage of the future human, Quilley, to one of the female Cro-Magnon elders, Nan. Quilley requests of his new bride that the remaining Neanderthals be welcomed into the Family, and it is possible that there might have been children created as the result of Neanderthal/Cro-Magnon unions within this hybrid human group.[7]

One of the most interesting tensions in the story is over the definition of "human." Specifically, Osterberg views all "natural" humans (all those who do not embrace genetic and chemical engineering) as backward and inferior brutes, in contrast to her Hy-Bractors. By this definition, there is no difference between Neanderthals, Cro-Magnons, and modern humans such as Rose. Indeed, since members of all three of these groups peaceably co-exist as members of the Family in the end, they come to learn that they indeed have far more in common with each other than their initial stagist view of each other suggested.

The storyline of Jack and Das's adventures in the 21st century are recounted in a series of journal entries from each man's perspective. Just as Leela's arc was meant to mimic the tale of Pygmalion as reflected in *My Fair Lady* (Orthia 2013, 281), Das initially plays the role of Eliza Doolittle to Jack's Professor Higgins. While Jack originally describes Das as perhaps "covered in fleas, but he's just another human" (Roberts 2005, 30), his journal entries highlight the differences between Das and an anatomically and culturally modern human. While his posts are written in a humorous tone, they represent a clearly stagist point of view and hence they paint the usually accepting Jack in a rather prejudicial, and hence negative, light. For example, Jack enjoys modernizing Das, despite the fact that he "isn't quite a human," explaining that while the Neanderthal is capable of learning how to read, write and handle math "thanks to the TARDIS," some subtleties of human behavior and language prove difficult for Das, including humor, irony, sarcasm, innuendo, and fiction, including lying, similar to the Neanderthals of Auel's novel (*ibid.*, 90–91).

For his part, Das's viewpoint provides an interesting lens through which to view 21st century English culture, and begs the question as to which of the two men is actually the most astute. While for the most part Das appreciates this century, he believes "cutlery ranks with socks as one of the most pointless things made by humans" (Roberts 2005, 113). He also deems the way humans "rush and jump about all the time" to be unattractive, and refers to Jack's enjoyment of "danger and fighting" as "stupid" (*ibid.*, 114; 235). He also calls modern humans "idiots" for having difficulty understanding one of the basic tenets of quantum mechanics, "that a thing changes when you're looking at it, which is obvious" (*ibid.*, 177).

Das meets and marries Anna Marie O'Grady, whom Das finds very beautiful, the opposite of his "hideous—thin as a stick" sister-in-law (*ibid.*, 235). Jack and Anna Marie's family consider her to be quite homely, Jack noting if "there is any trace of Neanderthal genes left in the human race, well, he found it all right," as she had a "face only a mother or a Neanderthal could love," again, a reference to the concept of mate-recognition (*ibid.*, 235–236). Das is thrilled with the prospect of having children with his new wife, adding "Jack says this will be possible" (*ibid.*, 236). In fact, the possibility of offspring brings the Doctor satisfaction, knowing that "through Das, just a piece of that strange world would live on" (*ibid.*, 250). This particular aspect of the plot is especially interesting given the pessimistic scientific viewpoint concerning interbreeding circa 2005.

It is interesting to note that Jack's efforts to clean up Das and turn him into a modern man are reminiscent of a famous 1939 illustration by anthropologist Carleton Coon of a Neanderthal for his book *The Races of Europe*. To bolster his argument that fashion such as wardrobe and haircut accentuate external differences between groups of humans, Coon sketched a clean-shaven Neanderthal dressed in typical businessman attire of the day. The facial features are distinctively Neanderthal, "heavy-jawed, crude-faced, but by no means more brutish than men met every day in any civilized country" (Trinkaus and Shipman 1993, 403–405). In this viewpoint, you can both take the Neanderthal out of the Paleolithic, and, to some extent, the Paleolithic out of the Neanderthal, supporting the viewpoint that they are just a slightly different form of ourselves. In the end, the fundamental question therefore becomes, "By what criteria do we adjudge ourselves and others to be human?" (Graves 1991, 513).

Conclusion

Trinkaus and Shipman (1993, 409) note of the controversial history of our interpretation of the geologic record, "Neanderthals were the mirror-like fossils to which everyone looked for evidence of human nature—and found it. What they have revealed, more than their own lives, is the lives of those who have gazed at them and pronounced. It has been, for humans, a journey of revelation and self-discovery, an exercise in ogling the fun-house mirror."

They further explain that "each generation projects onto Neanderthals its own fears, culture, and sometimes even personal history. They are a mute repository for our own nature, though we flatter ourselves that we are uncovering theirs rather than displaying ours" (*ibid.*, 399). Such is their ultimate role in the universe of *Doctor Who*, to force us to contemplate human savagery, not of Neanderthals, but of so-called modern humans.

At the end of *Only Human*, Quilley muses of his request that the Neanderthals be welcome into the Cro-Magnon tribe, "He couldn't change history. But he could help make this small part of it more civilized—more *humane*" (Roberts 2005, 251). While this sentiment, and Captain Jack Harkness's attempts to civilize Das (un)comfortably fit with Lindy Orthia's (2013, 272) accusations of blatant stagism, the Seventh Doctor's (as well as Ace's and Rose's) acceptance of Neanderthals as more human—more *humane*—than our own *Homo sapiens sapiens*, and respectful embracing of Neanderthal culture, provide welcome counterpoints.

In terms of their behavior, "Neanderthals have vacillated—in scientists' views—from brutish, glowering fiends to a religious, gentle, and caring family members and back again. Where does the truth lie?" (Trinkaus and Shipman 1993, 399). Clearly in the universe of *Doctor Who*, the truth appears to be that we *are* Neanderthals, and Neanderthals *are* us. In the words of the Ninth Doctor (espousing his typical stagist viewpoint of humanity as hopelessly primitive in relation to his superior Timelord abilities), the average human is merely a "stupid ape blundering on top of this planet" ("Rose," 2005). We are "brilliant, terrible, generous, cruel" but "never boring" (Roberts 2005, 202). In the end, perhaps that will serve as a fitting epitaph for our species at the end of *our* history, when evolution inevitably relegates us to the fossil record.

NOTES

1. There are two alternate spellings, Neanderthal (which will be used in this essay, except in relevant quotations) and Neandertal.

2. This essay will use the terms Cro-Magnon, *Homo sapiens sapiens*, anatomically modern human, and modern human synonymously, in the biological sense.

3. In addition, the Tenth Doctor (David Tennant) meets Neanderthals briefly in the four-page comic story *Snow Globe* (2010).

4. The entire series of commercials can be found at https://www.youtube.com/watch?v=x8o_YqzMBoo.

5. For more information on the changing interpretations of Neanderthal characteristics, see Trinkaus and Shipman (1993) and Drell (2000).

6. For consistency, dialogue will be cited from the novelization in cases where it is identical with the aired episode; dialogue found only in the novelization will be clearly noted as such.

7. There is also a romance in the story between a future human, Reddy, and a Nean-

derthal, Ka, but it is presumed that they are killed in an attack by the Cro-Magnons on the Neanderthals.

BIBLIOGRAPHY

Alterman, Peter S. 1978. "Aliens in Golding's *The Inheritors.*" *Science Fiction Studies* 5, no. 1: 3–10.
Angier, Natalie. December 22, 2008. "A Highly Evolved Propensity for Deceit." *New York Times.* Available at http://www.nytimes.com/2008/12/23/science/23angi.html?_r=0. Accessed April 10 2016.
Asimov, Isaac. 1959. *Nine Tomorrows.* Greenwich: Fawcett Publications.
Auel, Jean M. 2011. *The Clan of the Cave Bear.* New York: Bantam Books.
Berman, Judith C. 1999. "Bad Hair Days in the Paleolithic: Modern (Re)Constructions of the Cave Man." *American Anthropologist* 101, no. 2: 288–304.
Currat, M., and L. Excoffier. 2004. "Modern Humans Did Not Admix With Neanderthals During Their Range Expansion Into Europe." *PLOS Biology* 2, no. 12: e421.
DePaolo, Charles. 2000. "Wells, Golding, and Auel: Representing the Neanderthal." *Science Fiction Studies* 27, no. 3: 418–438.
Drell, Julia R.R. 2000. "Neanderthals: A History of Interpretation." *Oxford Journal of Archaeology* 19, no. 1: 1–24.
Duarte, Cidália, et al. 1999. "The Early Upper Paleolithic Human Skeleton from the Abrigo Do Lagar Velho (Portugal) and Modern Human Emergence in Iberia." *Proceedings of the National Academy of Sciences* 96: 7604–7609.
Farrington, Ian. 2004. "Observation" in *Short Trips: Life Science*, edited by John Binns. Maidenhead: Big Finish Productions. pp. 61–66.
Gardner, John, and John Maier. 1985. *Gilgamesh.* New York: Random House.
Gibbons, Ann. 2014. "Neandertals and Moderns Made Imperfect Mates." *Science* 343: 471–472.
Graves, Paul. 1991. "New Models and Metaphors for the Neanderthal Debate." *Current Anthropology* 32: 513–541.
Green, Richard E., et al. 2010. "A Draft Sequence of the Neanderthal Genome." *Science* 328: 710–722.
Hamilton, Anne. 2005. "Popular Depictions of Neanderthals." *Totem* 13, no. 1: 85–92.
Harmes, Marcus K. 2013. "Religion, Racism and the Church of England in *Doctor Who*" in *Doctor Who and Race*, edited by Lindy Orthia. Bristol: Intellect. pp. 199–212.
Harvati, Katerina. 2010. "Neanderthals." *Evolution Education and Research.* doi: 10.1007/S12052-010-0250-0. Accessed April 10, 2016.
Larsen, Kristine. 2013a. "Everything Dies: The Message of Mortality in the Eccleston and Tennant Years" in *Doctor Who in Time and Space*, edited by Gillian I. Leitch. Jefferson, NC: McFarland. pp. 157–174.
Larsen, Kristine. 2013b. "They Hate Each Other's Chromosomes: Eugenics and the Shifting Racial Identity of the Daleks" in *Doctor Who and Race*, edited by Lindy Orthia. Bristol: Intellect. pp. 235–250.
Mellars, Paul. 1996. *The Neanderthal Legacy.* Princeton: Princeton University Press.
Noonan, James P., et al. 2006. "Sequencing and Analysis of Neanderthal Genomic DNA." *Science* 314: 1113–1118.
Orthia, Lindy A. 2013. "Savages, Science, Stagism and the Naturalized Ascendency of the Not-e in *Doctor Who.*" In *Doctor Who and Race*, edited by Lindy Orthia. Bristol: Intellect. pp. 271–287.
Peel, John. 1991. *Timewyrm: Genesys.* London: Doctor Who Books.
Platt, Marc. 1990. *Doctor Who Ghost Light.* London: Target.
Roberts, Gareth. 2005. *Only Human.* London: BBC Books.
Sanderson, Ivan. 1967. *Things.* New York: Pyramid Books.
Sankararaman, Sriram, et al. 2014. "The Genomic Landscape of Neanderthal Ancestry in Present-Day Humans." *Nature* 507: 354–357.
Shreeve, James. 1995. *The Neandertal Enigma.* New York: William Morrow.

Smith, Kerri. 2007. "Modern Speech Gene Found in Neanderthals." *Nature*. doi:10.1038/news. 2007.177. Accessed April 10, 2016.

Sullivan, Shannon. n.d. "The Return of the Neanderthal." *Doctor Who: The Lost Stories*. Available at http://www.shannonsullivan.com/doctorwho/lostrz.html. Accessed April 10, 2016.

Tattersall, Ian. 1995. *The Last Neanderthal*. New York: Macmillan.

Trinkaus, Erik, and Pat Shipman. 1993. *The Neandertals*. New York: Alfred A. Knopf.

Wells, H.G. 2008. *The Grisly Folk and the Wild Asses of the Devil*. Gloucester: Dodo Press.

White, Michael. 2015. "How Our Understanding of Neanderthals Has Dramatically—and Rapidly—Shifted." *Pacific Standard*. Available at https://psmag.com/how-our-understanding-of-neanderthals-has-dramatically-and-rapidly-shifted-d20531ec369b#.vm0azowpl. Accessed April 10, 2016.

Wilford, John Noble. 1999. "Discovery Suggests Man Is a Bit Neanderthal." *New York Times*. Available at http://www.nytimes.com/1999/04/25/us/discovery-suggests-man-is-a-bit-neanderthal.html. Accessed April 10, 2016.

Wong, Kate. 2015. "Neandertal Minds." *Scientific American* 312, no. 2: 36–43.

The Dark Heart of the Village

Doctor Who *in the 1970s and the Problematic Idyll*

PETER LOWE

> "Come along Jo," said the Doctor brightly. "We've arrived."
> Jo yawned. "Culverton?"
> "Culverton." He glanced round again at the serene village, still bathed in the rosy glow of sunset.
> "Seems quiet enough."
> —Mark Gatiss, *Last of the Gaderene*

> It was useless for the Doctor to struggle as he was bound to the Maypole.—Barry Letts, "The Daemons"

The image of the Doctor, a man responsible for saving many planets and cultures, taken prisoner at that most English of village focal points—a Maypole—calls into question the role that such symbols of national and cultural identity were to play in the program's 1970s incarnation. Rather than represent what was enduring and secure, its writers used the idyllic English village as a location where surface tranquility masked hidden dangers. Indeed, the more serene the village looked, the greater the likelihood that it was already in the hands of a malevolent force. This re-purposing of the village motif was, to a large extent, made possible by the values inscribed into the location (and readily understood by *Doctor Who*'s British audience) by the propaganda of the Second World War, when England's villages had been invoked as the purest and best embodiments of the way of life that was most at risk from Nazi tyranny and, as such, most in need of defense. If an English village were to fall into the hands of Hitler's forces, Government propaganda of the early 1940s had made clear, it would be more than a loss of territory; it would be a loss of some part of the nation's soul. Twenty-five years after the end of the War, this village idyll became, in the world of *Doctor Who*, the most dangerous place imaginable. The difference, as this essay explores, is that in adventures like "The Daemons" (1971), "The Android Invasion" (1975), and the "Third Doctor" novel *Last of the Gaderene* (2000) what is at stake in the battle for the English village is not just the fate of a country, but of the planet itself. As Britain struggled to come to terms with the shifting global politics of the post–World War II order, *Doctor Who* invoked the idea of the threatened village in order to explore themes of invasion and conquest far beyond the scope of the German plans of 1940. In doing so, the series also articulated wider concerns about how accurate that wartime propaganda had really ever been, and whether Britain had become a place in which time-honored locations and figures of cultural authority were actually those least worthy of the public's trust. Nostalgia for "village life" may triumph at the end of each adventure, but in the 1970s *Doctor Who* made sure it had been given a thorough interrogation first.

"Your Britain": World War II and the 1970s

At a time when news reports carried a prevailing sense of the nation's political, economic, and social stagnation alongside anxieties about its declining global role, it seemed in its television schedules that Britain was regularly under threat in the early 1970s. On Friday evenings, at least, viewers could be assured that the men of the Walmington-on-Sea Home Guard would do their bit to see to it that Nazi ambitions went unfulfilled. The heroes of Captain Mainwaring's platoon in the BBC comedy series *Dad's Army* (1968–1977) were hugely popular figures in the national culture, and have gone on to generate in the past 40 or so years a following akin to that of another defender against implacable enemies, who provides this volume with its subject. Like *Dad's Army*, *Doctor Who* was a program happy to draw upon established motifs in its adventures, and the sense of an embattled Home Front pervades many of the adventures of the Third Doctor (Jon Pertwee) who put in his shift in inter-planetary defense work in an early evening slot on Saturdays.

Looking back from the insecurities of the early 1970s to Britain's more easily celebrated "finest hour," *Dad's Army* offered a light-hearted way of enjoying the Second World War in the knowledge that with the attendant fear of Nazi invasion safely in the past the rhetoric and symbolism of the period could be turned to comic effect. As has been noted, its "class consciousness, cultural conservatism [and] deep sense of nostalgia" (Sandbrook 2007, 793) proved reassuring amongst an audience comprising both those who had experienced the War firsthand and those born afterwards, enjoying vicariously the humor of Britain's often surreal War effort. The very real and pressing anxieties of the summer of 1940 and its aftermath were replaced by the "Don't panic!" catchphrase of Clive Dunn's Corporal Jones.

In an earlier period, when the prospect of a Nazi invasion was actually discussed more in terms of its likely date than its likelihood, it had been deemed necessary to remind the populace of exactly what was at stake if Britain were to find itself in a fight for its survival on home ground. In 1942 the artist Frank Newbould was commissioned by the Army Bureau of Current Affairs to supply images for a series of propaganda posters linked through the slogan "Your Britain: Fight for It Now." One of these images shows Salisbury Cathedral, framed by trees while another, entitled "South Downs," takes the viewer to Sussex, where a shepherd and his flock make their way homeward to a farm set in a valley. No indication of modernity is visible in these images: instead, as Sir Roy Strong has noted, such visions of England root ideas of national identity in forms that are "of course patriotic, [but] also peaceful, romantic, and tranquil" (Strong 2011, 147). Newbould's posters made Britain a land where timeless ways of life endured in time-honored surroundings: the very things that would be lost if an invading army were to violate such spaces.

The other two images in the series make this point perfectly. In "Oak Tree" we see the tree in question dominating the image, its size suggestive of its age and endurance. Underneath it, cyclists enjoy a rest and picnic in the shade, and ducks paddle in a small pond. Behind the tree we can make out the buildings of a village green, and in the right of the image a church is visible (the flag of St George flying from its tower) and to the right of the church there is the village pub, in front of which two figures can be seen enjoying the good weather and, presumably, a beer as well. Such a composite image fits with the idea of "Deep England" proposed by Patrick Wright as a reference point for notions of national identity: the symbol of a way of life captured in buildings that suggest continuity in the midst of change (Wright 1985, 81). These thoughts recur in the final image in the series, where the village was identified as Alfriston (in East Sussex) and the village green was depicted playing host to the annual fair. The trees and the spire of the church are clearly visible in the background, but in this case we focus more on the swing-boats and carousels in which the residents are enjoying the fine summer afternoon, the weather in an idealized Britain being uniformly (and perhaps unrealistically) pleasant. In the foreground a woman laughs as she holds balloons for sale, whilst on the right of the picture a woman in red dances energetically with a man in a dark grey suit as an accordionist plays. The contrast with contemporary images of life in Nazi Germany, with its manufactured "celebrations" of support for the regime, could hardly be more pronounced. Here, Alfriston Fair *is* England, and in much of the propaganda of the time England, and particularly the South-East of England, was itself being used as a synecdoche for "Britain." Fight for it, the posters urged, or see it lost.

Whether people in other parts of Britain would have felt quite so attached to a village fair in Sussex was, in the context of the time, not an issue. Villages like Alfriston functioned symbolically, their power reliant, as Jed Esty has argued, upon the viewer "seeing national life as something utterly familiar and knowable, yet also charmed" (Esty 2004, 80). In a time when vulnerability was interwoven with value, many people needed little persuasion to make this interpretative link. Two years before Newbould's posters these thoughts had been articulated in the magazine *Picture Post* when the 13 July 1940 issue was published under the title "What We Are Fighting For." Unsurprisingly, the village, as a location and a symbol, featured heavily in the magazine's pages. One view of an English village, in which a shepherd drives his sheep through the empty street past the church, is reproduced with the title "Sunday Afternoon in England: All Is Peace" (Anon. 1940, 10) On the opposite page the caption "Sunday Afternoon in Germany: All is Peace" (Anon. 1940, 11) shows massed ranks of *Sturmabteilung* (SA) men marching through the flag-lined streets as bystanders look on. Presented as they are on opposite pages, it is easy, for the reader looking back and forth between the images, to mentally place the marching men in the English village and, in doing so, to imagine a situation in which the German reality could swiftly become an English one.

The image of the picturesque village recurs in several *Doctor Who* adventures, but rather than stand as a symbol of stability these stories rely upon a disturbing lack of connection between the surface appearance and the reality beneath. In his study of "Englishness" as a social construction David Matless has read the village as standing, in British culture of the 1930s and 1940s "for community and harmonious class coexistence under benevolent authority" (Matless 1998, 125). As if to explore the darker possibilities that such a view excludes, however, in both "The Daemons" and "The Android Invasion" we see the superficially tranquil village as a site already taken over by an invasive alien presence.

Such village adventures fit with *Doctor Who*'s change of "location" in the 1970s, as more Earth-based stories were required after the Doctor (Patrick Troughton)'s banishment to the planet as a punishment at the close of 1969's "The War Games." Jon Pertwee's Third Doctor was mostly occupied not in travelling the galaxy, but in defending Earth from the dangers that would come to visit it, like a cosmic Home Guard standing firm against a host of threats from "abroad." In this he would work with the forces of the United Nations Intelligence Taskforce (UNIT) under the command of Brigadier

Alistair Gordon Lethbridge-Stewart (Nicholas Courtney), a man whose military thinking exasperated the Doctor but whose access to weaponry often came in useful in a crisis and whose reserves of available personnel meant that there were always soldiers on hand to be killed by invading aliens. Tellingly, if the Doctor and UNIT provided Earth with its Home Guard, then many of the Third Doctor adventures also made use of another banished Time Lord, the Master (Roger Delgado). As a character, the Master stood in as a "fifth column" already on the planet and looking to subvert its defense and leave it vulnerable to invasion from outside (as in 1971's "The Daemons") or by those creatures latent within (as in 1972's "The Sea Devils"). To gain control of an English village, however, the Master employs one of his most devious identities, working from inside the vicarage to bring the world to an end.

"The Daemons": Don't Trust the Vicar

"The Daemons" fits perfectly into the format of subverting the village from within, using the quaint English village of Devil's End (in reality Aldbourne in Wiltshire) to explore the evil behind the idyll. In the opening scene the viewer sees the village green in the midst of a thunderstorm, the church briefly illuminated by lightning as a figure reluctantly leaves the warmth of the village pub (The Cloven Hoof) before following his dog into the churchyard only to die "of fright" when confronted by an as yet unidentified presence there. This is not, we quickly appreciate, the peaceful space of Newbould's images. Playing with the idea of rural superstition conjured up in the village's name, "The Daemons," suggests that folk-tales of witchcraft and magic may originate in more terrifying realities.

Doctor Who had often balanced elements of fantasy and science-fiction in its storylines, but the Earth-bound adventures of the Third Doctor were seen by Barry Letts, who took over as the program's producer in 1970, as a means to probe deeper into the role that superstitions play in enabling people to process what could sometimes literally be *alien* concepts and experiences. In keeping with Letts' stated desire to "bring mythology back" into the program, "The Daemons" uses the village motif to represent community and to explore how such tightly-woven communal ties facilitate the Master's plans (Leach 2009, 33). In a story that echoes the earlier success of the BBC's *Quatermass and the Pit* (1958–1959) the Doctor finds that the mythology surrounding Devil's End frames a threat not only to the village but to the world. Whereas other adventures would draw on what John Tulloch and Manuel Alvarado describe as "the science-fiction discourse of the empirical present interrupted suddenly and fearfully attacked by alien invaders" "The Daemons" would also show how events of that nature in the past become, over time, woven into the mythologies that shape the village community, before breaking out again in the present as an example of "the 'sleepy villages and cities of England attacked by alien virus and war machine' syndrome" found in novels like H.G. Wells's *The War of the Worlds* (Tulloch and Alvarado 1983, 105).

As the Doctor and Jo Grant (Katy Manning) arrive, archaeologist Professor Horner (Robin Wentworth) is about to conclude an excavation of the ancient burial mound outside the village, convinced that there will be treasure within. Meanwhile, the vicar, Mr. Magister ("the Master" in Latin form) prepares to summon the Devil, or at least an alien being called a Daemon, whose reappearance throughout Earth's history has led to his being seen as *the* Devil, through a series of rites in the crypt of the church. When the mound is breached, fittingly late at night in an excavation broadcast live on television, we learn that the "burial mound" was, in fact, a buried spacecraft, and the "opening" of its hatch releases an energy burst that kills those in the immediate vicinity. The village is effectively overcome, then, by the superior weaponry of an invader—in this case one that has been dormant near the village for some time: something that is later manifested in the appearance of a heat barrier that surrounds Devil's End and makes exit or entry into the village impossible. With the massed UNIT troops watching from outside the village for most of the story, only the Doctor, Jo and UNIT officers Benton (John Levene) and Yates (Richard Franklin) can foil the scheme from inside. Fear abounds, as they are unsure, with the village under the Master's control, who can be trusted and who should be seen as an enemy. Outwardly tranquil as it remains, Devil's End becomes a location where appearances conceal darker truths, as though the picturesque village of Second World War propaganda was, unknown to the viewer, already packed with German agents, captured by the enemy without its capture having been noticed by the locals.

To reinforce this sense that superficial order, in the world of *Doctor Who*, is not to be trusted, one highly symbolic scene sees the Doctor trapped and taken prisoner in the course of that most English of rituals—a Morris dance. With the events of "The Daemons" playing out over April 30 and May 1 the "May Day" celebrations and dancing (performed in the program by the local group of Headington Quarry Morris Men) *could* be seen as the embodiment of the traditional way of life that the village space nurtures, were it not for the fact that the participants are being controlled by the Master's malevolence. To the modern viewer it may well be said that the sight of these dancers, with bells on their costumes and sticks with which to "hit" those of their peers, often carries a hint of menace, but as the Doctor finds himself surrounded by them the blows from the sticks become actual ones, and the ribbons that surround the village Maypole are used to wrap him like binding ropes.

In a village so inverted that Morris dancers can become agents for the controlling evil the usually reliable figure of the vicar can equally become a dark magician. Although the Master attempts to harness and direct the psycho-kinetic energy that is required to summon the Daemon, the creature is far more powerful than the Master imagines him to be, being in fact the last of a species of highly developed aliens studying humanity at close quarters, occasionally nudging its progress if they feel it requires "help." The Doctor's fear, on realizing what has been set in motion at Devil's End, is that the Daemon will, in the final analysis, prove beyond the Master's control, destroying the Earth like "any scientist [would] do with an experiment that fails" (Letts 1974, 85). Whereas the English village was once understood to be representative of the nation, the fate of Devil's End is, ultimately, destined to be the fate of the planet itself. Thus, in one of the show's most audacious special effects, "The Daemons" ends by blowing up the village church to save humanity. Shocking as this may appear, however, the idea of destroying the village to save it had actually already been woven into the rhetoric of Second World War defense that *Doctor Who* was creatively re-cycling in its village adventure.

The Cost of Resistance: "Saving" the Village by Destroying It

The placement of the Master as a parish vicar reminds the viewer of the centrality of the Church as both building and institution to the life of the English village. The 1935 book *Parish Churches of England*, published in the highly popular series of "English Heritage" titles by the firm of B.T. Batsford, spoke of the historical definition of "the parish" as "the community of a fixed area, organised for Church purposes and recognising as its communal and spiritual centre the church fabric" (Cox and Ford 1944, 2). Newbould made prominent use of churches in his propaganda art, and in the Second World War the distinction between British Christianity and the subversion of the religious impulse into the secular religion of Nazism was central to Britain's idea of itself as superior to its would-be-conqueror and engaged in the defense not only of its land but of the values that were encoded into its religious life. That the ringing of church bells had been designated the best way of alerting the populace to an invasion attempt in progress only cemented this link more completely in the national consciousness.

"The Daemons," however, explores the subversion of this idea: the vicar is an agent of the forces of darkness and the church provides the locus for bringing the Devil / alien to life. As though to problematize this further, the church itself is built on top of a far older sacrificial site, described in the novelization of the story as a chamber where the wall paintings are "all depicting the secret ceremonies of the old witch religion, literally thrust into the darkness of the underground by the light of Christianity" (Letts 1974, 32). Appearances, so useful in the visual language of propaganda, are shown to belie darker realities beneath. In the village as seen through the prism of *Doctor Who* we should trust the local white witch more than the vicar.

In the story's denouement the Daemon's energy proves too powerful for the Master to harness and the church itself explodes as it fails to contain the forces released within it. Rather than stand for the unshaken village community, then, the church is blown up (and the Daemon with it) so that the village may survive. From a conservationist standpoint, this poses something of a problem, but the explosive finale to "The Daemons" taps into what a contradiction always present in the rhetoric of wartime defense: that the unspoiled idyll may indeed need to be fought over (sustaining damage in the process) if it, or the freedom for which it functions as a symbol, is to be preserved.

In the midst of the Second World War a feature on "The Land We Are Fighting For" appeared in the July 6, 1940, issue of *Picture Post*. This essay argued strongly that the villages of Devon (and by extension England) "are no place for the Gestapo" (Anon 1940, 29) but at the same time acknowledged that backing up this view entailed thinking of the ways in which the narrow streets and winding lanes of the village might need to be made useful for those planning its defense. In an article decorated with views of the villages of Kersey (Suffolk), Wilmcote (Warwickshire), and Broadhembury (Devon) the reader is told that with invasion probably imminent the defense of the village is not solely something to be left to the armed forces: it could also be something that the village can do for itself, using its very fabric as fortification. "The deathly transformation of an English village into a Nazi outpost, depends quite simply on whether Nazi tanks and cyclists can force the main street," readers are told. "Whether they can do that depends on how the people in each town and village act this very day" (Anon. 1940, 29). A lack of action is a surrender of the village and its people—"your school and your church, your pub and your garden, your homes and *yourselves*" (Anon. 1940, 29). "Trench your garden," the article concludes, "learn to shoot, prepare a barricade from the school across to the pub, and you can save yourself by your exertions, and civilisation by your example" (Anon. 1940, 29). It was not enough in such a situation to simply see the village as an idealized space: truly fighting *for* it may entail seeing it as a battleground.

It was for the purpose of civil defense—and later in the War for the purpose of training troops to capture villages in France and beyond—that the Government appropriated some villages for use as training facilities for the military. One such tale informs Patrick Wright's study *The Village that Died for England*, which views this policy through the example of the Dorset coastal village of Tyneham. An official pledge to "restore" the village to its inhabitants after the War went unfulfilled, and Tyneham remains in the possession of the Government to this day, ostensibly no longer being in a condition in which its former residents could repossess it and still in the middle of an artillery firing range. It stands, in Wright's analysis, both as the embodiment of Newbould's village idyll and at the same time an English village "lost" without having been taken by an enemy, existing today only as a well-maintained ruin, accessible for brief interludes when the modern military is not using it and its environs for target practice. Although the village's sense of community could be invoked as integral to its defense then, the War showed that larger governmental forces could supplant that community with officialdom, relying on the "need to know" procedures in place in times of emergency to rebut the concerns of the displaced.

In the world of *Doctor Who* Stephen Cole and Justin Richards would draw upon the fate of Tyneham in their 2001 novel *Shadow in the Glass*, as the Sixth Doctor (Colin Baker) and a retired Lethbridge-Stewart attempt to unravel the mystery of why the Dorset village of Turelhampton, evacuated in haste in the closing days of the Second World War, should still be off-limits and guarded by troops in 2001. When the mystery surrounding Turel-hampton also leads the Doctor to a plot (supported by alien interference) by a revived Nazi movement to complete the plans unfulfilled in 1939–1945 the symbolic role of the village is once again placed at the heart of anxieties concerning British identity and defense, particularly acute when the situation is controlled by governmental officials whose actions are themselves suspicious. In times of threat, when it becomes harder to differentiate between "friendly" troops and hostile ones, an air of state control can prove as hard to penetrate as the heat barrier in "The Daemons" that cuts Devil's End off from the outside world.

"The Android Invasion": Don't Trust the Military

The village of Devesham in 1975's "The Android Invasion" provides an example of how outward tranquility can mask worrying levels of official, and alien, manipulation, rendering the idyll a highly disturbing one as the Fourth Doctor (Tom Baker) and Sarah Jane Smith (Elisabeth Sladen) explore it. The residents behave strangely, and the normal rhythms of life are jarring. Sarah is convinced that the erratic TARDIS has, finally, returned her to Earth, but although the physical signs appear conclusive the Doctor remains doubtful, doubts seemingly justified when mysterious figures in white overalls and helmets concealing their faces open fire on the new arrivals and another figure, this time wearing what should be the far more reassuring garb of "a corporal in the British Army" (Dicks 1978, 12) throws himself over the lip of a quarry as the Doctor and Sarah look on in horror. If the navigation systems on the TARDIS are accurate (a feat rarely achieved, as viewers of the show will recall) then this "Earth" is only convincing on the surface and its realism is not to be trusted.

Sarah, a journalist, remembers Devesham as a village she had visited two years earlier to research a story, and if the first sighting of it is visually in keeping with the images already familiar via other channels, its emptiness creates a growing feeling of unreality alongside the outward order. Writing in 1945, when the war was close to being won and Newbould's posters had served their purpose, Humphrey Pakington, in his study of *English Villages and Hamlets* made it the "first essential" of a good village that it should, "so to speak, read as a whole, and thus give the impression that the life lived therein is that of a community" (Pakington 1945,13). Devesham arguably reads "as a whole," but its too-precise appearance gives rise to anxiety, as though it has everything *except* the life that ought to be organically part of its fabric. Entering what should be its heart, the Doctor and Sarah find "a traditional village green complete with war memorial, thatched cottages, old-fashioned shops, and an appropriately rustic-looking village inn…. But there wasn't a single human being to be seen" (Dicks 1978, 15).

The Doctor wonders whether this gap between appearance and reality may be explained through the presence of the nearby Space Research Center. Thus, he deduces, the men in white overalls are wearing protection against nuclear contamination, the villagers have been moved elsewhere, and the "dead" soldier was suffering from radiation sickness. An official hand, in other words, has emptied the village for its own good in the wake of an atomic accident—a recurring anxiety in the adventures of the 1970s which are informed by, although often referencing only obliquely, the nuclear stand-off of the Cold War and the recurrent anxieties that atomic energy may have environmental consequences beyond those foreseen by its governmental supporters. As Alwyn Turner observes in discussing another environmentally-themed adventure, "The Green Death" (1973), the inclusion of such storylines was evidence of how children's television was very much a forum for writers and viewers to confront and consider the "politically charged times" in which they were composed (Turner 2008, 55). In the wake of the Watergate scandal in the United States, viewers could readily believe that when government, the military, and big business were involved nothing was beyond credibility. The powers of governmental and military authority could, therefore, account for the eeriness of Devesham if they had intervened in its life so comprehensively in response to the kind of crisis that would necessitate treating it as their real world counterparts did the village of Tyneham.

Just when an explanation seems to have been found, though, the villagers return like automata before taking up their positions and coming "to life" within the physical space, but this "normality" only masks an even stranger truth. The village of Devesham (in reality East Hagbourne in Oxfordshire) has been taken over, it appears, by robots and the Space Research Center on its outskirts—"a vast, sprawling ultra-modern building, all glass and concrete" (Dicks 1978, 26)—is eerily deserted when it should be a heavily-guarded installation. To add to the sense of the uncanny the Doctor, enquiring after Brigadier Lethbridge-Stewart (UNIT are, of course, involved in providing security for the Center) is told that he is "away in Geneva" and that Colonel Faraday (Patrick Newell) is in charge in his stead. Indeed, one of the things that makes Devesham confusing is the issue of who is absent and who is there when they ought not to be. Sarah tells the Doctor, for example, that although "Guy Crayford" (Milton Johns) is in charge of the Space Center he was given up for dead two years earlier when his prototype spacecraft disappeared during a test flight.

Attempting to piece together contradictory evidence, the Doctor finds himself in the village pub, drinking pints of ginger pop (English beer not being, perhaps, as popular among Time Lords as among other characters) and carefully critiquing the ways in which its "order" is superficial. The dartboard is in mint condition, although the landlord tells the Doctor that the pub is busy on "darts club nights," and the calendar has no months to follow from that in which the Doctor seems to be at the moment. This is the idea of the "timeless" English village taken to its extreme: Devesham becomes not only a place where it seems that time has "stood still," but one in which there is no prospect of its moving forward either.

It becomes clear as the story unfolds that "Devesham" is in truth a *simulacrum*—a village constructed, with the surrounding countryside, on an alien world in order that the warlike Kraals can prepare for their invasion of Earth and settlement of the planet after they have wiped out the human race using a lethal virus. In this instance, then, the idyll is a military training base, its veracity resting on its having been designed using the actual memories of someone who knows the original from which the replica is created, the still-alive Guy Crayford, kidnapped by the Kraals and, in the belief that the people on Earth had abandoned him, providing his alien allies with the information they need to advance their invasion plan. In effect, Crayford is like a modern version of a wartime English traitor, helping the Nazis to prepare for their invasion by reconstructing the very model of their target village. As in "The

Daemons" the emphasis in "The Android Invasion" is on the maintenance of external order and appearance while behind the scenes the village, and the whole world, is subverted from within.

In this case, however, the population of the village (and the Space Center nearby) are to be regarded as expendable: the androids will serve only a short-term purpose until the Kraals have completely installed themselves. They will "populate" the village, substituted for its regular inhabitants, until the invasion is successful. Outwardly, Devesham will function as normal, but once again its very normality will be deceptive, concealing from view its having already been taken. To add a further sense of urgency to the plot, the fake Devesham, its training purpose having been served, is poised to be eradicated by "a matter-dissolving bomb" (Dicks 1978, 70) prior to the Kraals' embarkation for Earth. In this crisis the Doctor must not only get to Earth in time to save the real village (and the wider planet) but must ensure that he is not in its simulacrum when it is itself destroyed—a fate that looks increasingly likely when he taken prisoner and bound (with imitation ivy from the Kraals' imitation village) not to a Maypole this time, but to the (imitation) granite pillar of the war memorial on the village green.

"The Android Invasion" works so well as a story because it not only charts the Doctor and Sarah's experience of the uncanny "Devesham" on the planet of Oseidon but then has the Doctor accompany the Kraals to Earth in an attempt to foil the invasion for which the replica village was the training base. One "Devesham" is destroyed (like Tyneham) as a prelude to the conquest of another such village, having served its purpose in training the invading force on how to fit seamlessly into such a space. If the Kraals' plan were to succeed we could invoke the *Picture Post* story of 1940 and imagine another idyllic view with the caption "Sunday afternoon in Devesham: all is peace" underneath, as the androids prepare the Kraals' new home for them.

Given that the viewer has already seen how deceptive "order" and "reality" can be, it is odd to find the story concluding in the *real* Devesham, featuring many of the *real* versions of the characters seen as robots in the fake village alongside their duplicates; a denouement rendered more thrilling by the fact that the Kraals have produced android versions of the Doctor and Sarah, so until the end of the story we are never wholly sure whether we are watching the authentic characters or not. The more something looks credible, the story reminds its viewers, the less we should be prepared to trust it. Fortunately, in the final analysis the deceptions work to the advantage of Earth. "Soon," we are told at the close of the narrative, "life in the Space Research Center—and in Devesham village—would return to normal" (Dicks 1978, 126); whatever "normality" is in such places. Lethbridge-Stewart will be back from Geneva, and all will be well until the next invasion attempt.

"Last of the Gaderene": Don't Trust Anyone

In the years when the program was off the air, *Doctor Who* was kept alive by the many novels that made use of the show's past in new storylines—providing fans with the television serials they had never had as familiar characters were inserted into new, but at the time same familiar, situations. Mark Gatiss's "Last of the Gaderene" (2000) brought the Third Doctor and Jo Grant back to explore strange occurrences at a rural aerodrome and, in a plot that made full use of the show's early-1970s plot devices, located in the quiet surroundings of the East Anglian country village of Culverton an alien plan to invade and colonize the earth by the insect-like Gaderene. As a novel written, as it were, 30 years after the context within which we may imagine its content filmed and broadcast, and then harking back to a time a further 30 years earlier in its plot, *Last of the Gaderene* provides a fascinating case study in *Doctor Who*'s capacity to both articulate and generate nostalgia. Indeed, in his introduction to the novel Gatiss readily acknowledges that its animating force is both the nostalgia of its 1970s-era plot for the certainties of the Second World War and his own nostalgia for the "magical childhood time" when such adventures were part of the television schedule—"the great constant" in the "little lives" of himself and his friends (Gatiss 2000, v).

As if to foreground this sense of shifting historical and cultural relevance, when the reader enters the story Culverton aerodrome is about to be closed down by order of the Ministry of Defence amidst the shifting geopolitics of the Cold War. The local handyman, Jobey Packer, first encountered standing poised to hammer the closure notice to its gates, was once himself a soldier serving from home in the Second World War, and he still regards the village of Culverton very much as Newbould's posters would have wanted him to do. It remains, after three decades of peace, "his little village. Safe, secure, always the same" and fulfilling its propaganda role in peacetime as it had in more perilous years (Gatiss 2000, 8). "There was the green with the old pump," Packer thinks, "the post office with its subsiding wall, the hotchpotch of cottages and houses clustered around the russet-coloured church as though seeking sanctuary" (Gatiss 2000, 8). The aerodrome, too, fits into this pastoral world: although constructed to house a fighter squadron in the Battle of Britain, its post–War life under the command of Harold Tyrell has been (as Tyrell recalls prior to his own leave-taking) one where emergencies have been rare. An air-show to celebrate the Coronation in 1953, and a "dramatic rescue" when cargo planes had been dispatched "to the aid of a stricken tanker off the coast" (Gatiss 2000, 9) in the mid–1960s seem to have been the high points in a life of quiet irrelevance until the Ministry's budgetary cuts finally caught up with the outpost and Culverton, like Britain itself, felt the need to put aside its wartime role.

The sense of the Second World War as a conflict still within reasonably recent memory enables Gatiss to use characters like Wing Commander Alex Whistler, resident of Culverton, decorated pilot, and opponent of the "men from the ministry" who have condemned the aerodrome to closure. When his housekeeper informs him that a private concern may be interested in buying the aerodrome he is skeptical, and when the village is suddenly filed with ranks of mysterious black-uniformed men he finds himself questioning the reports he has heard about plans for the future. When Whistler contacts his old friend Lethbridge-Stewart in search of information, however, the Brigadier finds that Legion International, the new owners of the aerodrome, "seem to have friends in high places" (Gatiss 2000, 59) and that their actions are shrouded in secrecy. Again, this is not necessarily a worrying sign, but the Brigadier's high level of security clearance makes the official obfuscation a little more worrying. Returning to the program's early–1970s period for his novel, Gatiss also invokes the recurrent anxiety of that time, the sense that there were what James Chapman calls "recurring themes of conspiracy and cover-up" amongst the human characters even before the viewer encountered any alien threat (Chapman 2013, 82). Legion International promises an aerodrome reborn as a civilian and cargo airport, with all the economic benefits that such a change will entail, but the heavily guarded convoys of equipment seen entering the compound in the dead of night suggest something else entirely.

As in "The Daemons" the fear here is that the takeover has already been enacted, and that superficial order is actually evidence of Legion International's success. When Whistler takes one of the young men of the village, Noah, with him one evening to attempt to penetrate the aerodrome and find evidence of what is going on Noah sees the Legion staff acting "as though they own the village" because, in essence, they already do. Whistler, a veteran of a time in which such a thing was once highly possible, is clearly prepared to resist this "invasion," if such it is, as if it were a continuation of the 1939–1945 struggle. "A lot of my pals gave their lives to defeat this kind of behaviour," he tells Noah, "I'm not about to let another lot of blackshirts take up where the old ones left off" (Gatiss 2000, 79). The difference this time around, though, is that there is no external enemy towards whose actions one can position one's resistance. With Legion's influence permeating the higher levels of governmental life there can be no trust that "those in power" will act for the greater good: indeed, quite the reverse seems to be the case here. If Culverton is to be saved it will have to save itself, with some help from the Doctor, of course.

The idea of the village captured by enemy subterfuge (aided, on occasion, by internal treachery) and then "liberating" itself recurs in much of British cinema from the Second World War, and most memorably in the 1942 film *Went the Day Well*, where the residents of Bramley End (in reality Turville in Buckinghamshire) must save themselves from the German commandos that have seized the village and the traitors in their own ranks who have helped them do so. At a time when propaganda was a matter of national importance, carefully constructed and disseminated by very official channels, there remains in works like this a belief that the organic community of the village is its own best defense. The global nature of the War is on too large a scale to comprehend, but the village, associated as it is with the quiet traditions of centuries of communal life, is something that can be imagined, threatened, defended, and preserved: a microcosm of the nation in a form that can more readily be understood. Many residents of Gatiss's Culverton, like those other, real villages, have rarely lived anywhere else, and for all the promotional attention given to the imminent rebirth of their aerodrome, there remain enough residents with a sense of suspicion directed to "outsiders" strong enough to make Legion's task more of a challenge.

Several storylines in Jon Pertwee's time as the Doctor drew upon a mounting sense of anxiety as to the amount of "secret" power and influence wielded "behind the scenes." Cabals of scientists, government ministers, industrialists, and military chiefs were often found behind situations that either produced crises of their own accord—as in 1970's "Inferno," 1973's "The Green Death," or 1974's "The Invasion of the Dinosaurs"—or created an opportunity for the Master to intervene and manipulate the situation for his own ends—as in the 1971 stories "The Claws of Axos" or "The Mind of Evil." As James Chapman notes, such adventures take place in "a Britain that seems full of "restricted areas": atomic research centers, monitoring stations, biochemical plants, and all manner of secret military installations" (Chapman 2013, 82). The public is rarely informed as to the nature of what is going on, but rather than encourage viewers to trust the suave civil servant the Doctor (although making the most of the access that his UNIT affiliation affords him) probes behind the orderly façade to uncover the invariably shocking truth. In Dominic Sandbrook's phrase, "barely a week went by without the Doctor infiltrating some top-secret research establishment, often in defiance of the government and the military, and uncovering a terrible elemental threat to the world's existence" (Sandbrook 2010, 205). The state, so all-pervasive in wartime, was now all too often part of the problem and its claims to be acting in the interest of the populace began to seem very suspect. In such a situation, the idea of the village community as a more "honest" alternative to officialdom gains credibility. Local knowledge is to be preferred to official pronouncements, although you are in trouble indeed when you find yourself faced, as the police constable's wife Helen Trickett does, by "a middle-sized man with swarthy, saturnine features and a neat, pointed beard" (Gatiss 2000, 176) telling you that he is the Master and demanding your obedience: proof that the village is not inviolable by any means.

With their slogan "Getting us where we want to go" Legion are indeed going to put Culverton on the map, but the aerodrome is to be a transport hub for alien life rather than for humans. As in "The Android Invasion," when the technology is in place it will enable the Gaderene to leave their own dying world and make their way across space to Earth. Early pieces of the transport apparatus arrived in Culverton during World War II, mistaken for bombs in amongst the raids of the Luftwaffe, but now the aerodrome is wholly in Legion's hands and the process of transfer is nearing completion. As the villagers are turned into cocoons for alien life forms and a giant worm-like creature comes to life in the marshland beside the aerodrome, fighting for "Your Britain" becomes once again more akin to fighting for Earth's survival. The Gaderene's world is dying, and the Master has guided them towards Earth in order to give them control over the planet. "Isn't that what we all fight to defend?" he asks the Doctor as the final battle rages, subverting the patriotic discourse of the Home Front, "Hearth and home?" (Gatiss 2000, 286). Caring nothing for the humans of Culverton, the Master offers the Gaderene a new "hearth and home" in an English village, and the planet that goes with it.

For a novel so rich in echoes of World War II, it is no surprise that in the denouement we should see the Wing Commander Whistler flying a Spitfire to break apart the inter-dimensional vortex through which the Gaderene hope to cross to Earth. Once again, the village has been defended against invading forces, although the village is, once again, not only a village, or even a synecdoche for the larger nation, but rather the arena within which the fate of Earth itself is briefly at stake, and ultimately preserved. The clean-up operation after the decisive battle will take some time, arguably, but Culverton is intact at the close of the novel as both a village and as a community; albeit one, like Devil's End, with a new and strange chapter to add to its shared history, one that gives the villagers something to talk about in the pub, perhaps.

Conclusion: Trust the Local Beer

At the close of "The Daemons" we find ourselves, as though in one of Newbould's posters, on the village green. The alien invasion threat has been defeated, the Master's influence has been broken, and we are, once again, in the symbolic and spatial heart of the village community. It is springtime, May Day in fact, and the Morris dancers (now no longer agents of evil) perform in time-honored fashion as the Doctor, Jo, and several of the assembled UNIT personnel join in with varying degrees of awkwardness. The village, Britain, and indeed the Earth itself, have been fought for and defended: until next time, or next Saturday evening. As the music swells the synchronized dance steps suggest a return to order in everyone's lives. Not everybody is a keen dancer, though. When asked if he would like to join in, Brigadier Lethbridge-Stewart replies to Captain Yates that he would be better celebrating in another of the village's traditional locations. "That's kind of you," he tells Yates, thoughtfully surveying the green, "but I think I'd rather have a pint" and he sets off for the pub as the scene fades into the closing titles. Newbould, who made the village pub an integral part of "Your Britain," would surely have approved of the need for a beer once civilization itself had been fought for and secured. Having explored the possibility that sometimes the village's outward tranquility was not always to be trusted, then, the *Doctor Who* adventure of the 1970s concludes with a return to the very images of order that it had subverted, making use of the symbolic properties of the village green—whether in reality or on an old wartime poster—and allowing its audience to let forth a deep sigh of nostalgia once the danger of invasion had passed.

BIBLIOGRAPHY

Chapman, James. 2013. *Inside the Tardis: The Worlds of Doctor Who*. London: I.B. Tauris.
Cole, Stephen, and Justin Richards. 2001. *Shadow in the Glass*. London: BBC Books.
Cox, J. Charles, and Charles Bradley Ford. 1944. *The Parish Churches of England*. London: B.T. Batsford.
Dicks, Terrance. 1978. *Doctor Who and the Android Invasion*. London: Target.
Esty, Jed. 2004. *A Shrinking Island: Modernism and National Culture in England*. Princeton: Princeton University Press.
Gatiss, Mark. 2000. *Last of the Gaderene*. London: BBC Books.
"The Land We Are Fighting For." 1940. *Picture Post* 8, no. 1. 6 July.
Leach, Jim. 2009. *Doctor Who*. Detroit: Wayne State University Press.
Letts, Barry. 1974. *Doctor Who and the Daemons*. London: Target.
Matless, David. 1998. *Landscape and Englishness*. London: Reaktion Books.
Newbould, Frank. "Your Britain: Fight for It Now" (Salisbury Cathedral Poster) Available at http://www.iwm.org.uk/collections/item/object/20271. Accessed 21 November 2016.
Newbould, Frank. "Your Britain: Fight for It Now" (South Downs Poster) Available at http://www.iwm.org.uk/collections/item/object/20289. Accessed 21 November 2016.
Newbould, Frank. "Your Britain: Fight for It Now" (Alfriston Fair Poster) Available at http://www.iwm.org.uk/collections/item/object/20275. Accessed 21 November 2016.
Newbould, Frank. "Your Britain: Fight for It Now" (Oak Tree Poster) Available at http://www.iwm.org.uk/collections/item/object/20272. Accessed 21 November 2016.
Pakington, Humphrey. 1945. *English Villages and Hamlets*. London: B. T. Batsford.
Sandbrook, Dominic. 2007. *White Heat: A History of Britain in the Swinging Sixties*. London: Abacus.
Sandbrook, Dominic. 2010. *State of Emergency: The Way We Were: Britain 1970–1974*. London: Allen Lane.
Strong, Roy. 2011. *Visions of England*. London: Bodley Head.
Tulloch, John, and Manuel Alvarado. 1983. *Doctor Who: The Unfolding Text*. London: Macmillan.
Turner, Alwyn. 2008. *Crisis? What Crisis? Britain in the 1970s*. London Aurum.
"What We Are Fighting For." 1940. *Picture Post* 8, no. 2. 13 July.
Wright, Patrick. 1985. *On Living in an Old Country*. Oxford: Oxford University Press.
Wright, Patrick. 1996. *The Village that Died for England: The Strange Story of Tyneham*. London: Vintage.

FILMOGRAPHY

Doctor Who and the Android Invasion. Broadcast 22 November–13 December 1975. Director: Barry Letts. Writer: Terry Nation. BBC Television.

Doctor Who and the Daemons. Broadcast 22 May–19 June 1971. Director: Christopher Barry. Writer: Guy Leopold. BBC Television.

Doctor Who and Environmentalism in the 1960s and Early 1970s

MARK WILSON

At just after 5:15 p.m. on the evening of Halloween, Saturday, October 31, 1964, approximately eight million people across Britain turned on their television sets and watched the first episode of the second season of *Doctor Who*, "Planet of Giants" (Howe and Walker 2013, 73). Not only was this the first story to air on Halloween night, it was also the first time the program had dealt with "eco-catastrophe" (Wood and Miles 2006, 94). Two years earlier, in September 1962, American biologist Rachel Carson's work *Silent Spring*, warning about the uncontrolled use of pesticides, had been published. The writer of "Planet of Giants," Louis Marks, "like many people, had read" Carson's book, and the story was partly inspired by it (Wood and Miles 2006, 98).

This essay discusses environmental awareness in post-war Britain, in particular with the rise of new conservation and environmental-themed television programs, and the influence of the ideas expressed in *Silent Spring*, which appeared in Britain in February 1963. Carson's work has been described as the book that launched the modern American environmental movement (Guha 2000, 69). However, in Britain, environmental awareness grew more slowly than it did in America. The theme of the environment is considered through three case studies of *Doctor Who* stories—"Planet of Giants," "The Green Death" (1973) and "Invasion of the Dinosaurs" (1974). These stories reflect wider issues pertaining to the environment at the time (concern about pesticides and pollution): "Planet of Giants" represents the first time the Doctor "went green" while "The Green Death" is a more overtly environmental story which can be compared to "Planet of Giants." "The Green Death" was also "one of the very few *Doctor Who* stories that had an overtly 'topical' point to make" (Wood 2009, 372) (although "Planet of Giants" also made a topical point, this was more hidden within the story). The third story, "Invasion of the Dinosaurs," offers an alternative environmental narrative to "The Green Death," yet it too sends out the message that the world is in danger because of mankind's impact on the environment.

These stories also reflect the politics and culture of post-war Britain. Their different approaches to "eco-catastrophe" comes in part from the periods when they were aired on screen (Wood and Miles 2006, 94). In the 1960s, environmental awareness was still developing in Britain; by the early 1970s, it had become central to British society, hence the use of the term "environmentalists" in "The Green Death." The period saw an increase in new environmental-themed television programs, feeding the British public with pictures of wildlife at home and abroad. For many people, this was their first introduction to wildlife, often in their own homes, through television programs such as *Look* (see below [Sheail 1998, 126]. Whilst "Planet of Giants," to an extent, fits this narrative, it also offered something new. The story was not set on a distant planet or faraway land but on contemporary earth, signaling to the viewer that perhaps all was not well with nature on their doorstep as a result of pesticide use. The stories were also influenced, in part, by leading environmental books at the time [*Silent Spring* and "A Blueprint for Survival," respectively. Goldsmith, Allen, Allaby, Davoll and Lawrence, 1972]).

New Awareness of Environmental Issues

By the beginning of the 1970s, environmental awareness in Britain had become central to British society. Not only had the Department of the Environment been established, but pressure groups such as Friends of the Earth were emerging, the United Nations held its first environment conference, the Queen mentioned the environment for the first time in 1970, in her speech made to Parliament, and it had begun to appear in political party literature and speeches (Veldman 1994, 4–5, 210; Beckett 2009, 234–243; House of Lords 1970). It was within this context that "The Green Death" appeared. Yet environmental awareness did not suddenly appear in Britain, fully formed, in 1970. Instead, there had been a long history of environmental alarm, with early concern for the natural world exhibited in the 19th century by opposition to railway construction in the Lake District and the establishment of organizations such as the National Trust (established in 1895). The inter-war period was characterized by the emergence of new pressure groups, campaigning for the right to roam and protecting the countryside from urbanization;

these included the Ramblers' Association (founded in 1935) and the Campaign to Protect Rural England (CPRE, then known as the Council for the Preservation of Rural England, established in 1926). Another phase in the growth of environmental concern developed during the post-war period. A number of new but important considerations set this period apart from previous years—technological advances in the form of new media such as television, which could be used in getting messages to a vast number of people; a number of environmental disasters which provided evidence to the public of the devastation of the natural world; and consumerism, which advanced both people's awareness and the tools of destruction with regard to the environment (Sheail 2002, 257–263).

This period saw destruction of the environment on a scale not seen since the Industrial Revolution. With this destruction came new awareness and concern about the natural world. The post–World War II period was distinctive; 1945 did not merely mark the end of a war which had destroyed much of the natural environment in Britain. It also saw optimistic ideas of a "brave new world" emerge, the birth of a new era with the "implementation of universal, collectivist welfare" and a more focused concern for environmental problems (Evans 1992, 93; McKay and Hilton 2009, 4). It was in this period that conservationism really took hold, with its proponents seeking "to conserve the environment as a resource for human enjoyment and accordingly emphasised the protection and conservation of flora, fauna and different wildlife habitats" (Nehring 2005, 395–396).

In 1949, the British government established the Nature Conservancy (NC), a non-governmental organization which offered independent scientific guidance to the government. The Conservancy was also involved with informing and educating the public about environmental issues (Bocking 1997, 13–14). While it had a relatively low profile, "the young Nature Conservancy was presented with public relation gifts by the failure of the chemical industry to anticipate how sensitive public opinion would be about spraying with toxic products, and of other interests on oil spills, nuclear power stations, fires on forests, heath and moorland, encroachments on common land and river pollution" (Nicholson 1987, 98).

Gradually, as environmental ideas began to influence more people and an environmental consciousness grew in society, the general public became increasingly alarmed about "the catastrophic London smog of 1952, the deteriorating conditions of many rivers, and the … indiscriminate use of pesticides" as well as widespread pollution of the natural world (Rootes 2009, 207). The destruction of the environment, changing attitudes towards nature, and more general concerns about standards of living also grew after the war, setting this period apart from earlier years. The lives lost and sacrifices made during World War II forced people to reassess social priorities. As the welfare state was born, and quality of life improved in post-war Britain, society had more to engage with and think about in relation to nature in various guises.

By the mid–1960s, environmental thinking shifted from a human-centered concept into a more inclusive bio-centric approach. During this period ownership of many household items such as fridges, washing machines, and cars, became commonplace. A reduction in working hours to five days a week meant that people had time, money and the means to travel, opening up the opportunity to visit national parks and the countryside. People "now wished to escape, if only for a weekend or two, from their everyday milieu of factory or farm, city or suburb. Nature, whether in the form of forests to walk through, beaches to swim from, or mountains to climb" became a way to escape civilization (Hilton 2003, 3–4, 309; Veldman 1994, 4–5). Even sub-consciously, people's experience of nature helped to develop the emerging environmental awareness as people experienced wildlife and nature in its natural habitat.

It was within this context that both Carson's work was published and *Doctor Who* first aired on British television screens. On its publication in Britain on February 14 1963, *The Times* described *Silent Spring*, as "a social study, eloquent, sincere—and alarming" (Anon, *The Times* 1963: 15). The book, a work of popular and partisan science, presented neatly for public consumption, provided a critique of uncontrolled pesticide use, with its central idea about ecosystems—the interconnectedness of all living things. It was instantly successful, becoming a best-seller translated into languages. Rebecca Solnit states that "To read its early passages is like listening to God call the world into being during the days of its creation, even if this is only the world of environmental ideas" (Solnit 2003). In Germany it was a best-seller for many months, and there was a sharp increase in membership of conservation organizations. In Sweden it ushered in modern environmentalism. Supporters included both President John F. Kennedy and Prince Philip (Guha 2000, 71–73).

Silent Spring offered a critical assessment of the indiscriminate use of pesticides and increased public awareness in the United States of the harmful effects of chemicals on the natural world, as well as criticizing the uncontrolled advance of science and technology. Before this, few books had been as successful in delivering this message to the American public (Lutts 1985, 211). Although Carson described several pesticides (a catch-all term for insecticides, herbicides, fungicides, etc.), she focused on one in particular—dichlorodiphenyltrichloroethane, an insecticide known commonly as DDT. DDT only came into widespread usage at the end of World War II, when it was seen as a miraculous product, having been used successfully during the war to prevent soldiers acquiring insect-borne diseases. After the war, it went on general release in the United States.

The first encounter between conservationists in Britain and pesticides was as early as 1952, when the Nature Conservancy told Parliament that the use of chemical sprays on roadside vegetation was having a detrimental effect on wildlife (Morrison 1952). The year 1960 brought reports of deaths, not just of birds, but also of foxes. The image "of half-blind foxes eating grass, touched a tender nerve in the countryside" (Nicholson 1987, 46–47). As the National Parks Commission Annual Report for 1960 commented, "The growing public concern about the effects of the use of toxic chemicals on wild life was reflected in the considerable publicity given last spring to the mysterious deaths of large numbers of birds, allegedly due to the use of toxic sprays" (Nicholson 1987, 47–48; National Parks Commission 1960, 50). This growing concern is reflected in the Doctor's role, in "Planet of Giants," where he states "that it's 'wrong' to kill worms and bees, as they play vital roles in the growth of things, and seems to believe in the correctness of the natural order. He even speaks of the 'life-force'" (Wood and Miles 2006, 96).

In preparation for the first United Nations Environment Conference, held in Stockholm in 1972, a report by the Nature Conservancy noted that as the 1950s progressed, "there was growing concern [in Britain] that the increasing use, especially as seed dressings, of new and highly toxic organochlorine insecticides (dieldrin, aldrin, heptachlor) was causing widespread and catastrophic deaths of wild birds."[1] This was all before *Silent Spring* was published. Throughout the 1950s the dangers of pesticides on wildlife were becoming apparent. In 1952, the Agriculture (Poisonous Substances) Act had been passed and the following year questions were raised in Parliament about the toxic effects of chemical sprays (House of Commons, 1953). Although this was mainly to protect workers from potentially dangerous chemicals, it does demonstrate that government officials were aware of the toxic nature of chemicals.[2] The problem was that chemicals that had been cleared had only been approved to be used in specific circumstances. There was nothing to prevent someone safe behind protective clothing using them, spraying a lethal dose in a moment (Davy 1963, 21). By 1957 the Conservancy was receiving complaints from across the country concerning the indiscriminate and widespread spraying by councils (Sheail 1985, 6–15).

The result of these spraying exercises was an increase in bird mortality. Two years before Carson published *Silent Spring*, the Nature Conservancy established the Toxic Chemicals and Wildlife Division, to investigate the deaths of these birds (Graham Jr. 1970, 83–86). The Conservancy even commented on the publication of a British edition of *Silent Spring*. The book, it argued, was "a severe attack on the indiscriminate use of chemicals to control agricultural pests and diseases, and although mainly concerned with the situation in the U.S.A., some of the criticisms and conclusions may be of wider application." It finished by claiming that there was increasing public concern about the widespread use of pesticides, a sentiment echoed in the National Parks Commission Annual Report of 1960 (National Parks Commission 1960, 50; Nature Conservancy 1963, 46).

The Ecologist's "A Blueprint for Survival" published in Britain a decade later was arguably even more influential. "Blueprint," initially produced as a special edition magazine and later developed into a best-selling book, detailed destruction of the environment (including that done by pesticides) and offered solutions to saving the planet from destruction. "The Green Death" echoed many of its arguments (this is mentioned on the extras of "The Green Death" DVD, released in the UK in 2013). "Blueprint" sold 75,000 copies in Britain, and was translated into 16 different languages (Jorgensen 2012, 11). In terms of its context and responses, as well as how far-reaching it was, "Blueprint" could be considered to be a British *Silent Spring*. In terms of writing style, it was not a direct descendent and Carson's work was more eloquently written than that which appeared in *The Ecologist*. However, just as Carson inspired the writer of "Planet of Giants," "Blueprint" inspired the writers of "The Green Death" and "Invasion of the Dinosaurs." If the British reception of both "Blueprint" and *Silent Spring* are compared, then it seems that "Blueprint" had a more immediate, direct impact. Pesticides feature in the analysis in "Blueprint" and whilst *Silent Spring* is not mentioned in detail, DDT is discussed. In Britain, concern for the environment was already a cultural discussion by the time *Silent Spring* arrived, as popular culture, such as television programs, increasingly deployed environmental themes.

Environmentalism and Television: Reaching a Mass Audience

Television has often played a part in informing and educating the British public about environmental issues. In 1963, for example, the World Wildlife Fund was established partly on the back of a television documentary called *S.O.S. Rhino* (1961) (Walshe, Bevan, Sealy and Phillipson 1999, 88; Schwarzenbach 2011, 50–51). The years after World War II saw television become a dominant part of the public's leisure time, overtaking radio as the main form of entertainment by the end of the 1950s. Between 1951 and 1954, the number of television sets that people owned in Britain doubled to three million, with the transmission signal reaching 90 per cent of the population by 1955 (Cain 1992, 64; Williams 2004, 1, 7, 14; Abercrombie 1997, 148). From the 1960s onwards, people in Britain spent more of their free time watching television than on any other activity. Some evidence of the growth of television comes from television's share of all advertising expenditure, which rose from 6 percent in 1957 to 22 percent three years later in 1960. Moreover, by that year nearly all newspapers included television listings (Abercrombie 1997, 148; Williams 2004, 95–96).

In 1961, the Nature Conservancy handed over evidence to the Pilkington Committee on Broadcasting. In it, they argued that broadcasting environmental impact information over television: "Is especially suited to the mass dissemination of information about ... conservation and can be used to educate all levels in the earth and life sciences and conservation. Without education only limited and inadequate advances in conservation are possible.... Broadcasting ... can make a vital contribution towards the growing problem of the wise use of leisure and of mutual understanding between competing claimants for the use of our limited area of land and water" (Nature Conservancy Annual Report 1961, 61).

As Max Nicholson, head of the Nature Conservancy for much of the 1950s and 1960s, states, "No appraisal of the advance of environmental conservation" in Britain "should fail to pay tribute to the outstanding, and indeed decisive, contribution of this group [the media] to the rapid acceptance of the message of the movement, and indeed to the enrichment of the message itself" (Nicholson 1987, 80).

Nature television programs have "proved a major British contribution to the worldwide movement," and without programs such as these, the environmental movement "would be much less enthusiastic and well informed, and also more narrowly limited. They are vividly perceived by each individual, and their message is quickly and faithfully embodied in the social conscience" (Nicholson 1987, 80). Since television was increasingly popular, David Attenborough, a BBC producer during the 1950s, suggested to his superiors that there should be regular natural history programs "about wildlife in the British countryside" (Attenborough 2010, 44–46, 59–60).

It was Sir Peter Scott, the presenter of many of these programs, who "convinced sceptical media magnates that nature and its conservation could draw and hold audiences comparable to almost any other programmes" (Nicholson 1987, 166). Scott presented the long-running series *Look* (on air 1955–1981). The very first episode was broadcast on June 14, 1955. It proved so successful that two years later the BBC established its Natural History Unit (Evans 1992, 99). *Look* challenged prevalent ideas about nature, with each episode focusing a different topic. The voiceover in the title sequence stated, "It's time to look at a different world—outside the realm of human affairs— a world of grace and beauty—with its own kind of comedy—a world of danger and mystery—that challenges our understanding—at this world—the untamed life of nature" ("*Look* No. 3: 'Land of the Flamingo,'" F.20, Papers of Sir Peter Scott, Cambridge University Library). A world of danger and mystery could equally apply to the miniature world which the Doctor and his companions faced in "Planet of Giants."

Nicholson, head of the Nature Conservancy from 1952 to 1966, described *Look* in particular as placing conservation issues within the public's consciousness. The program was responsible for introducing animals to people in their own homes and, crucially, instructing people "how to enjoy them" (Sheail 1998, 126). Whilst television was a relatively new medium, the fact these programs dealt with these issues indicates that an environmental consciousness was developing. By watching them, people became more educated about the natural world, meaning they were more likely to put what they had seen into practice.

The appeal of such programs possibly stems from the production style of them. "Television seems to be describing the world as it is" (Abercrombie 1997, 26; Fiske 2013, 67). The plots of both "Planet of Giants" and "The Green Death" took place in contemporary Britain, therefore providing audiences with examples of how the environment was—or could be—destroyed in *their* world, not the world of an alien species. They were describing the world as it is, with chemical pesticides being used and with pollution and groups trying to halt it. "This claim is enhanced by the feeling that television is operating in the present, unlike any other medium" (Abercrombie 1997, 26). While television does not convey to audiences reality in full, it does go some way towards realism—giving an impression of reality (Bousé 2000, 5–7). Programs depicting realistic stories or programs with stories which have elements of realism, such as nature conservation serials or series like *Doctor Who*, offer a view of the real world, and as such there is a sense that there are no authors. "The form conspires to convince us that we are not viewing something that has been constructed in a particular fashion by a determinate producer or producers" (Bousé 2000, 27). Television is a "cultural forum," allowing issues to be raised and commentary to occur on real-life events, yet sometimes providing contradictory messages in one particular show (Newcomb and Hirsch 1983). In the realm of science fiction, however, the "integration of social values [such as environmental protection] may be the most critical element that allows science fiction programing to resonate with its viewers" (Jorgensen 2012, 12). This can be seen below in discussion of "The Green Death" which reflected social values developing in Britain at the time, such as pollution. The letter written to the BBC from Gamlen Chemicals about "The Green Death," is evidence of this (the company was unhappy with the story as they thought it might negatively impact their work since the story had a similar-named company in it).

Doctor Who *and the Environment*

Doctor Who was first broadcast in 1963, a time when subject-specific television programs were becoming more prevalent. The series followed this trend by using the science fiction as a medium to describe current environmental problems in a fantasy setting. In *Doctor Who Live: The Next Doctor*, broadcast on BBC One in August 2013, comedian Rufus Hound commented that science fiction allows people to look at human problems with a degree of distance from them. The Doctor talks to the audience about life, death and the environment and understands these issues which seem fantastic but which are written in a way that the audience can relate to. Although the Doctor does not have any particular political bias, he (that is, the Third Doctor) is seen by many to be a moral hero standing up for what is right (in both "The Green Death" and "Invasion of the Dinosaurs," the Doctor has a sense of what is right and wrong. Even though he opposes the environmentalists' work in "Invasion of the Dinosaurs," he acknowledges *why* they are doing it. As he says to the Brigadier, "It's not the oil and filth and the poisonous chemicals that are the real cause of pollution, Brigadier. It's simply greed." The First Doctor was not typically characterized as a hero, yet even he recognizes that it is wrong to kill bees and worms and the like, and that something should be done to stop DN6) (Jorgensen 2012, 12). Dolly Jorgensen also describes how research has shown that audiences are not confused or lost by cultural commentaries that appear in scripts: interviews with fans who had watched the 1974 *Doctor Who* adventure "Monster of Peladon" revealed they were acutely aware of social commentary in the adventure about issues relating to class and gender (Jorgensen 2012, 12; Tulloch 1995, 67–85).

Three stories in particular are worth mentioning in relation to *Doctor Who* and the environment in the 1960s and early 1970s. "Planet of Giants," adopted an environmental theme for the first time. "The Green Death" was a moralistic tale nine years after "Planet of Giants," which reflected ideas in British society at the time about pollution and protecting the natural world. "Invasion of the Dinosaurs" is almost the reverse of "The Green Death"; here, the environmentalists are the bad guys. Yet there is still a strong environmental message tied up in the narrative of that particular story.

"Planet of Giants" involves the First Doctor, his companions Ian (William Russell), Barbara (Jacqueline Hill), and his granddaughter Susan (Carole Ann Ford) finding themselves shrunk to a minute size and stuck in a garden where a deadly insecticide has been sprayed, killing everything it has touched. The Doctor and his companions discover a laboratory where the insecticide has been produced, and eventually destroy the formulae before returning to the TARDIS and regaining their normal size. "Planet of Giants" was the first *Doctor Who* story to be entirely set on contemporary Earth. This allowed the viewer to look at pesticides "with a fresh eye" and perhaps even understand better the dangers they present (Wood and Miles 2006, 94).

The story is clearly influenced by Carson's analysis in *Silent Spring*. For instance, the Doctor describes the insecticide as killing "indiscriminately."

This was something Carson also warned about (indeed, the tenth chapter of her work is titled "Indiscriminately from the Skies"). Just as the Doctor and his companions make alerting the authorities of the eco-disaster that DN6 will cause their top priority (Wood and Miles 2006, 96), Rachel Carson wrote her best-selling book to alert the world to the eco-disaster that uncontrolled use of pesticides, such as DDT, would cause. Barbara and Susan both question the Doctor on the ethics of killing creatures such as bees and worms. The Doctor's response, that both are vital for the growth of things, again echoes Carson's when she variously describes the importance of living things, including bees and worms, which had both been affected by insecticide use (Carson 1962, 15, 63). Carson's focus was on several organochemical insecticides, with one in particular, DDT, described as being particularly dangerous. Similarly, in "Planet of Giants," the fictional insecticide is called DN6. Not only was DN6 lethal, and deadlier than radiation, it had been made "everlasting," and was likely "to seep into the soil and start killing all the animal life," not just insects, as it was originally intended (Wood & Miles 2006, 98). Though the very title of *Silent Spring* comes from the idea that, when all the birds have died due to their exposure to pesticides, the spring will be silent, Carson's work focused on many different animals and plants which were affected by chemicals, not just birds. She warned of the likelihood of chemicals in soils entering the food chain, chemicals which might have been used decades before, but a residue of which still persisted (see Carson 1962, 147–152 for chemical residues in food). Indeed *The Times* reported on August 16, 1969, that penguins in Antarctica were found to have significantly raised levels of DDT in their bodies as a result of eating contaminated fish (17). In 1963, Julian Huxley noted that pesticides did not just affect birds; he described how they affected all living things (Davy 1963, 21). "Planet of Giants" aired at a time when environmental awareness, in Britain, was developing. Just as in wider society the environment was not yet front-and-center, the story included a number of concerned citizens whose focus was to raise awareness. Barbara, for instance, resolves "to stop DN6" over her own health worries (Wood and Miles 2006, 96).

As noted in *About Time: The Unauthorized Guide to Doctor Who*, "Planet of Giants" is evidence of a sense "that the commercial, consumer society of early 1960s Britain is the measure of all things. In this … story, it's shown to be fragile" (Wood and Miles 2006, 99). As Britain entered the 1960s, newspaper articles described environmental problems across the country. Already, the great London smog disaster, in December 1952, had caused the public to think about the negative effects of industrialization. This had continued throughout the decade with stories of water pollution in British waterways and rivers (Anon. *The Times* 1950, 5; Anon. *Daily Mirror* 1951, 7). In America, Rachel Carson's seminal work was inspiring a new generation of activists who now saw the world itself as in peril and needing to be protected—from ourselves. In the context of this uncertain world, came *Doctor Who*.

Doctor Who is science fiction. Unlike documentaries or other genres, science fiction offers viewers a view of the present through allegory. An article in the journal *Progress in Human Geography* argues that certain aspects of science fiction writing "have received widespread academic praise for their recognition and ... [understanding] of the sociospatial processes underlying the postmodern condition now prevalent in western societies, and their future visions of the new spatialities this condition will evoke" (Kitchen and Kneale 2001, 20). The appeal of science fiction, the article continues, is that it creates a sense of "estrangement" in the participant, whether reader or viewer, but with science fiction, unlike works of fantasy, the genre seeks plausibility by "balancing the fantastical with a scientific rationale that domesticates the implausibility of the narrative" (Kitchen and Kneale 2001, 21).

In "Planet of Giants," when the Doctor's companions ask him about all the insects and other creatures which were dying, and whether it was wrong, the Doctor replied "quite so. Both [worms and bees] are vital for the growth of things." The program put to use "science fact" in a "science fiction" setting, which, as Jorgensen notes above with regards audience awareness of events in the series, was effective in getting its message across to the audience. Having read Carson, Marks used her narrative—about the potentially dangerous use of pesticides—as a reference for his story and in the character of the Doctor; whilst his attitude is sometimes arrogant, he does state on several occasions why it is wrong to kill creatures indiscriminately. In this way the First Doctor reflects Carson's work. As noted in *The Television Companion*, the idea of shrinking the Doctor and his companions was originally considered to launch the series. This did not happen, but the idea remained for a future story. What Marks brought to the table, specifically, was the environmental theme, from *Silent Spring* (Howe and Walker 2003, 75).

Nine years after "Planet of Giants," the political landscape of Britain had changed considerably, with regards to the environment. By now, environmental concern was central to British society—the Department of the Environment had been created; the first United Nations Environment Conference had been held; and the Green Party had just been formed in Coventry, as PEOPLE (Veldman 1994, 206; Beckett 2009, 136–137, 234–243). It was during this period, in 1973, that a very different, more overtly environmental *Doctor Who* serial aired—"The Green Death." Following the death of Welsh miner, whose body was glowing green, the Doctor and Jo Grant (Katy Manning), arrive, meet environmentalist and Nobel laureate fictional scientist Professor Clifford Jones (Stewart Bevan) and begin to investigate. Local chemical company Global Chemicals, which claims their new refining process can produce 25 percent more fuel from any amount of crude oil, were responsible for this and other deaths, as well as creating large maggots from the process. The story dealt with contemporary environmental issues, covering deforestation in the Amazon, as well as connecting to *Silent Spring* with debates over pesticides and events like the *Torrey Canyon* oil spill, which occurred in March 1967. BBC producer Barry Letts had read "Blueprint" and was concerned about the fate of the world. He was so influenced that he decided to base a *Doctor Who* story on some of the themes the book raised and thus "The Green Death" was born. The story's writer, Robert Sloman was similarly affected by reading the book (Letts was also a writer of this story but was not credited, due to being a producer also).[3]

Like "Planet of Giants," "The Green Death" was set in contemporary Britain and involves people more concerned with profit than environmental protection. It is clear from the beginning of the first episode of "The Green Death," where the Doctor's and (by extension) the viewer's sympathies should lie. Jo Grant describes Jones as a younger version of the Doctor, who himself comments upon how good it is to finally meet the scientist as he has followed his work closely. One of the first lines of the story is uttered by Jo who reads a newspaper article about Global Chemicals' new refining process exclaiming, "Don't they know how much pollution it will cause?" A little later she comments, "It's time the world awoke to the alarm bell of pollution" (Jorgensen 2012, 15). She goes on to tell the Doctor she intends to help Professor Jones since he is "fighting for everything that's important." Jo's raised consciousness is therefore put into a news and media context, reflecting the trending issue of environmentalism in the wider society, one where a real government scientist described the environment in Britain in 1970 as being "more topical than sex" (Barr 1970, 2). The Minister for Ecology mentioned in the story indeed reflects real-life Secretary of State for the Environment, established in 1970.

As with "The Green Death," the writers for "Invasion of the Dinosaurs" had been inspired by "Blueprint," and although this story portrays the environmentalists as antagonists, rather than the heroes, their beliefs are still shown in a positive light, even though their actions are meant to be questionable. Jorgensen argues that the "Doctor's environmental message is that we cannot adopt quick fixes to reach our long-term environmental goals. The Doctor consistently approves of the environmentalist ends put forward in these series … but disapproves of his antagonists' means" (Jorgensen 2012, 21–23). This is as true for "Planet of Giants" as it is for "The Green Death" and "Invasion of the Dinosaurs." The Doctor, seen as an "eco-activist," connects together ecological and anthropological issues and argues for change in society. He encourages humans to change their behavior. *Doctor Who* does not try to persuade viewers to take a certain point of view, rather gives them the means and opportunities to form their own conclusions (Jorgensen 2012,

23–24). The Doctor therefore supports their ideology, but not their actions (the environmentalists wanted to use a time machine to return London to a time before the Earth became polluted, so civilization could begin again. A by-product of this was the dinosaurs which appeared). In both stories, it is clear that the producers wanted to promote the issues and offer alternatives to problems, and also encourage the audience to think along the same lines.

Though "The Green Death" is a work of science fiction, the story had a link to the real world. Two letters in the BBC Written Archives provide evidence for this realism. The first, dated June 25 1973, comes from the Sales Manager at chemical company Gamlen, writing to the BBC claiming that after "The Green Death" had aired, there had been some comparisons between themselves and the fictional Global Chemicals organization portrayed in the story. The response, dated June 29 from the Head of Television Administration Department at the BBC to the Sales Manager points out *Doctor Who*:

> Is a science fiction series which owes its existence to the fantastic situation created involving time travel, visits to other worlds, battles with Daleks and other monsters etc. Anyone watching the programme would realise that any organization depicted was part of this fantasy and did not relate in any way to reality. In view of this I cannot conceive that the reputation of Gamlen Chemicals has suffered in any way by association with the fictitious "Global Chemical" organization. It is also worth noting that the loggia featured in the program consists of a "G Chemicals" superimposed on a symbolic representation of the world, whereas your loggia appears to be a white G on a black background. It seems to me that there is quite a clear difference between the two symbols and there should be no cause for confusion [Letter from Head of Television to Sales Manager, T65/71/1, BBC Written Archives Centre].

The fact Gamlen Chemical Company felt the need to write to the BBC at all demonstrates the effect that this story had: Gamlen's concern not to be associated with Global Chemicals is significant as they surely would not have bothered to object were the series not so popular. The fact any real company was compared to the fictional organization at all, also shows that people questioned real scientific organizations as a result of the story. In addition, the BBC also wrote a fictional newspaper article which was published to coincide with the first episode of the story, describing the situation as favorable to Global Chemicals and that the government had "rightly ignored" the "crackpots" of Jones and his team and Wholewheel (the scientific body which Jones and his team worked for).[4]

In dealing with ill effects of chemical pollution as a by-product from energy production, "The Green Death" takes the standard "renewable energy good, non-renewable bad" stance. The apparently stereotypical hippies who appear with Professor Jones, who have long hair and live in a commune, were given some character depth (in order to legitimize the characters and the environmental theme, rather than the viewer seeing them simply as hippies):

one is a mathematician who studied probability factors of a projected future ecology; another worked on windmill designs, having previously worked on supersonic aircraft design; and Jones himself was investigating protein-rich mushrooms which could feed the world (similar to foods like quorn today).

Although the environmentalists are the antagonists in the "Invasion of the Dinosaurs," the Doctor does sympathize with them. He states, "Look, I understand your ideals. In many ways I sympathise with them. But this is not the way to go about it." He also claims, "It's not the oil and the filth and the poisonous chemicals that are the real cause of pollution, Brigadier. It's simply greed." "Invasion of the Dinosaurs" reveals a darker side to environmentalism, with people developing "Operation Golden Age," a plan to return Earth to an era before industrial development, prompted by concerns over the pollution levels of the planet. Within the story the audience are shown films depicting the results of human activity on nature; the first shows black sludge that has been dredged, with the voiceover describing how pollution began in the Industrial Revolution, with chemicals poisoning air and water. In the second film, dead fish are shown in water full of rubbish, with the voiceover stating that heavy metals such as mercury have been found in fish, and that the life of the seas is becoming stagnant, stinking and without life. The third film deals with the issue of population, detailing how humanity is overcrowding the planet and therefore destroying it through pollution (Jorgensen 2012, 15–16).[5] Through these films, therefore, viewers were shown contemporary environmental problems. Although this story is often known as "the one with the awful dinosaurs," they are really only window dressing to what is another story "about the problems of pollution and the lengths to which mankind might go to try to solve them" (Howe and Walker 2013, 459).

Conclusion

Environmental awareness in Britain developed over a long period and from different roots. One of the main methods of dissemination of environmental ideas in the post-war period, was television. Through television sets, ideas about the natural world, images of wild animals, and the plight they faced, entered homes across Britain. Programs such as *Look* raised environmental awareness by introducing ideas into the public's consciousness about the natural world. As Britain entered a new decade of the 1960s, the whole country had already experienced several environmental problems and this had continued throughout the decade with news of polluted waterways across the country. The use of pesticides in gardens and on roadsides across Britain also worried many people. Then, two years after Carson's work had begun to inspire a new generation of activists who saw the world itself as in danger and needing protection, the BBC began to air the second series of *Doctor Who* with a story which echoed much of Carson's book.

As Tat Wood and Lawrence Miles claim, "Planet of Giants" is evidence of a sense that commercialization in the early 1960s (that is, in contemporary society), may not be so good after all (Wood and Miles 2006, 99). This was also something which Carson argued. She was never fully anti-pesticides, but rather was against them being used indiscriminately. Whilst *Silent Spring* was not the only influence for the story (the 1957 film, *The Incredible Shrinking Man* and television programs like *Dixon of Dock Green* [1955–1976] also influenced the story), as an "eco-sermon" the format of the program "works" (Wood and Miles 2006, 101). Being shrunken and seeing the world in minuscule allows the Doctor and his companions—and by extension, the viewer—to appreciate more the effects that this insecticide will have, not just on insects but on everything.

But it was not until nine years later, when environmentalism had moved to the center of British society, when the series took a more overtly "green" tone, with the story "The Green Death" which sought to entertain *and* enlighten viewers about a topical, important and contemporary issue which faced Britain at the time—that of pollution. Both "The Green Death" and "Invasion of the Dinosaurs" deal with contemporary issues which were complex and had no obvious or easy answer. While *Doctor Who* was not the only program which sought to cover environmental issues in the 1960s and early 1970s, it is clear that such issues were an influence both on the writers of the program and its wider audience.

NOTES

1. "Management of Wildlife as a Natural Resource," p. 27, prepared for the Stockholm Conference, 1972, The Nature Conservancy, FT8/9, The National Archives (hereafter TNA), London.

2. Agriculture (Poisonous Chemicals) Act 1952, Chapter 60 15 and 16 Geo 6 and 1 Eliz 2—http://www.legislation.gov.uk/ukpga/Geo6and1Eliz2/15 16/60/introduction. Accessed March 12, 2016.

3. "The Green Death" DVD Extras, "The One with the Maggots" and "Richard Sloman Interview," released in the UK on August 5, 2013.

4. Memo from Barry Letts (Producer) to Don Shaw regarding newspaper article for *Doctor Who* story "The Green Death," March 9 in T65/71/1—The Green Death, WAC. Also "Government Go-Ahead for Global" (no other information but presumably typed copy of newspaper article), in T65/71/1—The Green Death, WAC.

5. There is mention of an increasing public concern for pollution in the 1970 annual report of the Natural Environment Research Council. The report also notes that the "growing public apprehension of the impact that modern society is having on the natural environment has been sharply underlined … by the problem of pollution." See The Natural Environment Research Council Annual Report, 1970, p. 2, FT6/15, TNA. As a result the government even established a special commission to look into this problem—the Royal Commission on Environmental Pollution. See "Information and Advice" Policy Compendium, The Nature Conservancy Council, FT8/9, TNA. The Nature Conservancy became separate to the Natural Environmental Research Council in 1973 with the formation of the Nature Conservancy Council.

ARCHIVES

House of Commons Debates

House of Commons Debate, "Chemical Sprays (Toxic Effects)," February 19, 1953, vol. 511 cc1448–9—http://hansard.millbanksystems.com/commons/1953/feb/19/chemical-sprays-toxic-effects. Accessed March 12, 2016.

House of Lords, "The Queen's Speech," July 2, 1970, vol. 311 cc9–13—http://hansard.millbanksystems.com/lords/1970/jul/02/the-queens-speech. Accessed March 12, 2016.

Morrison, J. House of Commons Debate, "Toxic sprays (Research)," November 20, 1952, vol. 507 c187W—http://hansard.millbanksystems.com/written_answers/1952/nov/20/toxic-sprays-research. Accessed March 12, 2016.

Legislation

Agriculture (Poisonous Chemicals) Act 1952, Chapter 60 15and 16 Geo 6 and 1 Eliz 2—http://www.legislation.gov.uk/ukpga/Geo6and1Eliz2/15 16/60/introduction. Accessed March 12, 2016.

Newspaper Articles

"Bevan Joins Tories in River Bill Protest." 1951. *Daily Mirror*, June 1, 7.

"Dirty Rivers." 1950. *The Times*, November 17, 5.

"Environment: More DDT in Antarctic Penguins." 1969. *The Times*, August 16, 17.

"When the Sedge Withers and No Birds Sing." 1963. *The Times*, February 14, 15.

Brien, Alan. 1970. "London: Of Man, Rats and the Absurd." *The New York Times*, April 6, 48.

Davy, John. 1963. "Menace in the *Silent Spring*." *The Observer*, February 17, 21.

BBC Written Archives (WAC)

"Government Go-Ahead for Global" (no other information but presumably typed copy of newspaper article), in T65/71/1—The Green Death, WAC.

Letter from Head of Television Administration Department to Sales Manager at Gamlen Chemical Company, 29 June 1973, in T65/71/1—The Green Death, WAC.

Letter from Sales Manager at Gamlen Chemical Company to the BBC, 25 June 1973, in T65/71/1—The Green Death, WAC.

Memo from Barry Letts (Producer) to Don Shaw regarding newspaper article for *Doctor Who* story "The Green Death," March 9 in T65/71/1—The Green Death, WAC.

R9/7/71—Audience Research Reports—Television—General Chronological September & October 1964—Week 45—Doctor Who "Planet of Giants," WAC.

Cambridge University Library (CUL)

"*Look* No. 3: 'Land of the Flamingo,'" program synopsis and running order," F.20, Papers of Sir Peter Scott, GB0012, CUL.

The National Archives (TNA)

"Information and Advice" Policy Compendium, The Nature Conservancy Council, FT 8/9, TNA.

"Management of Wildlife as a Natural Resource," prepared for the Stockholm Conference, 1972, The Nature Conservancy, FT 8/9, TNA.

The National Parks Commission, Eleventh Annual Report, 1960, COU 1/11, TNA.

The Natural Environment Research Council Annual Report, 1970, p. 2, FT6/15, TNA.

The Nature Conservancy Annual Report, 1961, FT 6/11, TNA.

The Nature Conservancy Annual Report, 1963, FT 6/13, TNA.

Bibliography

Barr, John. 1970. "Environment Lobby." *New Society* 384: 209–211.
Carson, Rachel. 1962. *Silent Spring*. Boston: Houghton Mifflin.
Goldsmith, Edward, Robert Allen, Michael Allaby, John Davoll, and Sam Lawrence. 1972. "A Blueprint for Survival." *The Ecologist* 2, no. 1: 1–43.
Graham, Frank, Jr. 1970. *Since Silent Spring*. London: Hamish Hamilton.

Secondary Sources

Abercrombie, Nicholas. 1997. *Television and Society*. Cambridge: Polity Press.
Attenborough, David. 2010. *Life on Air: Memoirs of a Broadcaster*. London: BBC Books.
Bate, Jonathan. 2001. *The Song of the Earth*. London: Picador.
Beckett, Andy. 2009. *When the Lights Went Out: Britain in the Seventies*. London: Faber & Faber.
Bocking, Stephen. 1997. *Ecologists and Environmental Politics: A History of Contemporary Ecology*. New Haven: Yale University Press.
Bousé, Derek. 2000. *Wildlife Films*. Philadelphia: University of Pennsylvania Press.
Burt, Jonathan. 2002. *Animals on Film*. London: Reaktion Books.
Cain, John. 1992. *The BBC: 70 Years of Broadcasting*. London: BBC Books.
Crowson, Nick, Matthew Hilton, and James MacKay, eds. 2009. *NGOs in Contemporary Britain: Non-state Actors in Society and Politics Since 1945*. Basingstoke: Palgrave Macmillan.
Evans, David. 1992. *A History of Nature Conservation in Britain*. London: Routledge.
Fiske, John. 2013. "Moments of Television: Neither the Text nor the Audience." In *Remote Control: Television Audiences and Cultural Power*. Edited by Ellen Seiter, Hans Borchers, Gabriele Kreutzner and Eva-Maria Warth. London: Routledge. pp. 56–78.
Guha, Ramachandra. 2000. *Environmentalism: A Global History*. London: Longman.
Hall, Stuart. 1975. "Encoding and Decoding in the Television Discourse." *Centre for Contemporary Cultural Studies—Media Series No. 7*, September: 1–19.
Hilton, Matthew. 2003. *Consumerism in 20th Century Britain*. Cambridge: Cambridge University Press.
Howe, David J., and Stephen James Walker. 2013. *The Television Companion: The Unofficial and Unauthorised Guide to Doctor Who*, Vol. 1. Prestatyn: Telos.
Jorgensen, Dolly. 2012. "A Blueprint for Destruction: Eco-Activism in *Doctor Who* During the 1970s." *Ecozona* 3: 11–26.
Kitchin, Rob, and James Kneale. 2001. "Science Fiction or Future Fact? Exploring Imaginative Geographies of the New Millennium." *Progress in Human Geography* 25, no. 1: 19–35.
Lear, Linda. 1997. *Rachel Carson: Witness to Nature*. London: Macmillan.
Lutts, Ralph H. 1985. "Chemical Fallout: Rachel Carson's *Silent Spring*, Radioactive Fallout & the Environmental Movement." *Environmental Review* 9: 210–225.
McKay, James, and Matthew Hilton. 2009. "Introduction." In *NGOs in Contemporary Britain: Non-state Actors in Society and Politics Since 1945*. Edited by Nick Crowson, Matthew Hilton and James McKay. Basingstoke: Palgrave Macmillan. pp. 1–20.
Mitman, Gregg. 1999. *Reel Nation: America's Romance with Wildlife on Film*. Cambridge: Harvard University Press.
Morley, David. 2013. "Changing Paradigms in Audience Studies." In *Remote Control: Television Audiences and Cultural Power*. Edited by Ellen Seiter, Hans Borchers, Gabriele Kreutzner and Eva-Maria Warth. London: Routledge. pp. 16–43.
Nehring, Holger. 2005. "The Growth of Social Movements." In *A Companion to Contemporary Britain, 1939–2000*. Edited by Paul Addison and Harriet Jones. Oxford: Blackwell. pp. 389–406.
Newcomb, Horace, and Paul M. Hirsch. 1983. "Television as a Cultural Forum: Implications for Research," *Quarterly Review of Film Studies* 8: 44–55.
Nicholson, Max. 1987. *The New Environmental Age*. Cambridge: Cambridge University Press.
Ritvo, Harriet. 2009. *The Dawn of Green: Manchester, Thirlmere & Modern Environmentalism*. Chicago: University of Chicago Press.

Rome, Adam. 2003. "'Give Earth a Chance': The Environmental Movement and the Sixties." *Journal of American History* 90: 525–554.

Rootes, Christopher. 2009. "Environmental NGOs and the Environmental Movement in England." In *NGOs in Contemporary Britain: Non-State Actors in Society and Politics since 1945.* Edited by Nick Crowson, Matthew Hilton and James MacKay. Basingstoke: Palgrave Macmillan. pp. 201–221.

Schwarzenbach, Alexis. 2011. *Saving the World's Wildlife: The WWF's First Fifty Years.* London: Profile Books.

Seiter, Ellen, Hans Borchers, Gabriele Kreutzner, and Eva-Maria Warth, Eva-Maria, eds. 2013. *Remote Control: Television Audiences and Cultural Power.* London: Routledge.

Sheail, John. 1985. *Pesticides and Nature Conservation: The British Experience, 1950–1975.* Oxford: Oxford University Press.

Sheail, John. 1998. *Nature Conservation in Britain: The Formative Years.* London: The Stationary Office.

Sheail, John. 2002. *An Environmental History of Twentieth-Century Britain.* London: Palgrave.

Solnit, Rebecca. 2003. "Three Who Made a Revolution." *The Nation*, March 16. http://www.thenation.com/article/three-who-made-revolution#axzz2c2vbR2EG. Accessed March 12, 2016.

Tulloch, John. 1995. "'Through a Little Bit of Poison into Future Generations': *Doctor Who* Audiences and Ideology." In *Science Fiction Audiences: Watching Doctor Who and Star Trek.* Edited by John Tulloch and Henry Jenkins. London: Routledge. pp. 67–85.

Tulloch, John, and Henry Jenkins, eds. 1995. *Science Fiction Audiences: Watching Doctor Who and Star Trek.* London: Routledge.

Veldman, Meredith. 1994. *Fantasy, the Bomb and the Greening of Britain: Romantic Protest, 1945–1980.* Cambridge: Cambridge University Press.

Walshe, Tom, Colin Bevan, Ruth Sealy, and Naomi Phillipson. 1999. *A Knight on the Box: 40 Years of Anglia Television.* Norwich: Anglia Television Limited.

Wheeler, Michael, ed. 1995. *Ruskin and Environment: The Storm-Cloud of the Nineteenth Century.* Manchester: Manchester University Press.

Williams, Jack. 2004. *Entertaining the Nation: A Social History of British Television.* Stroud: Sutton.

Winter, James. 1999. *Secure from Rash Assault: Sustaining the Victorian Environment.* Berkeley: University of California Press.

Wood, Tat. 2009. *About Time: The Unauthorized Guide to Doctor Who 1970–1974 Seasons 7 to 11,* 2d ed. Des Moines: Mad Norwegian Press.

Wood, Tat, and Lawrence Miles. 2006. *About Time: The Unauthorized Guide to Doctor Who 1963–1966 Seasons 1 to 3.* Des Moines: Mad Norwegian Press.

FILMOGRAPHY

Dixon of Dock Green. 1955–1976.

"The Green Death," broadcast between May 19 and June 23, 1973. Third Doctor. Director: Michael E. Briant. Writers: Robert Sloman and Barry Letts.

The Incredible Shrinking Man. 1957. Director: Jack Arnold. Writer: Richard Matheson

"Invasion of the Dinosaurs," broadcast between January 12 and February 16, 1974. Third Doctor. Director: Paddy Russell. Writer: Malcolm Hulke.

Look. 1955–1981.

"Planet of Giants," broadcast between October 31 and November 14, 1964. First Doctor. Director: Mervyn Pinfield. Writer: Louis Marks.

Appendix.
Adventures Referenced

"The Android Invasion." 1975. Director: Barry Letts. Writer: Terry Nation. BBC.
"Asylum of the Dalek." 2012. Director: Nick Hurran. Writer: Steven Moffatt. BBC.
"The Attack of the Cybermen." 1985. Director: Matthew Robinson. Writer: Paula Moore. BBC.
"The Awakening." 1984. Director: Michael Owen Morris. Writer: Eric Pringle. BBC.
"The Aztecs." 1964. Director: John Crockett. Writer: John Lucarotti.
"Battlefield." 1989. Director: Michael Kerrigan. Writer: Ben Aaronovitch. BBC.
"The Beast Below." 2010. Director: Andrew Gunn. Writer: Steven Moffat. BBC.
"Before the Flood." 2015. Director: Daniel O'Hara. Writer: Toby Whitehouse. BBC.
"The Big Bang." 2010. Director: Toby Haynes. Writer: Steven Moffat. BBC.
"Black Orchid." 1982, Director: Ron Jones. Writer: Terence Dudley. BBC.
"Carnival of Monsters." 1973. Director: Barry Letts. Writer: Robert Holmes. BBC.
"Castrovalva." 1982. Director: Fiona Cumming. Writer: Christopher H. Bidmead. BBC.
"The Caves of Androzani." 1984. Director: Graeme Harper. Writer: Robert Holmes. BBC.
"The Celestial Toymaker." 1966. Written by Brian Hayles and Donald Tosh. Directed by Bill Sellars. BBC.
"A Christmas Carol." 2010. Director: Toby Haynes. Writer: Steven Moffat. BBC.
"City of Death." 1977. Director: Michael Hayes. Writer: David Agnew (Douglas Adams, Graham Williams, and David Fisher). BBC.
"The Claws of Axos." 1971. Director: Michael Ferguson. Writer: Bob Baker and Dave Martin. BBC.
"Cold Blood." 2010. Director: Ashley Way. Writer: Chris Chibnall.
"Curse of Fenric." 1989. Director: Nicholas Mallett. Writer: Ian Briggs.
"The Curse of the Fatal Death." 1999. Director: John Henderson. Writer: Steven Moffatt. BBC.
"The Daemons." 1971. Director: Christopher Barry. Writer: Guy Leopold (Barry Letts and Robert Sloman). BBC.
"Day of the Doctor." 2013. Director: Nick Hurran. Writer: Steven Moffat. BBC.
"The Deadly Assassin." 1976. Director: David Maloney. Writer: Robert Holmes. BBC.
"Dinosaurs on a Spaceship." 2012. Director: Saul Metzstein. Writer: Chris Chibnall. BBC.
"Earthshock." 1982. Director: Peter Grimwade. Writer: Eric Saward. BBC.
"The Edge of Destruction." 1964. Directed by Richard Martin and Frank Cox. Written by David Whittaker.
"End of the World." 2005. Director: Euros Lyn. Writer: Russell T. Davies. BBC.
"The End of Time." 2009. Director: Euros Lyn. Writer: Russell T. Davies. BBC.
"The Evil of the Daleks." 1967. Director: Derek Martinus. Writer: David Whitaker.
"Face of Evil." 1977. Director: Pennant Roberts. Writer: Chris Boucher. BBC.

"The Faceless Ones." 1967. Director: Gerry Mill. Writer: David Ellis and Malcolm Hulke. BBC.

"The Fires of Pompeii." 2008. Director: Colin Teague. Writer: James Moran.

"The Five Doctors." 1983. Director: Peter Moffatt. Writer: Terrance Dicks. BBC.

"Genesis of the Daleks." 1975. Director: David Maloney. Writer: Terry Nation.

"Ghost Light." 1989. Director: Alan Wareing. Writer: Marc Platt. BBC.

"The Girl in the Fireplace." 2006. Director: Euros Lyn. Writer: Steven Moffat. BBC.

"The Girl Who Died." 2015. Director: Ed Bazalgette. Writer: Jamie Mathieson and Steven Moffat. BBC.

"The Greatest Show in the Galaxy." 1988–1989. Director: Alan Wareing. Writer: Stephen Wyatt.

"The Green Death." 1973. Director: Michael E. Briant Writer: Robert Sloman and Barry Letts. BBC.

"The Gunfighters." 1966. Director: Rex Tucker. Writer: Donald Cotton.

"The Highlanders." 1966–1967. Director: Hugh David. Writer: Elwyn Jones and Gerry Davis. BBC.

"The Horns of Nimon." 1979–1980. Director: Kenny McBain. Writer: Anthony Read. BBC.

"The Impossible Planet." 2006. Director: James Strong. Writer: Matt Jones. BBC.

"Inferno." 1970. Director: Douglas Camfield and Barry Letts. Writer: Don Houghton. BBC.

"Invasion of the Dinosaurs." 1974. Director: Paddy Russell. Writer: Malcolm Hulke. BBC.

"The King's Demons." 1983. Director: Tony Virgo. Writer: Terence Dudley. BBC.

"Last of the Time Lords." 2006. Director: Colin Teague. Writer: Russell T. Davies. BBC.

"Marco Polo." 1964. Director: Waris Hussein and John Crockett. Writer: John Lucarotti. BBC.

"The Mark of the Rani." 1985. Director: Sarah Hellings. Writer: Pip and Jane Baker. BBC

"The Masque of Mandragora." 1976. Director: Rodney Bennett. Writer: Louis Marks. BBC.

"The Mind of Evil." 1971. Director: Timothy Combe. Writer: Don Houghton. BBC.

"The Mind Robber." 1968. Director: David Maloney. Writer: Peter Ling and Derrick Sherwin.

"The Myth Makers." 1965. Director: Michael Leeston-Smith. Writer: Donald Cotton. BBC.

"The Pandorica Opens." 2011. Director: Toby Haynes. Writer: Steven Moffat.

"Planet of the Giants." 1963. Director: Mervyn Pinfield and Douglas Camfield. Writer: Louis Marks.

"Planet of the Ood." 2006. Director: Graeme Harper. Writer: Keith Temple. BBC.

"Pyramids of Mars." 1975. Director: Paddy Russell. Writer: Stephen Harris (Lewis Greifer and Robert Holmes). BBC.

"The Reign of Terror." 1964. Director: Henric Hirsch and John Gorrie. Writer: Dennis Spooner. BBC.

"Resurrection of the Daleks." 1984. Director: Matthew Robinson. Writer: Eric Saward. BBC.

"Robot of Sherwood." 2014. Director: Paul Murphy. Writer: Mark Gatiss. BBC.

"The Romans." 1965. Director: Christopher Barry. Writer: Dennis Spooner.

"The Satan Pit." 2006. Director: James Strong. Writer: Matt Jones.

"The Savages." 1966. Director: Christopher Barry. Writer: Ian Stuart Black. BBC.

"The Sea Devils." 1972. Director: Michael Briant. Writer: Malcolm Hulke. BBC.

"The Shakespeare Code." 2007. Director: Charles Palmer. Writer: Gareth Roberts. BBC.

"The Sound of Drums." 2007. Director: Colin Teague. Writer: Russell T. Davies. BBC.

"Spearhead from Space." 1970. Director: Derek Martinus. Writer: Robert Holmes. BBC.

"State of Decay." 1980. Director: Peter Moffatt. Writer: Terrance Dicks. BBC.

"The Tenth Planet." 1966. Director: Derek Martinus. Writer: Kit Pedler and Gerry Davis. BBC.

"Terminus." 1983. Director: Mary Ridge. Writer: Stephen Gallagher. BBC.

"The Three Doctors." 1972–1973. Director: Lennie Mayne. Writer: Bob Baker and Dave Martin. BBC.

"The Time Meddler." 1965. Director: Douglas Camfield. Writer: Dennis Spooner. BBC.

"The Time Monster." 1972. Director: Paul Bernard. Writer: Robert Sloman (and Barry Letts). BBC.

"The Time Warrior." 1973–1974. Director: Alan Bromley. Writer: Robert Holmes. BBC.

"Timelash." 1985. Director: Pennant Roberts. Writer: Glen McCoy. BBC.

"Tooth and Claw." 2006. Director: Euros Lynn. Writer: Russell T. Davies. BBC.
"The Trial of a Time Lord [Mindwarp]." 1986. Director: Ron Jones. Writer: Philip Martin. BBC.
"The Two Doctors." 1985. Director: Peter Moffatt. Writer: Robert Holmes. BBC.
"The Underwater Menace." 1967. Director: Julia Smith. Writer: Geoffrey Orme. BBC.
"Underworld." 1978. Director: Norman Stewart. Writer: Bob Baker and Dave Martin. BBC.
"An Unearthly Child." 1963. Director: Waris Hussein. Written by Anthony Coburn. BBC.
"The Unicorn and the Wasp." 2008. Director: Graeme Harper. Writer: Gareth Roberts. BBC.
"The Unquiet Dead." 2005. Director: Euros Lyn. Writer: Mark Gatiss. BBC.
"Vengeance on Varos." 1985. Director: Ron Jones. Writer: Philip Martin. BBC.
"Vincent and the Doctor." 2010 Director: Jonny Campbell. Writer: Richard Curtis. BBC.
"The Visitation." 1982. Director: Peter Moffatt. Writer: Eric Saward. BBC.
"The War Games." 1969. Director: David Maloney. Writer: Terence Dicks and Malcolm Hulke.
"The Web Planet." 1965. Director: Richard Martin. Writer: Bill Strutton.
"The Wrath of the Iceni." 2012. Director: Ken Bentley. Writer: John Dorney. Big Finish.

About the Contributors

Carey **Fleiner** is a senior lecturer in classical and early medieval history at the University of Winchester. Her research interests include film and television depictions of the Romans, and the cultural influence of the music of Ray Davies and The Kinks. Her publications include *"Optima Mater"* in *Royal Mothers and Their Ruling Children* (2015).

Marcus K. **Harmes** is a senior lecturer at the University of Southern Queensland in Australia. He is the author of *Doctor Who and the Art of Adaptation* (2014). As a small child he was terrified when watching "The Greatest Show in the Galaxy" and "The Curse of Fenric," and *Doctor Who* has remained an object of fascination ever since.

Karen **Hellekson** is an independent scholar who has published widely on science fiction and fan studies, including *Doctor Who* and alternate history. She is the founding coeditor of the academic journal *Transformative Works and Cultures* (http://journal.transformativeworks.org/).

Rhonda **Knight** is a professor of English at Coker College, where she teaches medieval and early modern literature. She has published articles on varied topics, including Gerald of Wales, *Sir Gawain and the Green Knight*, and several mystery writers. This is her second contribution to a volume on *Doctor Who*.

Kristine **Larsen** is a professor of astronomy at Central Connecticut State University. Her teaching and research focus on the intersections between science and society, including gender issues in science and depictions of science in popular media. She is the author of a book on Stephen Hawking and co-editor of one on Neil Gaiman.

Peter **Lowe** is a senior lecturer in English literature at the Bader International Study Centre (Queen's University Canada), Herstmonceux Castle, East Sussex. His research interest focus on the literature of the twentieth century, particularly the poetry and prose of the Modernist period. He is the author of *Christian Romanticism* (2006) and *English Journeys* (2012).

Susana **Loza** is an associate professor of critical race, gender, and media studies at Hampshire College. Her publications include "Playing Alien in Post-Racial Times," "Vampires, Queers, and Other Monsters," and "Hashtag Feminism, #SolidarityIs ForWhiteWomen, and the Other #FemFuture."

Aven **McMaster** teaches in the Ancient Studies Department at Thorneloe University at Laurentian. She enjoys finding ways to connect *Doctor Who* to her teaching and research, which includes language, Roman and Greek literature, and Roman culture. She cohosts two podcasts on literature and language: The Endless Knot Podcast, and As We Like It.

Dene **October** is a senior lecturer at University of the Arts London. He leads modules in *Doctor Who* by Design and Fan Cultures. He is the author of several articles and a monograph on *Doctor Who*. He also writes about David Bowie and has several publications on the artist's media, performance and legacy.

Andrew **O'Day** received his Ph.D. in television studies from Royal Holloway, University of London. He is the editor of *Doctor Who: The Eleventh Hour* (2014) and of the forthcoming volume *Doctor Who: Twelfth Night*. He has also contributed articles to a range of edited collections on *Doctor Who*.

Mark **Sundaram** teaches at Laurentian University. He has created a video series about etymology, literature and history on the Alliterative YouTube channel, and he also cohosts The Endless Knot podcast, featuring conversations and interviews on those topics, along with the As We Like It podcast on film adaptations of Shakespeare.

Ramie **Tateishi** is the program director of the M.A. in film studies program at National University. His work on film, television, and popular culture has appeared in journals such as *Asian Cinema*, in collections such as *Fear Without Frontiers* (2003), and *The Language of Doctor Who* (2014).

Mark **Wilson** teaches English in Beijing. He writes about environmental disasters, such as the Great London smog disaster (1952) and the impact on Rachel Carson's *Silent Spring*, environmental pressure groups, and television programs have had in raising awareness on environmental issues.

Index

Ace 108, 113–14, 156–161, 165
Adaptation 8–9, 14–16, 23, 26, 29*n*4, 35, 42–43, 132–138, 141, 143–146
Adric 5, 12*n*2
Agency 118–120, 127, 129, 130; audience 15–16, 19, 21, 24, 27
Alternate history 118, 120, 121, 126–129; genetic theory of 118, 120, 128
Amnesia 21, 26
"The Android Invasion" (1975) 169, 171, 176–179; village location in 171, 176–179
Archive 25, 108, 125, 142, 200*n*1; BBC written 3, 12*n*1, 29*n*3, 30*n*15, 73*n*1n2; junking, missing, wiped 13, 20, 23–24, 27–28, 29*n*3
Arthur, King of Britain 5
Asimov, Isaac *see* "The Ugly Little Boy"
"Asylum of the Daleks" (2012) 5
Atlantis *see* Mythology
"Attack of the Cybermen," (1985) 99
Audience reception, classical 63, 70, 71, 74*n*15
Auel, Jean *see The Clan of the Cave Bear*
"Auld Mortality" (2003) 120, 124, 126, 128
"The Awakening" (1984) 7, 92–100
"The Aztecs" (1964) 4, 16, 26, 29*n*11, 64, 73*n*9, 80, 94, 97, 98, 149

Baker, Colin 4, 118, 176
Baker, Tom 4, 43, 102, 122, 176
"Ballad of the Last Chance Saloon" (song) 85
Barry, Christopher 61, 62, 73*n*6, 73*n*7, 74*n*14, 74*n*15, 76*n*55
Bartock, Danny 53
"Battlefield" (1989) 2, 5
Baverstock, Donald 3
Bayldon, Geoffrey 120, 121, 124
BBC 87–90, 197–199; and anti-commercial bias 87–90; Audience Research Reports 16, 29*n*5, 71–72, 75*n*52, 76*n*57, 89–90; books 102, 109; education and 2, 15–16, 20; Eighth Doctor Adventures range 109, 112, 113, 116; family entertainment 13; national culture 1, 26; Past Doctor Adventures range 109, 116; Radiophonic Workshop 17; sales 23; stor-

age 23, 28, 30*n*15; studios 21; written archives 3, 12*n*1, 29*n*3, 30*n*15, 73*n*1n2
"The Beast Below" (2010) 11
Beckles, Sir Hilary 56, 58
Beelzebub 99
"Before the Flood" (2015) 11
Benton, Sergeant 39
"The Big Bang" (2010) 3
Big Finish 35, 44–45, 120, 127, 130*n*2
"Black Orchid" (1982) 4
Blood Harvest (1994) 115
A Blueprint for Survival 187, 191, 197, 199
Bolter, Jay David, and Grusin, Richard 14, 19, 21
Boudica 35, 44–45
Boule, Marcellin 150–151, 154, 157
Brantlinger, Patrick 51, 52, 55, 59
Briggs, Ian 139, 142
Britannicus, step-brother to Nero 67, 69
British Broadcasting Corporation *see* BBC
Brown, Perpugilliam (Peri) 112
Bryant, Peter 104
Bush, Melanie 120, 128, 129

Cambridge Latin Course see Latin
Cambridge University 36
Camera 14, 50, 83, 86–87, 93, 98; frame mobility 20–22, 29*n*2
Campbell, Joseph, monomyth 42
Capaldi, Peter 5
"Carnival of Monsters" (1973) 93
Carpenter, John 142
Carry on, Cleo (1964) 63, 67, 72
Carry on Cowboy (1965) 87
Carry On series 38
Carson, Rachel 186, 189–191, 194–196, 199, 200
"Castrovalva" (1982) 94
Casualties of War (2000) 116
Causality 118
Cause and effect 118–120, 128–130
Cavaliers 96
"The Caves of Androzani" (1984) 93

209

"The Celestial Toymaker" (1966) 27
Chancellor Goth 94
Chaplet, Dodo 82, 85
Chatterton *see* Chesterton, Ian
Chesterfield *see* Chesterton, Ian
Chesterton, Ian 2, 13, 24, 37, 61–64, 68, 71, 97–98, 194
Christie, Agatha 5
"A Christmas Carol" (2010) 5
Churchill, Winston 5, 7
"City of Death" (1977) 2, 4
The Clan of the Cave Bear 149, 155–156, 163
Clanton, Billy 83
Class 6, 36, 38–40, 50–51, 53, 112, 158, 169, 171, 194; as demonstrated by classical education 36, 38–40; of characters within *Doctor Who* 39–40, 46n1n3
Classical civilization, field of scholarship 37–41, 43–44; taught in schools 37, 40–43, 63
Claudius, Emperor of Rome 64, 69, 74n25, 75n35, 75n44
"The Claws of Axos" (1971) 182
Cleopatra (1963) 7, 63
"Cold Blood" (2010) 61
Collings, David 120
Colonel Wolsey 94, 95–96, 97, 98
Colonialism 47, 50; British 6, 9, 51, 53–58; European 52, 54
Colorblindness 48–49
Comedy, in *Doctor Who* 6–7, 52, 63, 65, 74n18
Constructivism 41, 43
Control (character) 157
Costume 48, 62, 80–83, 84, 94, 173
Cotton, Donald 3, 79
Courtney, Nicholas 38, 46n3, 120, 172
Cro-Magnons 148–150, 152–154, 156–157, 161–163, 165
Cromwell, Oliver 94
The Curse of Fenric (1989) 3, 133, 134, 136, 137, 138–144
"The Curse of the Fatal Death" (1999) 3
Cusick, Ray 61, 73n8

Dad's Army (1968–1977) 169–170
"The Daemons" (1971) 38, 98–99, 168, 169, 171, 172–176, 183–184; village location in 171, 172–176, 183–184
Daleks 4, 70, 71, 122
"The Daleks' Master Plan" (1965–66) 4
Darvill, Arthur 44
Das 148, 162–165
Davies, Russell T. 5, 10, 40, 43
Davis, Gerry 79
Davison, Peter 4, 135
Davros 122, 123
"The Day of the Doctor" (2013) 5, 26
"Deadline" (2003) 120, 125, 126
"The Deadly Assassin" (1976) 94
Deleuze, Gilles 22

Delgado, Roger 38, 172
Demons 99
Deracialization 49, 54
The Devil 99
Dickens, Charles 5
Dicks, Terrance 46n3, 46n4, 102–16
"Dinosaurs on a Spaceship" (2012) 5
Dixon of Dock Green (1955–1976) 200
The Doctor (character): first 1, 4, 14–16, 20, 24, 26, 37, 61, 63, 66, 67, 82, 84, 104, 107, 118, 120, 124, 128, 194; second 5, 7, 72, 103–6, 107, 112, 114–15, 124, 148, 156; third 38–39, 104–5, 106, 118, 119, 121–124, 128, 130n3, 169, 171–174, 180–183, 194; fourth 2, 4, 42–44, 122, 176–179; fifth 4, 12n2, 148, 161–162; sixth 7, 106, 112, 118, 128, 176; seventh 107–9, 113–14, 120, 128, 148–149, 156–161, 165; eighth 109–11, 113–14, 128; ninth 5, 149, 162–163, 165; tenth 5, 39–40, 43, 52–56, 130n2, 165; eleventh 5, 11, 44; twelfth 5
Doctor Who: audience expectations 5, 7, 62, 63, 64, 73n6, 73n8; class and gender studies 6, 9; genre 18–19, 24, 47, 92, 132, 137, 142, 194—alternate history 118, 120–121, 126, 129, "celebrity-historicals," 5, 10, fantasy 94, historical fiction 98, gothic 94, 98, mystery horror 99, "pseudo" historical 4, 6, 15, 93, 94, 96–97, 99, 100, "pure" historical 2–4, 6, 7, 10, 15, 93–94, travel log 93; media studies 5–6, 8–10; mission statement 3–4, 11, 62, 74n14; program history 1, 2–4, 7, 8, 10; time line 120, 122, 125, 128; *see also* fans and fandom
Doctor Who (1996) 109
Doctor Who Unbound (2003, 2005, 2008) 118–121, 125, 129, 130
Dorney, John 44

Earp, Wyatt 84
"Earthshock" (1982) 2, 99
Eccleston, Christopher 5
"The Edge of Destruction" (1964) 23
Education 15, 18, 35–36, 38–41, 62, 63, 64, 65, 73n9; class and status 36, 39, 40, 45; classical in Britain 3, 43, 62–64, 73n2; history of in Britain and Wales 35–36; *see also* BBC; class
Egyptology 99
The Eight Doctors (1997) 102, 109–10, 115
Elizabeth I, Queen of England 5
Emma 3
Emmerson, Steve 116
"End of the World" (2005) 2, 5
Endgame (2000) 102, 111, 112–14
English Civil War 93, 94, 96, 100
Enkidu 159–161
Environment 186–200
Eugenics 156, 163
"The Evil of the Daleks" (1967) 10, 116

Evolution 150–151, 153–159, 161–163, 165
"Exile" (2003) 119, 123, 124

"Face of Evil" (1977) 2
"The Faceless Ones" (1967) 116
fans and fandom 9, 10, 70, 74*n*15, 102–17, 125–126, 180, 194; discussion 20, 24, 25, 28; fan-historians 28, 134; recordings 13–14, 28; reconstructions 6, 9, 10, 13–14, 19–24 26–27, 28;
Fawkes, Guy 95
Feminist theory 37, 44
Fenn-Cooper, Redvers 159
"Fires of Pompeii" (2008) 39–41, 43, 61, 70, 72, 73
"The Five Doctors" (1983) 93, 105, 115
Focalization 22
Ford, Carole Ann 15, 97, 118, 120, 194
Foreman, Susan 7, 15, 17, 20, 24, 26–27, 97, 118, 120, 124–126, 194, 195
Foss, Eric 50–51, 59
Francis, Derek 61, 66–67, 70
Franklin, Richard 42
Freud, Sigmund 41, 73
"Full Fathom Five" (2003) 127
A Funny Thing Happened on the Way to the Forum (1964) 66, 72

Gallifrey 7, 106, 115, 118, 120, 124–126
Gargoyle 99
Gatiss, Mark 121, 180
Gaunt, Simon 18–19
"Genesis of the Daleks" (1975) 122
Genetic engineering 162–163
Genre 18–19; *see also* Doctor Who
Gérôme, Jean-Léon 64, 75*n*34
"Ghost Light" (1989) 148–149, 152, 156–159
Ghost Light (novel) 148–149, 151–152, 156, 158–159
Ghost stories 133, 138, 140, 141, 142
Gilgamesh 159–161
Gillan, Karen 41
"The Girl in the Fireplace" (2006) 5
The Girl Who Died (2015) 143
Gogh, Vincent van 5
Golding, William *see The Inheritors*
Grant, Jo 38–39, 173, 180, 196, 197
Great London smog 188, 195
Great Man (theory of history) 119, 123–130
"The Greatest Show in the Galaxy" (1988) 8, 132, 135
Greek 38, 38; quotations in 38; teaching of 36
"The Green Death" (1973) 177, 182; companion in 196, 197; environment in 194, 196, 197, 198, 199
The Grisly Folk (1921) 149, 154
Gunfight at the O.K. Corral (1957) 81, 85
"The Gunfighters" (1966) 7, 27, 78–90; "Ballad of the Last Chance Saloon" (song) 85; cinematography 85–87; conception of 79–81; costuming 82–83; reception of 87–90; set design 86–87; Western accents 83–85

Halbwachs, Maurice 25
Halpen, Klineman 51–52, 54–55
Hamlet 98
Hampden, Jane 95, 96, 97–98, 99
Harkness, Jack 162–165
Hartnell, William 2, 4, 16, 26, 27, 37, 61, 63, 104, 118, 124, 134
Hashashins 15
"He Jests at Scars" (2003) 120, 127–129
Hegel, Joseph 17
Heriot, Zoe 103–104
"The Highlanders" (1966) 4
Hill, Jacqueline 61, 66
History 1–11, 92–98; alternate history 118, 120, 121, 126–129; as an analytical tool 5–6, 10; classical 6–7, 35–38, 45, 57–58; engagement with 5–6, 29*n*3*n*4, 56, 79–84, 134–134
Holliday, Doc 82, 86
Holmes, Robert 106, 115
Homo sapiens sapiens see Cro-Magnons
Hood, Robin 5
"The Horns of Nimon" (1979) 42, 46*n*4
Horus 99
Hughey, Matthew 49, 52, 54, 56, 57, 59
Hulke, Malcolm 102, 103–4, 107
Humans, anatomically modern *see* Cro-Magnons
Humor *see* comedy/history
Hurt, John 127
Hussein, Waris 21, 28*n*2, 29*n*7
Hutchinson, Sir George 93–98, 100
Hypermediacy 19–20

Identity, British 35, 36, 38, 44–45, 46*n*1, 48–51, 171, 174, 176, 181, 187–196, 199
Imperialism 48, 50, 53, 58; British 50, 54–55; European 47, 49, 50
"The Impossible Planet" (2006) 49, 50, 53, 60
The Incredible Shrinking Man (1957 film) 200
Industrial Revolution 97
"Inferno" (1970) 182
The Inheritors 149, 154, 156
"The Invasion of the Dinosaurs" (1974) 182; environment in 194, 197, 199, 200
Irongron 96, 97
Itxa 98

Jacobi, Derek 120, 121, 125, 126
Jaffa, Sir Ian of *see* Young man, tiresome
James, Montague Rhodes 140, 141, 142; *Ghost Stories of an Antiquary* (1904) 140
Jameson, Louise 44
Jason and the Argonauts (1963) 38, 43
Java Man 159
Jayston, Michael 120
Jenkins, Henry 23, 105, 107, 109, 111
John, King of England 97

Jones, Martha 3
Jovanka, Tegan 92, 95–97
Juliet Bravo (1980–1985) 125, 126
Jung, Carl 41

"The King's Demons" (1983) 4, 97
Kingston, Alex 44
Kneale, Nigel 142
Kublai Khan 18

Labyrinth 99
Lambert, Verity 2, 29n3, 62, 72, 73n2, 73n9, 74n14
Langford, Bonnie 120, 128
Last of the Gaderene (2000) 168, 169, 180–183; village location in 180–183
"Last of the Time Lords" (2006) 3
Latin 36–41; *Cambridge Latin Course* 37, 40–41, 43, 46n2; compulsory, in entrance requirements 36; quotations in 37–40; teaching of 36, 40; textbooks 37
Lavender, Isiah, III 47, 57, 59
Leela 44–45, 149, 163
Leiberman-Crelin hypothesis *see* Neanderthals, language
Leonard, David 55, 59
Leonard, Paul 116
Leonardo da Vinci 4
Lethbridge-Stewart, Brigadier Alistair Gordon 38–39, 120, 121, 172, 178, 181, 184
Letts, Barry 172
Levene, John 39
Lévi-Strauss, Claude 41
Liberal Humanism 48–49, 53, 57
Light (character) 157–158
Linx 96, 99
Literary Theory 37, 41, 43, 140
Little Hodcombe 92, 93, 94, 95
Littledale, Trevor 122
Lloyd, Innes 79, 80
Look 187, 192, 193, 199
Loose Cannon 20, 22, 26
Lucarotti, John 3, 13, 7, 21, 25, 28, 29n62, 74n10

Mackenzie, Inspector 158
Magistrate 96
The Making of Doctor Who (1972) 102, 107, 114
Malik, Sarita 49, 56, 59
Malus 93, 94, 95, 96, 97, 98, 100
Manning, Katy 38, 173
"Marco Polo" (1964) 3, 6, 13–30, 62, 70, 71, 74n10, 75n53, 93, 97, 98
"Mark of the Rani" (1985) 4, 97
Marks, Louis 3, 62
"The Masque of Mandragora" (1976) 3, 4, 62, 96–97
The Master 4, 38, 42, 97, 109, 121, 123, 172, 182–183
"Masters of War" (2008) 119, 121–124

Masterson, Bat 86
Matthews, Rev. Ernest 157, 159
McCoy, Sylvester 120, 135
McCrimmon, Jamie 103–4, 106, 114–15, 156
McLuhan, Marshall 13, 20
meddling 2, 139; memory *see* memory; milestone moments 26; myth *see* mythology; narrative 5–6, 14–17, 44, 143; production 9; public 9, 14–17, 26–27, 49; slavery *see* slavery
The Meddling Monk (character) 96
"The Meddling Monk" (1965) 4
Memory 13, 20–28
Mercurio, Solana 51–52
Mesopotamia 149, 152, 159–161
Metadrama 93, 96
Metafiction 92, 93–94, 94–98
Mills, Charles 49, 53, 59
"The Mind of Evil" (1971) 93, 182
"The Mind Robber" (1968) 5
Moffat, Steven 3
Molloy, Terry 122
Monroe, Marilyn 5
Morgus 93
"The Myth Makers" (1965) 2, 3, 38, 41, 79
Mythology 41–42; Atlantis 41–42; Jason and the Argonauts 42; monomyth 37, 42; Pandora 41; Theseus and the Minotaur 42; Trojan War 41, 69

Narrative 5–6, 7, 9, 13–19, 21–22, 26, 28–29n2, 35, 43–45, 47, 54, 57–58, 78, 82, 84, 87, 92–94, 96, 98–100, 102, 103, 109–110, 115–116, 133, 136, 139, 141, 143, 179, 187, 194, 196
Nathan-Turner, John 134
Nature Conservancy 188, 190, 191, 192, 193
Neandertals *see* Neanderthals
Neanderthals 8; anatomy 150–152, 154–155, 157, 159, 162, 164–165; culture 148, 151–152, 158–159, 161–162, 165; extinction 148, 153–154, 157, 160–163; genetics 148–149, 152–153, 164; intelligence 151–152, 154–155, 160, 162; interbreeding with Cro-Magnons 148, 152–154, 156, 161, 163–166; language 151–152, 154–155, 158, 162; position on human evolutionary tree 148–151, 154, 159, 162–165; religion 151–152, 154–155, 158–159; stereotypes of 149–151, 154, 156–157, 159–160, 162
Nefertiti 5
Nero, Emperor of Rome 7, 41, 61–77; actors who've portrayed 65–66; Christians, relationship with 61, 63, 64, 65, 66, 67, 68, 75n44; comedic portrayal 62, 64–65; cruelty 62, 67, 68–9, 72; film and television characterization 64–66; historical character 66–67; historical sources 65; "Mad Emperor" 72; mother (Agrippina), relationship with 64, 65, 66, 69, 73; musical

interests 64, 65, 67; popular image 63, 64, 67–68; sense of humor 68–69
Newbery, Barry 21, 86
Newbould, Frank 170, 183–184
Newman, Sydney 2, 3, 4, 12*n*1, 16, 62, 73*n*9
Nijhar, Preeti 49, 51, 52, 59
Nimrod 151, 157–160
Noble, Donna 39–40, 52–56
Norsemen *see* Vikings

"Observation," 148–149, 152, 154, 161–162
O'Neal, Siri 127
Only Human (2005) 148–150, 153–156, 162–165
Ood 6
Orthia, Lindy 48, 55, 59
Osterberg, Chantal 162–163
"Other" and "otherness" 6, 7, 8, 118, 124, 126, 160; alterity 118, 124, 130
Oxford University 36

"The Pandorica Opens" (2011) 41, 43–44, 61
Pastiche 98–99, 100
Peel, John 107–8
Pentangle 99
Performativity 16, 27
Pertwee, Jon 104–05, 118, 124, 169, 171
Pesticides 193, 194, 195, 196, 197, 199, 200
Picture Post (1938–1957, magazine) 171, 175, 179
Ping-Cho 14–17, 29*n*8
Pisa, Rustichello da 14, 18
"Planet of Giants" (1963) 8; companions in 194, 195; DN6 in 194, 195; environment in 193, 194, 195, 196, 197
"Planet of the Ood" (2008) 49, 50–52, 53–56, 59
Plautus 69, 70
Players (enemy) 105–106, 110–14, 115
Players (1999) 102, 106, 111, 112–13, 114
Polo, Marco 6, 13–30, 93
Pompadour, Madame de 5
Pompeii 39–40, 43
Pond, Amy 11, 41, 44
Positivist theory 41, 44
Postcolonial theory 6, 31, 37, 43–45, 46, 48, 49, 53, 55, 58, 60, 92, 98, 196
Postmodernism 92, 98–99, 100
Post-racialism 49, 53, 58
Pringle, Eric 92
"The Pyramids of Mars" (1975) 4, 99

Queen of the May 95, 100; and music 95; and spectacle 95
Quilley 163, 165
Quo Vadis (1951) 7, 38

Raaga 99
Racism 157–158, 163
Radiophonic Workshop *see* BBC

The Rani 97
Read, Anthony 42
Reception 5, 8–9, 16, 18–19, 27, 29*n*5, 70, 78, 89, 93, 191
"The Reign of Terror" (1964) 2, 3, 62, 63
Reith, John 15–16, 21
Remediation 6, 13–17, 22–24, 26–28, 29*n*4
Renaissance (Italian) 97
Representation 16
"Resurrection of the Daleks" (1984) 99
"The Return of the Neanderthal" 148, 156
Rieder, John 47, 49, 60
"Robots of Sherwood" (2014) 5
Role-playing 92–98
Roman era, signposts in media 63
Romans 35, 40–41, 44–45
"The Romans" (1965) 2, 3, 4, 37, 40–41, 61–64, 66–68, 70–73
Rome 37–40
"Rose" (2005) 165
Roundheads 96
Royalists 94
Runes and runic writing 136, 138, 139, 140, 141, 142, 143
Russell, William 37, 61

Sadok 99
Satan 99
"The Satan Pit" (2006) 49, 50, 53, 60
Scott, Peter 192
"The Sea Devils" (1972) 172
Season 6B 105–106, 109, 111, 112, 114–16
Sergeant Willow 94, 95–96
Seriality 15, 26–27, 29*n*4
Shadow in the Glass (2001) 176
Shakespeare, William 5, 38, 93, 98
"The Shakespeare Code" (2007) 5
The Sheriff of Fractured Jaw (1958) 87
Sherwin, Derrick 104
Sil 93
Silent Spring (1962) 186–187, 189–191, 194–197, 200; DDT in 189, 191, 195
Skaro 122
Sladen, Elisabeth 176
Slavery 49, 50–52, 53–55, 56–58; metaslavery 56–57; reparations for 54, 56–58
Smith, Josiah Samuel 156–159
Smith, Matt 5, 11, 44
Smith, Sarah-Jane 4, 176–177
Snow Globe 165
Song, River 3, 44
Sound design 17, 19–22, 29*n*7, 120–121
"Sound of Drums" (2006) 3
Soundtrack 9, 14, 29*n*2, 85
"Spearhead from Space" (1970) 106
Spooner, Dennis 3, 61, 62, 63, 74*n*13, 74*n*15, 134
Stagism 149, 156, 158, 161, 163, 165
Star Wars (1977) 42
"State of Decay" (1980) 115

Stephenson, George 4
"A Storm of Angels" (2005) 120, 124–126, 128
Studio constraints 20, 28n2, 29n9n10, 86, 104
Suetonius 64, 65, 69, 74n25, 75n28, 75n4
Sutekh 99
Swallow, Genevieve 125
"Sympathy for the Devil" (2003) 119, 121–124

Tacitus 65, 68, 69, 75n28, 75n44
TARDIS 1, 2, 4, 13–15, 17, 23–24, 27, 40, 43,
    46, 48, 55, 72, 82–84, 92, 94, 97, 100, 106,
    109, 115, 120, 122, 124–129, 152, 161–163, 177,
    194
Tate, Catherine 39
Taylor, Steven 82–85; Western accent 84;
    Western costuming 82–83
Tegana 14, 22, 25, 27
Telepathy 154–156
Television ownership 191
Televisuality 20–21, 23, 28
Tennant, David 5, 39, 43, 130n2
"The Tenth Planet" (1966) 104
Terence 70, 71
Terileptils 99
Terminus (1983) 134–135
Terunda 156
Thal 122
Third Programme (1946–1970) 79
"The Three Doctors" (1973) 105
Time Lords 103–104, 106, 107, 110, 114, 115
"The Time Meddler" (1965) 96
The Time Meddler (1965) 15, 96, 132, 133–134
"The Time Monster" (1972) 38–39, 41–42
"Timelash" (1985) 2, 4
Timewyrm: Exodus (1991) 102, 107–8, 113–14
Timewyrm: Genesys (1991) 107–08, 149–150,
    159–161
Tlotoxl 94, 98
"Tooth and Claw" (2006) 5
Tosh, Donald 79–80
Transmedia 15, 25, 27, 29n4
Transmodernism 17
Transparency 19–20, 24
"Trial of a Time Lord" (1986) 93, 128
Troughton, Patrick 4, 5, 10, 72, 97, 103
Troy see Mythology
Tucker, Rex 86
Tulloch, John 105, 107, 111
Turing, Alan 139–140
The Turing Test (2000) 116
Turlough 92, 96, 98, 161–162
"The Two Doctors" (1985) 105, 106, 114–15
Tyler, Rose 53–54, 162–163, 165
Tyneham, Evacuation of 176

The Ugly Little Boy (1959) 149, 154–155
"The Underwater Menace" (1967) 42
"Underworld" (1978) 42, 46n3, n4
"An Unearthly Child" (1963) 14

"The Unicorn and the Wasp" (2008) 5
UNIT 118, 121, 122, 171, 178, 183
United Nations Intelligence Taskforce see
    UNIT
"The Unquiet Dead" (2005) 5

Valeyard 120, 128, 129
"Vengeance on Varos" (1985) 93
Verney, Andrew 97, 98
Vicki 2, 61
Victoria, Queen of England 5
Vikings 4, 8; depictions of in film, television
    and music 138; Lewis chess pieces 139;
    longboats 136, 137, 138; in Northumbria
    134, 136–139, 141, 142; Ragnarok 135, 139–
    140, 143
Villages: English 7, 94–100, 168–184; idyllic
    8, 94–95, 96, 143, 168–169, 173; inversion of
    the idyllic 7, 8, 95, 96, 171–72, 174–83; nos-
    talgia and 7, 8, 96, 169; outsiders and 7, 8,
    98–99, 180–81; symbolism 7, 96–98, 143,
    170–71, 183–84
"Vincent and the Doctor" (2010) 5
Virgin Publishing 102; Virgin Missing
    Adventures range 109; Virgin New Adven-
    tures range 107, 109, 116
"The Visitation" (1982) 2, 99

War Doctor 127
"The War Games" (1969) 4, 61, 72, 102, 103–
    108, 110–12, 114–15, 171
"The War Machines" (1966) 132
Wareing, Alan 135
Warner, David 119, 121, 122, 130n3
Waterfield, Victoria 115
"The Web Planet" (1965) 21, 72
"The Wedding of River Song" (2010) 132
Weir, Arabella 119, 123
Wells, H.G. 4; see also "The Grisly Folk"
Whitaker, David 3, 62, 73n2
White Ignorance 49, 53, 55
White Innocence 53–55, 57
White Savior(ism) 52–57
White Supremacy 52, 54, 57
Who Recons 22
Whoflix 21
The Wicker Man (1973) 99
Wiles, John 79
Williams, Rory 44, 61
Wilson, Donald 38
World Game (2005) 102, 106, 112, 114, 115
World War II 96, 168, 169, 180
"Wrath of the Iceni" (2012) 35, 44–45
Wright, Barbara 2, 4, 16, 20, 24, 26, 61–64,
    66–68, 70–72, 94, 97, 149, 194, 195

Yates, Mike 42
Yetexa 94; tomb of 98
Young man, tiresome see Chesterfield